Cinemachines

Cinemachines

An Essay on Media and Method

GARRETT STEWART

THE UNIVERSITY OF CHICAGO PRESS [chicago and london]

The University of Chicago Press, Chicago 60637
The University of Chicago Press, Ltd., London
© 2020 by The University of Chicago
All rights reserved. No part of this book may be used or reproduced in any manner what-
soever without written permission, except in the case of brief quotations in critical articles
and reviews. For more information, contact the University of Chicago Press, 1427 E. 60th
St., Chicago, IL 60637.
Published 2020
Printed in the United States of America

27 26 25 24 23 22 21 20 19   1 2 3 4 5

ISBN-13: 978-0-226-65656-4 (cloth)
ISBN-13: 978-0-226-65673-1 (paper)
ISBN-13: 978-0-226-65687-8 (e-book)
DOI: https://doi.org/10.7208/chicago/9780226656878.001.0001

Library of Congress Cataloging-in-Publication Data

Names: Stewart, Garrett, author.
Title: Cinemachines : an essay on media and method / Garrett Stewart.
Description: Chicago : University of Chicago Press 2020
. | Includes index.
Identifiers: LCCN 2019021371 | ISBN 9780226656564 (cloth) | ISBN 9780226656731
(paperback) | ISBN 9780226656878 (ebook)
Subjects: LCSH: Cinematography. | Digital cinematography.
Classification: LCC TR850.S737 2019 | DDC 777—dc23
LC record available at https://lccn.loc.gov/2019021371

Contents

. . . .   PRELUDE: *Advance Press* 1

. 1   SNEAK PREVIEW: *Past the Apparatus?* 15

. 2   PRODUCTION NOTES: *Tech Specs* 39

. 3   FEATURETTE: *The Making of a Medium* 60

. 4   RERUN TRIPLE BILL: *Kinks of Comedy* 79

. 5   VFX FESTIVAL: *SF and Beyond* 106

. 6   OMNIBUS REVIEW: *On the Technopoetics of CGI* 124

. . . .   POSTSCRIPT: *Special AffX* 155

NOTES 179

INDEX 191

Prelude *Advance Press*

There is certainly a good deal of press in advance of this essay, scholarly and journalistic alike, to nudge it forward. Not just corporate bottom lines but recent academic books may tell us we're in a "postcinematic" culture. Videogame profits are vying, and hardly just as tie-ins, with box office or DVD receipts. More important for analytic discourse, the orientations of New Media theory are revising the focus of screen studies. But "cinema," whether waved goodbye to, or not, with the flourish of "post" in the vocabulary of New Media, is a name that cannot be restricted simply to exhibition in a theatrical venue. In narrative terms, the "cinematic" category of visual experience still references what it has traditionally meant: not so much attending *the* cinema, the designated movie house, as seeing *a* motion picture. Encapsulated there is the fact (rather than mode) of movie watching, though no longer "film going," that derives from an original sense of the *cinématographe* as kinetic visual event as well as mechanism.

No doubt about it, something is decidedly "behind us" in screen experience, and no hasty vernacular shorthand can compromise this recognition. "Post," our viewing certainly is—even when still cinematic. Despite the fact that curricular prose still speaks of "film courses," or commercial schedulers list "film screenings," not just "showtimes," the medial condition that *does* demonstrably antedate our current situation is celluloid, not cinema. Digitization—the generative work of pixel array rather than photo transparencies—marks the obvious, even when not visible, watershed in the developing formats of what I am calling, by portmanteau, *cinemachines*: a term meant to flag the intimate bond of technics and spectacle in any epoch of screen imageering. And the plural of the term (like the correlate "media" in this book's subtitle) bears the mark of historical transition in its own right: from one such machine to the next in line, from celluloid mechanics to digital electronics. What motion pictures are now is post-*filmic*, not postcinematic. And whether this is a shift in medium, or just in technical means (a renewed philosophical debate taken up shortly, but not soon to be settled), this difference in optical sequencing behind the framed view can have potent narrative consequences, making an on-screen difference linked to its historiographic determinants. There is no need to quibble, only to distinguish. In terms of material support, photographs in motion make for a different medium than single still images. That, by consensus. After the era of black and white imaging on screen, color stock may be thought of as a new medium, or not; less so, perhaps, anamorphic widescreen; maybe, or maybe not, the shift in substrate from 35 to 70 mm—but certainly the shift from photochemical to electronic storage and projection. From the sprocketed strip of photogram increments to the data compression of digital aggregates: thus has the cinemachine's founding seriality evolved along variant axes and at two different subliminal scales, two different medial underlays. To grant this is one thing; to think about it when watching is another. Hence the pixel reflex that focuses attention in the last two chapters.

Cinemachines: the very title may seem, and in fact is, a bit polemical. Because, at a knowing institutional glance, a tad retrograde—especially in the age of electronic game studies, social mediation, and the supersession of the theatrical motion picture by any number of mobile devices for image gathering as well as picture taking. Yet in the full century that falls between filmic and digital frameworks (and the differing nature of their individual frames), between the photogram and the Instagram, there remains a certain continuum whose story gets more interesting, rather than less, in the backlight—and backcast—of computer imaging. In recent academic discussion, however, the variable relations of cinematic technology to everything from ontology to narratology are increasingly losing ground to videogame ludology, neurobiology, and their posited common ground in affect study and proprioceptive engagement, all within the loose orbit of screen phenomenology. Sophisticated moving-image research, aimed at classic cinema as well, often presses ahead, that is, by treating the historical body of screen work—and mostly in the abstract (rather than the narrative concrete)—as a work both *on* and *of* the body of the spectator, as if induced in turn, in many a figurative evocation, by the screen's own body, its scrim a kind of fleshly integument.

On the whole, there is a vanishing choir to preach to in reaching through, past such dubious materialities, to technical questions of mediation, whether filmic or digital, in narrative cinema. But this at least allows discussion to economize. Any academic reader of this essay is likely to know what this writing is, in methodological terms, up against when advancing an approach through technics rather than somatics.[1]

It will be enough simply to make plain what still seems worth saying about cinematic spectatorship in light, reflected or otherwise, projected or LED-lit, of an apparatus that is mechanical before physiological—and of a medium with a good deal of demonstrable impact to be gained, in its narrative deployment, from not letting us forget this.

In the immediate run-up to the first *Star Wars* movie, no one can doubt that George Lucas, when founding in 1975 a digital effects studio under the trademarked name "Industrial Light and Magic," heralded a new era in screen production. But despite the catchy "industrial" as a surprise modifier for the more gossamer "light and magic," this branding didn't in itself pinpoint the breakthrough. Mechanical at base, lit incident on screen has always been an industrial operation, an engineered illusion— not least in its most "magical" effects. Lucas's computer-age watershed can thus offer a pivotal vantage point, angled back as well as forward. So let my plural term stand, in its implied historical spread. Cinemachines: an evolving modality of image generation for motion pictures, not just for the picturing of motion. *Apparatus* is a fine term as well, but refined (by high theory) out of uncontested parlance—and fallen into disuse as a neutral descriptor. Once dominating the field but long since marginalized or abandoned, apparatus *theory* (with its heavy burden of critique vis-à-vis the camera's channeling of a coercive and gendered gaze within the identificatory ruses of "suture") has left in its wake a certain blind spot in regard to the functional workings of the apparatus itself. It would be nice to think that what follows might bring back that simple term rinsed of tendentious ideological critique. For it's good to remember—despite the ideologically suspicious among the usual suspects in the pantheon of apparatus theory[2]—that cinema, then and now, has a specific apparatus in the everyday sense.

Recording, editing, and projection require geared mechanisms—the founding *cinématographe* performing all three functions at once—even as the resulting spectacle may emerge in turn as an engine of human desire, identification, and its potentially blinkering cultural stereotypes. If the times have left apparatus theory behind, with its claims for cinema's bourgeois constructions of the passive viewer, why would that seem to require any deliberate overlooking of the machine itself—or its descendants in digital electronics, on private as well as public screens? What reasonable objections can be raised, or resulting constraints imposed, to discourage *apparatus reading*, rather than a once entrenched, now discredited, apparatus theory—at least when the technology of a given film openly declares itself, if only by optical allusion? Which is really to ask: what benefit can be had from ignoring the evidence of our senses? Certainly when the normally invisible cinemachine seems to demand attention in its own right, whether by misfirings or other signs, one has already begun looking under the hood.

Let me anticipate how this might go by jumping ahead to my penultimate screen example first, the unexpected 2016 hit *Arrival* (Denis Villeneuve)—with a fuller discussion of this film eventually closing out the "Technopoetics" of the last chapter and followed up in the PostScript by the tracing out of certain further inferences of digital legerdemain from the director's next film, *Blade Runner 2049*. In a lower-profile mode, *Arrival* is a sci-fi narrative that, as screen realization, raises (and concentrates) almost every question to come in this essay about medial immanence in cinematic response—and does so, at one climactic point, from within the entrenched "special effects" context of its own genre. For there—in the specificity of these effects, within an underexplored tradition of film theory that sees all cinema as a "tricking" of vision—rests a typifying instance of this essay's recurrent evidence. *Arrival*'s alien visitation plot brandishes no high-tech forms of mediation on the part of the invasive and levitating motherships, but has them baffling earth's scientific community with the lack of intercommunicative circuits kept open among these separate hovering vessels. Their dozenfold benign flotilla—delivering a collective wake-up call from the future—thus emerges from the intricacies of plot (as if by default parable) as a collective interstellar medium in itself: a signal channel from the future, needing no second-order modes of coordinated transmission. Our guess at this emblematic function is only enhanced by the homebound "return" of the ships at the end: a return—by way of sheer optical reversion—to their conveyed status as an urgency millennially pending, whose time has not yet come. They go into astral hibernation before our eyes.

But how do we actually *see* in order to realize this—especially with so little valedictory *show* entailed? And how, in media-archaeological terms, can the mere fade-away of one vast craft after another in a puff of its own dematerialization rather than flight (its apotheosis, in effect, as temporal rather than spatial vehicle: again, as pure medium, more transmit than transport) manage to evoke a definitive lineage of technological film history as well as a cosmic future within the far horizons of the story's premise? How, that is, can *Arrival* microtool such departures with a sheer "atmospheric" (both nebulous and in fact sheer) digital version of the rudimentary lap dissolve in the conversion of vehicle to vapor?

Technical specifications for this imaging by the VFX (visual special effects) designer, as we'll later see, can only enrich its mystery—and the depth of its evoked media-historical backstory. Dated (say archaic) in optical evacuation, the return to millennial latency of the giant ships is rendered in a time-loop irony medial as well as thematic. Reverting to the earliest special effects of the cinematographic medium, here is the *arche*-trick of filmic cinema: the laboratory cross-fade of both ghostly materialization and phantasmal erasure. Moreover, within the fading ellipse of one giant lozenge-like ship after another, how, beyond this throwback technical allusion, might we find summoned to mind's eye something further about the long life of the apparatus? How might we be inclined in this way to register the shifting optic valence by which, in film history, such a dissolve (elliptical in the other sense)—though once a spectral effect within the framed scene—soon became a gesture of syntactic elision (…) in the maturing function of screen grammar? How, that is, might we intuit such a dual and, so to say, metamedial function—the conversion of ghostly machination to technical styleme—as reprised in the very grain of this later diaphanous trope for the once and still coming epiphany of an alien future?

Or to put the question more programmatically in the present essay's terms: how does a viewer's instinctive reaction to the hazy, phased-out texture of such a special effect—a digital evocation of a predecessor filmic technique—draw some part of its power from the cinemechanics (the asserted apparatus function) it exploits, transfigures, and rehistoricizes? We can, I promise, get closer to answers when, after intervening arguments, this screen narrative comes round again for a more extended interpretive discussion. I've introduced Villeneuve's film as an anticipatory "example," but in fact the methodological stakes of its consideration, here and later, render it less an instance of a device than an *exercise* in particular medial options or tendencies. Such moments, in current as well as classic films, register a *performance* of the apparatus rather than the simple proof of it. More than ever, perhaps, given the way VFX designers are to be numbered among the true auteurs of recent cinema, such effects thereby deliver up, and precisely from affect to interpretation, the legible (the "authored" and readable) as well as the merely visible. And often do so in the fashion of a rearview mirror, as well, on the historical vicissitudes of the apparatus.

Perhaps one critic above all, Jean Epstein, offers a fully conceptualized way of looking back on film history from the vantage, the virtualities, of the digital moment—without himself even catching wind of it from his final writings in the mid-1940s. In his most recently translated study, *The Intelligence of a Machine*, whose impact for questions of the apparatus will be detailed in the "Sneak Preview," all cinema is posited as an ontological "trick" effect. It is from this perspective that Epstein had in fact theorized the bitmap array of data compression, however indirectly, from the very position of his resolute insistence on the cellular discontinuity of the celluloid strip. This, then, the serial intermittence of the reeling spool, is our true point of launch: 10-9-8-7-6-5-4-3-2-1-0. Such a *quantified* count-down of the leader, flashing through the spinning intermittencies of the Maltese cross on the way to the file of exposed photograms, and then on their own way to screen projection, gives this essay its medium-deep lead in approach to screen *qualities*: photomechanical once, now pixel-driven in the i/o mode, whether just in the unseen codes of digital recording or in full CGI (computer-generated imaging).

Essay, yes. This volume, though bound, isn't exactly a traditional mono-graph. Its segmentations are not independently structured chapters meant to carve up some holistic field of concern, still less to gerrymander it into manageability. Nor do they amount to separate essays, standing free of each other. They are phases and facets of a single, newly exemplified pro-posal, noted in its inferences from film to film. Not notes *toward*, sketchy or provisional, they are annotations *on* a prevailing confluence of mediality and analytic attention—however much ceded at times to competing in-terpretive agendas—that remains inherent to a certain intensity of screen viewing. Or in the marketing and distribution lingo of commercial film-making from which they draw their figurative division of labor, with its own very different sense of a "publicity machine," these notes are the "rollout," instead, of a kind of methodological white paper. What they have in mind is a certain "retooling" of film studies: less ambitious, if perhaps no less contentious, than it may sound. In the face of affect studies and associated approaches—when "focused," as it were, not on screen materialization but on the spectatorial body[3]—this "retooling" is simply a (re)turn of attention to the machinic fabrication, the tool use, of the photogram or pixel as drivers in the underlying morphology of a narrative screen grammar. I speak in metaphor there, of course, with that linguistic analog, which is what I admittedly want to resist (too much metaphor in the method) in the widespread figuration of cinematic corporeality—rather than its sheer, and once quite literally so, plastic (and later pic-celled) materiality.[4]

In front of the screen, confronting it as we do, the thrill and the chill, the spine tingle and gut wrench, the clutch and lurch of excitation are all, of course, quite real. They constitute what we might call our visceral discernment of the audiovisual display. But the force of the image, as of the soundtrack, is preceded in all this by the technical innards of the machine itself. As will be unmistakable in our return to early German film criticism in the historical "Featurette" segment below, the film body has always been central to the cinematographic imagination. As the tandem weight of technology in these same Weimar discussions will make equally apparent, however, the moving body was understood early on, in such eye-opening encounters with a nascent if rapidly maturing medium, as the specular product (an image generated) rather than a figurative property (a corporeal surface in itself) of the screen process. What, by contrast, seems misleading about a contemporary emphasis on a carnalized medium has to do mainly with the materiality of the engineered image that such theory occludes, in contrast to the materiality it tropes as somatic. Underplayed there, too often, is the force of the machine—in a questionable deference to a fleshly optic. The results are becoming as tenacious as they may seem fallacious. As if in recoil from a body politic too immediately implicated (and abstracted) by the ideology of the apparatus in its previous theorizations, discussion has veered away to the body itself, both as trope for a quasi-haptic audiovisuality and as its neuromuscular topography in uptake. A tacit interactivity, it would seem, has insinuated itself, almost without saying so, as a broad new paradigm.[5] It's worth thinking again— in directions the first two preliminary chapters can only begin to lay out.

Under the coming rubric of "Sneak Preview," what is anticipated in its introductory remarks certainly snuck up on their author. I had no forethought of another book on cinema at this time. The case seemed closed: both on the postfilmic moment and on its implications for nonnarrative surveillance—and this within a dwindling academic commitment to narrative analysis itself.[6] But there is a tide that seems to be turning—and thus a renewed case worth *advancing*. In recent symposia and publications, it would appear that a gathering counterforce, if not a perfect storm, is pressing related issues back into relevance under impetus from certain unexpected new tailwinds. There are the still-arriving films themselves, of course, week by week, especially in the continually rebooted genre of Hollywood sci-fi. These are wide releases whose CGI spectacles have increasingly seemed fixated on the production values of their own VFX in ways not fully explored in recent historical accounts of such cinematic devices. Then, too, at the other end of the cultural spectrum, amid the growing hyphenate field of film-philosophy—with various resuscitations of theory forged at such an intersection—there is a second wave of interest in the specifically ontological (and therefore arguably technological) orientation of Stanley Cavell's film theory, in and out of explored sync with the continuing centrality of André Bazin's influential writings.

Into this current mix of new screen evidence and renewed philosophical considerations (with a major anthology on the subject of Cavell's film writing in the works as well) comes news from abroad in the form of two important translation projects, one a single brief monograph, one an entire journalistic treasure trove: first, as mentioned, the belated but welcome translation of Epstein's provocative short treatise, *The Intelligence of a Machine*, and then, the next year, the massive University of California Press edition of early German film criticism.[7] To that recovered Weimar archive, including its frequent meditations on the filmed body and face in their machinic transmission, we'll be working back later from Epstein's 1946 book—in view of the accumulating shelf of commentary on the French director's film theory that the translation has helped facilitate. This is, however, a building academic response that, to my surprise, tends to downplay Epstein's emphasis on all cinema as "special effect"—exactly what invites my own return to the issue. When I said above, in reaction to a blanket somatics of reception, that "it's worth thinking again," I had in mind, given its suggestive title, the broad philosophical parameters of *The Intelligence of a Machine*.

Epstein writes arrestingly of perception's own "special effect" (*truquage* in his spelling), quite apart from effects particular to cinema—though by association with the medium's own simulated continuum. That feature of his book anticipates an unacknowledged link between his view of the mentally constructed rather than coherently viewed image and, quite differently pursued, Christian Metz's apparatus theory of motion-picturing's essential cinematic "trick." Epstein and Metz together consolidate a sense of machinic mirage at the very core of the cinematic illusion that the readings ahead will often find masked on screen—even while indirectly symptomatized. This occurs, time and again, in the strident illusionism of local optic sleights of sight in a given narrative: a technological first cause getting flashed past, but quickly buried again, in its more blatant effects. These machinic (even when electronic) irruptions of course include, in the computer era that follows the writings of both Epstein and Metz, and of Deleuze as well, a whole new arsenal of computerized prestidigitations as well as former celluloid ruses. So full disclosure: had this been an exhaustive book rather than an essay, it might have been yet another compendium on the evolution of special effects. As an essay, however, its method can afford to intercept the changing face, and interface, of cinematic illusion on the perhaps paradoxically narrower score of screen motion's *wholesale* trickery.

And occasions for pursuing this line of thought have indeed kept presenting themselves lately by way of unexpected intersections. As exemplified by his own early cinematography in its flouting of bodily norms in a surrealist choreography of the image plane, Epstein makes an intriguing point—introduced early in *The Intelligence of a Machine*—that slapstick and avant-garde cinema are somehow cousin (even at times simultaneous) enterprises, each playing fast and loose with norms of corporeal motion. This idea leant, for me, an extra theoretical context to a recent Berlin conference on film's comic genre(s), whose umbrella title, "The Positive Negative," elicited, in the case of my own contribution, a look at the photomechanical subtext of selected screen comedies from the silent and sound era. In some of their most radiant hilarities, the "negative" chemistry of the photo strip, its dependence on the imprinted and developed photogram, is surfaced absurdly into these comic plots—just as, much later, the plus-minus operations of computer imaging can be found bursting the seams of all narrative transparency in more recent screen farce. It is thus that comedy, when turned *comedial*, can also help forge a link between the current influence of Bergson (in and around Deleuzian film scholarship) and that earlier French philosopher's famous separate work on verbal and visual laughter as "mechanization." Enter, again, the cinemachine—and its plural genealogy, from photochemistry to cybercircuitry.

So a certain inner pressure was indeed mounting, after all, for me to write again on cinema's divided history—and, in part, because various confusions still needed clearing away. Published the year after Epstein's *The Intelligence of a Machine* appeared in English, as it happens, a notable anthology called *Post-Cinema: Theorizing 21st-Century Film*—for all the frequent excellence of the contributions—has it, by title, just backwards. Much of twenty-first-century viewing is postcinema, to be sure—but not still constituted as "film," except when that term is taken as a nostalgic misnomer for digital moviemaking. My interest is not in subsuming the "postcinematic" into some broader term for image transmit that would include traditional movies along with the whole array of digital motion otherwise bombarding the small or mobile screen—as has been offered, for instance, with the term "animage."[8] By the very plural of cinemachines, I want instead, as indicated, to resist the prefix "post" altogether as applied to the cinematic image in any continued attention to narrative movie making, however much its digital constituents (decidedly postfilmic) may be featured and thematized. In contrast to *Post-Cinema*, therefore, *Cinemachines* began to imagine itself as returning to the debate in order to track what amounts to the retinal return of the suppressed. This includes not just the photogram always lost to view in one sense, while recovered in another by the so-called frame grab. It includes as well the constituent pixel, and beneath that, by inference, the unglimpsed algorithmic template of electronic screening as the cinemachine's latest generative function. For cinema persists as institution and as narrative form, regardless of what subsists in the film stock's former place. In this and other ways, my new explorations would inevitably remain attached to Deleuze's question about what computerized imagery would do to the function of the time-image in cinema, not what postcinematic video would do to perceptual temporality at large.[9]

The prospect of tackling again such issues was much on my mind when I was invited to take part in a symposium in 2017 at the University of Chicago on the film-philosophy overlap in classroom teaching. Even there, I soon realized that a notable emphasis on "technique" in Cavell's sense of screen disclosure was in danger of being overlooked in its tangential, but nonetheless tangible, medial inferences. I refer to the difference in *The World Viewed*—in all its considerable difference from Epstein's radical epistemology—between *the* world recorded as document and *a* world projected as fiction. So it was, there in Chicago, that interpretive commentary was again called forth, as instance from principle, in something of the "close reading" mode championed by Cavell himself—though only, in my own argument, when projected images are further conceived in light (thrown light) of their recorded form on the strip (or, since then, their digital mode of traced optic microdata). The process on screen by which the indexical is assimilated to the fictional, in Cavell's sense, must thus, in mine, find its counterpart one level down as well—in the predigital medium he wrote about, though not in these terms—when the automatized photo*gram*mar of the strip is visibly activated as the avowed syntax of the cinemato*graph*. In this regard, a more targeted return within Cavell studies to his concept (and brief catalogue) of "Assertions in Technique"—partitioned off as the penultimate chapter of *The World Viewed* (1971)—discloses an intuition more reverberant, as discussion ahead will suggest, than even Cavell may have intended. In such ways, a given *manifestation* of the celluloid track, as later of the digital file, can offer itself to cinemachinic analysis as, in the other sense, a *manifest* of vehicular contents in operational transmit: the medium having become the technical message.

All told, then, occasions and incitations were piling up: if not a perfect storm, at least the propellant force of uncharted crosscurrents in both the flood of ongoing narrative imagery, given the exponential sophistication and proliferation of VFX, and various impinging discourses on the matter—and materiality—of screen mediation. A further articulation of what I have called "narratography" at this new turn seemed in order. In its convergence of image with theoretical investigation, what I am here stressing as *apparatus reading* takes its cues from impulses operating between the lines of narrative, yet without ignoring the storylines that release them. So what is the plot of my own story, my own "essayed" account, of all this? Moving in film-philosophical terms from Epstein versus Cavell on the "trick" of the moving image (in chapter 1) through a debate with New Media understandings of the "postperceptual image" in a supposed postcinematic screen rhetoric (chapter 2), discussion next arcs back for historical context both to early German writing on the technical effects of filmic illusion (chapter 3) and to simultaneous experiments in what Bergson would have seen enacted as "mechanization" and its "interferences" in silent screen comedy (chapter 4). The essay then turns to contemporary trends in cyber technique and its pixel disclosures, when seen against the backdrop of earlier sci-fi (chapter 5) and then maximized in a wide gamut of diegetic "special effects" (chapter 6). At this point a ventured reconfiguration of Metz's theory for digital rather than filmic *trucage* (coined *digitage* here) leads to a coda on the particular "special affect" involved in any such hyperattuned "machinic" response. Explored there, as throughout, is a cognitive as well as interpretive stance—my own, since early days of filmgoing, but not mine alone—that is nerved for a techno/logical engagement with any facet of medial reveal, whether filmic or digital. This key of response to "assertions in technique," as to the attempted suppression of such devices, operates quite apart from a traditional aesthetics of reflexivity in the movies-about-movies vein (Vertov to Fellini and beyond). Instead, the recognitions thus incurred involve a closer registration of the cinemachine's own differing—and differential—substrates in narrative propulsion.

Apparatus reading is thus medial before textual. Its objects are not reflexive—self-*referential*—so much as engrained, formative, apparitional. And always mechanical as well as physiological. Hence this essay's methodological starting point: an assumption that reminders, even investigations, of this are often at their most exacting—as only the close work of screen reading can disclose—in the narrative execution of movie plots themselves, whenever the coils of their storytelling seem to meet a medial analysis halfway. How bluntly obvious this may sound can help vouch for the potential new yield from pursuing its ramifications in a scholarly climate progressively less concerned with such narrative matters. But this essay hardly proceeds in isolation. In its effort to steer forward in a manner as unencumbered as possible in the glossing of certain featured issues, the sometimes discursive nature of the resulting endnotes is meant to evoke the broader base of analytic and theoretical context by which the streamlining of the essay's methodological demonstrations is necessarily ballasted.

No scholarly storms, perfect or otherwise, need brewing, then, in order for critical notice to sweep up some of the latest screen evidence—and debate—for an assessment at once narratival and media-historical. Disciplinary sea swells aren't required. Stars don't have to align in order to encourage, now and then, a set of annotational asterisks—their "marginal" glosses organized partly in resistance to prevailing weather patterns. This essay marks out a constellation of several such flagged "asides" from dominant channels of pursuit, with each recharted course—and thereby new route of approach—offered as a brief chapter in response to ongoing developments from perspectives interlinked and eventually convergent. Commentary can be timely, one assumes, when bucking as well as cresting certain tides. In the latest academic emphasis on gamer protocols and participatory affect in various burgeoning sectors of digital screen studies, in all their physiological and cognitive overtones, the neighboring "format" of narrative cinema has increasingly been sidelined and underattended in its own adaptive forms. Given this lapse of "analysis" to which New Media studies inclines, its own unique precisions seem at times to be having an erosive—rather than their potentially invigorating—effect on interpretive scrutiny in other manifestations of the computerized image.

The tendency is surely reversible. It should be easy enough to recognize instead, especially with the examples waiting, how digital electronics—when contemplated from the bottom up, as a subnarrative feature, rather than from the instrumental top down, as an interactive function—can offer the missing bridge between media theory and narrative investigation. In such explorations of the changing cinematic apparatus, one can't sensibly repudiate or mute the sheer material differences unfolding over a time both historical, on the one hand, and, on the other, internal to the microtimed manufacture of each illusory image field, whether photogrammic or digital. Nor should one ignore, in methodological terms again, the interpretive joins between such once-wheeled, now further compressed and morphed, increments of the image—operating as technical baselines to any immanent motion—and those eroded or enhanced narrative arcs, short circuits, and cross-sparked ironies with which such technological underlays are often tactically entwined. Underattended, hence under-read, these effects may well be—at least in the current fashion of cinema analysis. But once noticed, once annotated, what do they *notify us of*? And how to respond to the very underside of display to which they sometimes yield access? With those questions any hermeneutics of the apparatus must always begin again— whatever fresh spurs to consideration arrive from other scholarly quarters.

No sea swells, riptides, or prevailing currents required, I repeat. No groundswells—just a continuing ear to the ground (or to the eddying disciplinary forces that define its outer shores). And hence the proverbial "occasional essay" as a result. In particular, and in sum—across important French and German translations, theoretical anthologies, symposium convergences, and the litmus tests of recent screen releases—it is certainly the case here that *occasions* critical, cinema-historical, media-theoretical, and film-philosophical have together conspired, when angled in on each other, to inspire a concerted new look at the workings of the cinemachines in question. And not the least of these occasions, on the thirty-fifth anniversary of the landmark sci-fi film *Blade Runner* (Ridley Scott, 1982), with whose photographic subtext I began my first book on cinema, is the appearance (the release and the very look)—an entire digitized epoch later—of the film on which this book closes, *Blade Runner 2049* (Denis Villeneuve, 2017). For here is a film that cries out, from within its technical finesse, for the kind of narrative response that only medial attention, otherwise so little focused on medial *reading* lately, can begin to exert on the specifically visual mysteries of its special effects—and humanoid affect. What the film provokes in response to its optical densities, it also tacitly advocates by way of a perceptual stance toward the screen image. It is the kind of call these pages would wish to answer. Given the climate change of current disciplinary investigations, the fact that the narratographic burden of this essay may stand quite to the side of dominant trends isn't to deny that margins and peripheries can help draw more definitive lines of debate.

What emerges most pointedly here is a renewed argument—in the era of cultural "overview"—for the more textured disclosures of *close looking*: looking, where the visible becomes further legible beneath plot. So yet again *reading*, in the sense of visual *interpretation*; but *close* here in the resultant sense of *deeper*: a peering beneath the visuals (because *through* them in both senses) to a glimpse of their motoring visualization—even if only inferred by virtuoso turns or optical disturbances on screen. This is what a recurrent focus on special effects is meant to *specify*. It is in this way that apparatus reading cuts through to the illusionist common denominator— the inherent special effect, the trick that *is* cinema—calibrated by each major historical, hence technological, phase of its cinemachines.

Academic terminology, certainly in the form of curricular rubrics, has struggled, for decades now, to render itself as determinate and encompassing as possible, straight through to the platform multiplications of New Media—even when its efforts at catch-up seem to let slide some of its founding priorities. The original and eventually tattered banner of institutional film studies, often restitched in the 1970s as film and television studies, has since been frayed further in various evolutions from moving image studies to such video- and game-inclusive rubrics as screen studies or film and media studies. But what has fallen away lately from a good deal of just such study itself—despite the medial infusion that the energies of theorized computer imaging might have been expected to inject, let alone the growing scholarly interest in image archaeology—is a close medial attention to the framed visual image in its tightly meshed narrative force. What has thus atrophied is exactly what once made cinema programs so eager for the spelling out of their discipline-specific scope. Screen study, that is, is less likely to be preoccupied these days with what is on screen than with how it got there, and not technologically but culturally, corporately: more with fixed iconology, say, than with the transient faceting of iconicity.

This isn't inevitable. And regret can best take shape in an exemplified counterproposal. With an original motivation no less compelling under current technical dispensations, the whole field of cinematic study arose to address the uniqueness of the moving image—in moving its own visual discourse along: the image, *legible* through its particular medial input, as it is materialized in and as screen depiction, actualized by machination. Apparatus reading is simply one name for a studious looking anew in this vein. Its terminological leverage in the coming chapters, as the illustrative distillation of medium and method at once, involves, in short, the concerted turning of the latter back on the former. That may sound like a predictable enough turn to take. But, by definition, surprise awaits. For you never know what you'll find—without actually looking.

1   *Sneak Preview*

PAST THE APPARATUS?

THAT MUCH SAID ABOUT MY PROMPTINGS TO BEGIN AGAIN, LET ME NOW ACTUALLY DO SO with two delayed "epigraphs": tandem machinic maxims three decades apart in the postwar screen era, yet each still on the near side of the digital turn in mainstream film production. It is between these formulations that the work of this essay is to unfold—and partly in order to move beyond them into the digital realm of cinema's new postfilmic condition.

> The cinematograph merely possesses the mandatory faculty to realize—to render real—the combination of space and time, providing the product of space and time variables, which means that cinematographic reality is therefore essentially the idea of a complete mode of location. Yet it is only an idea, an artificial idea, of which we can only affirm an ideological and artificial existence—*a kind of trick or special effect*. Nonetheless, this trick [*truquage*] is extremely close to the process by which the human mind itself conjures up an ideal reality for itself.
>
> —Jean Epstein, *The Intelligence of a Machine* (emphasis added)[1]

> Montage itself, at the base of all cinema, is already a perpetual *trucage*, without being reduced to the *false* in usual cases.
>
> —Christian Metz, "*Trucage* and the Film"[2]

Two embedded epigraphs, that is, on the "world" of moving pictures as sheer illusion: including in the first case, by analogy, the exterior world of pictured motion itself as its own merely "idealized" real; and in the second, a distinction between overt deception and a general fabrication. Within the sphere of cinema per se, two variant French spellings of *truc/qu/age*, one striking idea: that any local "trick" is a synecdoche for the medium all told. The Epstein translation renders the single phrase "trick" ("of a sort") by adding for clarification its more common English sense in "a kind of trick *or special effect*"—in any case, a faking of the real. The liberty of amplification is entirely apt, given Epstein's broad argument. Identified there is an inherent rigging of vision—and not just as regards the screen world, but, more striking yet in Epstein, the world's own cognitive screening: namely, the sensorial interface that always operates, well outside the movie theater, between us and those perceptions we accumulate in order to derive our sense of placedness—of space-time "location," here in the now. Epstein's radical point: we are only in the know about our whereabouts through mediation, necessary for the mind in "conjuring" a running image of what lies beyond it. Just as film is necessary for the screening of *its* world, or digitization since, so must the brain's electric medium override intermittence in order to picture the continuum of our world.

The point is, in short, as much epistemological as cinematographic. For consciousness involves a sense of embodied locus that is, in Epstein's view, as "artificial" as focalized continuity in the screen image: an experience of presence mentally constituted, indeed constructed, rather than directly received—in his terms "ideological" (idealized) rather than ontological. We are always taking the virtual for the actual. This is because only neural *constructs* make possible our access to any outside source of sensation. Movies replay this distance from immediacy at one further and absolute remove. In this sense, what filmic cinema tricks out on screen, by way of dissembled motion from its own celluloid movement, offers a screening of dubiety itself—and then, of course, its immersive undoing. This is a measure of the "intelligence" (Epstein's title) that the celluloid cinemachine imparts as well as embodies.

And so a third delayed and embedded epigraph is in order here, where again the idealities of the screen are found cognate with those of the human mental apparatus in the framing of reality. The axis that will mostly concern us, as it does both Epstein and Metz, is the one perpendicular to the throw of light, both on strip and screen: the plane of kinesis itself rather than the orthogonal axis of the reflected beam. But the latter illuminates its own field of artifice in the focus and resolution of the image itself. Here from prose fiction—complementing a book-length battery of narrational analogs on Salman Rushdie's part drawn explicitly from montage, camera angles, and zoom lenses to account for his shifting choice of focalization—is a sense of that other inherent illusionism of the screen image *as image*. And this is as much the case for the photomechanical grain of filmic cinema as for the pixelated texture of more recent projection. Such is the *trucage* of resolution itself, the distance-policed illusion of so-called optical fidelity.

Reality is a question of perspective; the further you get from the past, the more concrete and plausible it seems—but as you approach the present, it inevitably seems more and more incredible. Suppose yourself in a large cinema, sitting at first in the back row, and gradually moving up, row by row, until your nose is almost pressed against the screen. Gradually the stars' faces dissolve into dancing grain; tiny details assume grotesque proportions; the illusion dissolves—or rather, it becomes clear that the illusion itself *is* reality.

—Salman Rushdie, *Midnight's Children*[3]

In sum, for Rushdie as well as for both Epstein and Metz, cinema is, at base, a magic realism in its own right. What Epstein, as we'll see, means in part by the "mosaics" (10) of the film image are just those shuffled surfaces whose overall serial cogency risks disintegration in another way, as Rushdie suggests, when its exhibition protocols are breached. Look too closely—at life in the present, at the image in presentation—and its "dancing grain" is as much a demystification of inhabited reality as is the photogram chain or the digital file. One might say that cinema's fantastic "realism" exposes the world's own.

In the very broadest terms, then, concerning both human vision and its prosthetic machines, and to answer the triggering question of this chapter: one never gets past the apparatus. Worth remembering, too, in an earlier literary vein than Rushdie's magic realities, and concerning a debunked screen experience nearer to the origin of the new optic medium, how a character in Frank Norris's 1899 *McTeague* resists a debut experience of the "kinetoscope" with a Swiss-accented English that insinuates a pun on the dubious screen grain as well as its illusion of presence—insisting how "dot's nothun but a drick"[4]: a falsification of movement itself, with all those shimmering "dots" of light as lurking proof of the deception. Including a horse "that can move its head" (in reprise of Eadweard Muybridge's precinematic motion studies), the kinetic shadow play remains for this one skeptical viewer an inherent *trucage*, a "nothun" pretending to be something, "dricked" through and through.

Tricked Out / Space Doubt

Apart from the tropes of a philosophical prose fiction like Rushdie's, the thread of skeptical inference and critique in film-philosophy circles has a clear early touchstone in Epstein. According to just this epistemic premise

in the passage on "truquage" above—arriving in the second-to-last paragraph of Epstein's final chapter, titled "Irrealism"—we find lodged a central
concession about the "special effect" of recorded reality when manifested
on theater screens. Duping is constitutive. The point bears repeating, since
it is just this tricking of world coherence that can instruct us in "those
processes by which the human mind itself conjures up an ideal reality for
itself." Indeed, to pick up on Epstein's heavy iteration there, this is how
consciousness fashions its "irreal" (its virtual) notions of the "itself" per
se. Bearing down on this manifestation of the "virtual" can contribute to
a theoretical machinics of cinematic projection that is better calculated
to engage with those later electronic transforms that none of the major
philosophical thinkers we'll be engaging with alongside Epstein—Charles
Sanders Peirce, Henri Bergson, Gilles Deleuze, and Stanley Cavell—were,
of course, historically positioned to write about.

Yet Epstein came weirdly near—in what we might call his reciprocal
deconstruction of mind and motion picture, with substance and duration
each a "special effect" of perception on and off the screen. By the tenets of
"irrealism," all screen presence is never more than intermittence and probability. In this light, "the cinematograph brings us back to Pythagorean and
Platonic poetry: reality is but the harmony of Ideas and Numbers" (105).
Nor does Epstein stop there with his backcast to a mathematical idealism
at the basis of physical science and screen mechanics alike. Written on
the postwar eve of the computer revolution, his book's closing note seems
sounded in full theoretical anticipation of virtual reality—a terminology,
for him, quite the opposite of paradoxical. Since physics admits that it
"can only know reality" in "the form of numerical rules prescribing the
conditions under which reality is ultimately allowed to produce itself"
(105), then it is only these formulas that "create a specific and fictive zone
in space that is the locus of this extreme reality—and no one knows how
to get any closer to it" (105). The real is always, we may say, *screened from
us* by probabilities rather than met with present confirmation.

Film looms large as a new cognitive model. The "artificial" continuities
and coordinates thrown up by celluloid projection might thus be con-
strued as a mode of recognizing—and reckoning with, not numerically
but imaginatively—the fact of our epistemological remove from the world.
Such is a mode of thinking—with and through, and finally beyond—the
automatized intellection of *une machine*. Rather than merely represented by
projection, the world's ingrained virtuality is revealed in synchromesh with
it. Arriving decades later in screen production, the algorithmic basis of the
computer image offers the same potential analog for perception (or, in pixel

breakup, its travesty) but gets us no closer, in Epstein's sense, to the receding abstraction of the real—just, perhaps, more algebraically (if invisibly) attuned to the world's infinitesimally flickering field of intermittence. When Deleuze ended his career wondering whether the coming "numeric" basis of cinema would change everything in our conception of the time-image,[5] Epstein's proleptic answer might well have been: not "really."

Machination: Between Axioms and Praxis

Epstein: arguably the greatest theorist-practitioner of the cinema after Eisenstein. But always, in Epstein's case, on arguable grounds, even for his enthusiasts. His is a nest of propositions where theory and practice can seem to rub each other the wrong way—under the shadow of special pleading—in their seeming attempt at rapprochement. I thus turn to his newly translated work in light of a current "revival" that, even in the fullest endorsements, tends to minimize the strenuousness of Epstein's insight in one founding respect. Commentary has always tended to downplay in his writing, in favor of its more colorful and elusive ideas (especially *photogenie*), what Epstein stresses as the fundamental cinematic underlay: the malleable plasticity of the photogram band. Nor is it always recognized how this stress is pursued for its leverage, as well, on human perception more broadly. Operable discontinuity is the case not only for the motion picture (as the discontinuous moving of separate pictures) but, as we saw above, for the more fundamental intermittence, rather than unity, of material space and time in the physical universe—with the human body's own disparate molecular makeup, in addition to its periodic cognition, included.

When such respectively medial and countermetaphysical claims are eased to the side in commentary, Epstein's theory of cinema is sometimes discredited, or at least discounted, as the tendentious philosophical cover for a private aesthetic credo. The experimental director whose most famous film, for instance, fuses two Poe stories, "The Oval Portrait" and "The Fall of the House of Usher" (together assimilated both to the title of the latter and to a heady surrealist amalgam), can seem boxed in as the *philosophe* of his own visual initiatives—not least when the opening chapter of *Intelligence* identifies human bodies on screen, by subsection title, as "Uncanny Portraits" (1). His theoretical writing risks being quarantined in this way as the prose of a deft poet-polemicist seen to be privileging a uniquely cinematic lyricism steeped in the features of aberrant motion and composite imagery dear to his own directorial vision—rather than excavating thereby the true status of screen mediation. Yet his guiding claims are more pointedly technological than that—even before being tied to human vision and consciousness at large. This is why Epstein insists from the start on the graphic aggregates of the cinematograph: the photo-frames through which, in their very plasticity, indexical documentation can alone be transformed to mentation. And from there to the rethought poetry of motion.

Granted, when his theoretical pronouncements are lifted out of context, it is easy, with his signature film style in mind's eye, to put them down to his own visual proclivities—and thus partially to write them off. When in *La chute de la maison Usher* (1928) the painter protagonist touches up a canvas at brush tip only to inflict a telepathic sting on the cheek of his model, it is the kind of moment that would make skeptics doubt Epstein's more sweeping argument: his proposal not just about "uncanny portraits" but, almost by allegory, about the almost tele-tactile convergence of secondary visual representation and physical reality in the processing of the human eye. That the on-screen portrait has the same filmic status as the painter before it in this localized "truquage" may indeed seem more a *mere* trick than a medium-deep demonstration. And yet the double terminological sense of "frame"—both definitive and bedeviling for film studies—operates here precisely when Poe's oval, once squared off into an admittedly wavy and internally rippling specular bracket, may serve to remind us of that other work with, rather than within, frames whose mechanics, rather than manual brushpoint, engineers the temporality of screen image.

Whether or not all this may seem seeded in this one shot, it is by some such overassociation of theory with practice that the force of the former is easily lost in Epstein's approach. This is to say, again, that Epstein's pronouncements on the shared mediatory functions of mind and screen alike in *L'Intelligence d'une machine* can (too readily) seem a self-interested extrapolation from selective magic, singled out for promotion and over-read as the fundamental mechanics of perceptual intelligence.

The actual case isn't just otherwise, however, but rigorously so. And the framed portrait—submitting to the serial strokes of composition; made move only by physical as well as visual increments—makes this hard to miss. Epstein's sense of film's defining rudiments—slow motion, acceleration, close-up, and montage—is scarcely to be found compromised by his own maximal and eccentric use of them, but only if the horizons of his argument are kept in clear focus. With the Poe film still in mind, for instance, when Madeleine Usher's feverish hysteria is figured by tripled images of her face orbiting a vertiginous empty center, in a layered hallucinatory translucency in which one close-up exceeds the others slightly in scale, the medium certainly shows through in its conjuring mechanics: shows forth, that is, as too many frames at once for a singular image—the medium's sine qua non converted to aberration.

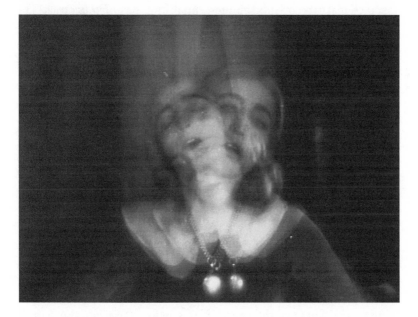

Figuring clearly enough a nonplastic spasm of psychic distress, nonetheless what we see imploded in a single framed space are the multiple images ordinarily strung out on the strip to project any and all motion. Film is showing its own hand in such an abandoned norm. But we needn't call this self-exposure *definitive*. No need to tie principle too tightly, as Epstein never himself does, to his own experiments. His pervasive claims for cinema as the dissolution and remolding of the recorded world and its mobile agents—a world whose own optical fungibility and intermittent signaling is only answered by the manipulable frames of celluloid itself— needn't appear selective and tactical, driven by agenda rather than genuine medial apprehension. Yet the claims bear interrogation, to be sure. This is the case, most famously, with variable speed, as distilled in the *Usher* film by a distended loop of the sister's decelerated physical collapse, in slower and slower descent: her falling body perceived as if from inside her own lost grip on consciousness. How can this anomaly be constitutive? Or ask: what are its tacitly obtruded mechanics meant to be thinking out, thinking through, for us in this event of mechanized "intelligence"?

Considering Epstein's stress on cinema's distinctive features, we may wonder why montage and the close-up (those definitive elements traced back through Griffith to Dickens by Eisenstein) wouldn't be more definitive, as ingredient features of cinema, than the anomalies of slowed or accelerated motion. What in the case of Madeleine Usher's fall, for instance, makes retardation quintessential, its effect an *intrinsic* trick? The answer is implicitly approached by Epstein only through interrogating the celluloid medium (or means) in particular, not the screen experience as normally managed by shot and montage. Slow motion is a second-order function of serial arrest on the strip. If the lock-step chain of photograms can be routinely overcome by split-second pauses matched to flickering disappearances—so as to produce the looks of a hug, a lunge, a gallop, you name it—it is through just that staggered seriality, by further internal duplication and thus prolongation, that the image can be slowed, say, to a float in descent. Or by sheer iteration stopped dead in its track(s)—so that the micropause that alone permits a resolution of the image on screen (rather than just a spooling blur) is recapitulated at the scale of the action itself in arrest.

Cinema, *because it is first of all film* (its image units discrete, variable, plastic) can thereby study, whether by stalling or skimming, the effects it produces. So far, Epstein. His point is that only film can *think* this for us, imagine what it would look like to hover in freefall—as well as to commute instantaneously between places, or for the eye to zoom in upon the speaking countenance. Only film has this quality with regard to the quantifications of time—or revise that, historically: only film and, in the conjoint perspective of this essay, its evolved substrate in digital imaging as well (its units discrete, variable, electronic). Whatever intelligence accrues to the motion picture's optic mechanism can be found inherited, via sometimes extreme genetic modification, by the systems of electronic imaging—TV broadcast, portable disk playback, online streaming, etc. After Epstein, cinemachines proliferate—and within a lineage not just worth tracing but often delineated by given films, as was the case earlier, for instance, when Epstein's *Usher* rehearses previous ontologies of painting and photo portraiture through the fantastic rectangle (rather than oval) of his plot's own picture plane. Seeing as much is the beginning of an apparatus reading—where scrutiny lets the machinic intelligence dictate its own terms of interpretation.

A moment more, then, on the theoretical inferences that *come to mind* from the machinery of Epstein's Poe film. Every bit as unique to cinema (as posttheatrical) as is slow motion (via retardation of the image file) is cinema's capacity for double or triple tracking: the overprinting of one image on another in the filmic era, their interlacing now in computer editing. In that facial palimpsest of Madeleine Usher's dissociative episode, film stops rationing images one at a time, thereby altering the ratio of simultaneity and sequence. In many ways Epstein's practice, as well as its theoretical codification, bears a superficially close resemblance, at this point, to the pioneering work of psychologist Hugo Munsterberg, who saw filmic montage as quite directly evocative of mental states and their combinatory operations.[6] What is *psychological* for Munsterberg, however, is to become more strictly *cognitive* in Epstein. Screen editing, for Munsterberg, evokes the work of shifting and fading attention spans, flashes of memory, laminates of association, shocks of distraction, and so forth. In his response to the new medium, technique becomes immediately figurative. Yet Epstein's theoretical claims end up being far more extreme than this general theory of film's mental equivalents might suggest. As we've seen, his stress on film's perceptual (rather than apparitional) basis is more painstaking and exact than Munsterberg's—and more far-reaching. But also more deepgoing: more concerned with the medial support as such. Beneath its manifestation of motion, film's intellective traction depends on the essential stillness of the film strip, awaiting the arbitrary and variable nature of its imposed motion. If Munsterberg advances, by title, a theory of *The Photoplay*, Epstein's is at base an account of the play of photos—and their broader epistemological inferences.

Here is his most straightforward assertion to this (defining) effect: "Outside the viewing subject there is no movement, no flux, no life in the mosaics of light and shadow that the screen always displays as stills" (10)—"stills" that, of course, appear to us only as they are vanished into action, their separate image cells sprocketed past the aperture. Mutatis mutandis, so with perception at large—with mutability indeed its essence as well. If Munsterberg's psychopoetics of cinema sees the field of projection operating like the mind in working over the world both present to it and past, Epstein's more unflinching subjectivism understands film operating like the world per se, as much itself on screen as it can ever appear to us: the world in its being worked up, constructed in process, by the mental operation, its coherence and continuity lent only by the human sensorium (and thus so elusively different from Deleuze's Bergsonian sense of the world's ontological form, beyond subjectivity, revealed in and as image). Any localized "special effect" thus helps keep honest this tricking of the screen all told—even while addressing by association the "idealizing" mind in the changeable flow of phenomena. In *Usher*, all those lyric waverings, overlays, and slowings tend to circle round on their own basis to testify more directly than usual, in their very abuse of the (recently established) cinematic norm, to the segmental nature of the filmic spool, becoming a descriptive poetry of the photo-chronic transcript.

On this score, Epstein minces no words from the start about the chopped-up nature of the substrate, for the most "striking wonder" of the new machine is that it "transforms a discontinuity into a continuity" (7), each virtual snapshot snapped past fast enough to smooth out this illusion. It is then that the trace of photochemical exposure time is pulled into a different time frame altogether as the serial lurch of gesture and motion, rendered in parable by Usher at work on his sister's portrait. At which point it is clear, if typically invisible—or, in other words, thought for us by the machine—that time is merely an abstraction from succession, just as space is abstracted from the contiguity of objects. In this respect, cinema's function as an "annex" of the "brain" in its role as "the alleged center of intelligence" (65) is the wising up of perception: a model for acknowledging the relativity and interdependence of supposedly separate a priori conditions. Here is how film images "bear a subtle venom" that Epstein insists has been given "little attention" in regard to its "corrupting" force (7), which is—in precisely the medium's "philosophical" use—to poison reality's facile assumptions for us. Thus, "having taught us the unreality of both continuity and discontinuity, the cinematograph rather abruptly ushers us into the unreality of space-time" (25)—when any such localized temporality is in fact merely a function of discrete images in their timed spacings. Effect to this cause, mirage of this machination, all cinema—like all supposed reality—is, again, a "special effect" of perception.

Photogenesis

Apart from any such neuropsychology of vision, Epstein is better known, if often vaguely understood, for his englobing and elusive concept of *photogenie*.[7] Not until the "time-image" of Deleuze, perhaps, has an abstraction attracted so much citation without pinpointed explanation. Compared to this, even Alexandre Astruc's "camero stylo" is transparency itself, no pun intended: indicating the writing in shadow (against light)—rather than in ink—accomplished by camera angle and montage in the inscription of a screen statement. One problem in grappling, instead, with *photogenie* is inherited from its watered-down vernacular version in "photogenic," as a term for the camera-friendly face. It is also worth noting, however, that "photogenic drawing" was once the name for the light-produced image of photography: the flip side, in a sense, of the term's biological specification as a "light-producing" animal or insect, like a firefly. Light-inscribed and light-generating: what could be a more perfect account of the cinematic apparatus in the circuit of projection, whether photogrammatic or digital?

But Epstein is after something else: more like a photogenius, or genius loci, of the screen plane's aura in response, a transference subtly personified in order to evoke its cognate relation to the automatically induced operations—and "intelligence"—of embodied perception itself. The photogenic body is not the on-screen star's but that of a tangible corporeal investment that receives and processes the image in an immersive somatics of response. This logic points to the true subversive force of his 1946 *L'intelligence*, as it plays out a leveling materialism of perception tout court, first on screen, then as a clarifying point of vantage on the virtual impressions of "real" life. The body is understood, to speak anachronistically, as its own kind of data processor, converting discrete signals into continuous impressions just like film does. It makes the world up—pieces it together out of its own supposed intake. Embodied cognizance manufactures the image it seems directly to view, generates in part what it wants to think it merely registers. In this light, *photogenie* amounts to something more like the photo*genetic* than the photogenic correlate of this epistemological process.

Well beyond any etymological allusions in Epstein's own admittedly opaque coinage, it is perhaps useful to think of his signature term—or to let the filmic machine of cinema think it for us—as the genie of diegetic mirage. As such, it is sprung from the lamp of projection, its aperture rubbed lightly—continually but not continuously—by the file of photograms. This is a genie conjured in and for itself (as disembodied image) but also by and for us in our own combinatory and compressive somatic sensorium. Body art: but strictly sensorial before otherwise affective or emotively entailed.[8] That sensorial basis is this essay's stress, narrowing the somatic paradigm to the primacy of the perceptual. But make no mistake. The machinic model in these pages is not proposed as exhaustive. Yes, the motion picture makes manifold corporeal demands on the spectator, and doles out corporeal rewards in comparable measure. Who doesn't, so to speak, *feel this way* about movies? But the fact that the bodies moving on screen impress upon our own a whole range of impulses and affects, intensities and perturbations, needn't lead to our forgetting that, even though eyes are body parts in themselves, the projector lens isn't, nor is the screen organic in the same way either. Somatic response needn't translate to screen metaphor. Eyes and ears—those linked organs of perception, ocular and auditory—locate the first corporeal dimension involved in any mediated encounter with the "special effect" of screen motion. Yet the projected image doesn't have a body just because its effects are broadly somatic, let alone a skin just because it can tingle ours—or bring that of its actors closely into view. Even in the variable slow-motion throes of a gothic *photogenie* like that of Epstein's Poe film, whatever the frame rate, ours is the only flesh meant to creep.

Epstein's sense of cinema's own processual fabrication of screen movement from mobilized photographs should make that obvious. These are not bodily tissues in their rotated transparencies, nor, it bears repeating, are they palpably embodied when their shadows hit the screen. No need for a sweeping haptic metaphor for the way their induced affect embraces us as more-than-mere-viewers, nerved and braced in our seats. Epstein's work in *The Intelligence* depends on a more strenuous epistemology, as we've begun to appreciate, than any such somatography of viewing might suggest. By his reasoning at its most extreme, live bodies in action, quite apart from the foursquare space of projection, are in fact comparable, as atomistic congeries, to the piecemeal chain of photo imprints that propel their equivalent on-screen representations. The body, too, must be renewed from molecular interval to interval as a coherent construct. Epstein is thus instructively positioned between Bergson and Deleuze in regard to the latter's one foundational demurral from the former (and much earlier) French philosopher's disdain for cinema. For Bergson, notoriously, any sense of *durée*, of temporal continuity, was dubiously simulated, rather than captured and reproduced, by the new medium he rejected. Where time is a function of motion in Deleuze's sense of the movement image on screen, Bergson saw the ersatz continuum of screen event as a misleading fabrication. What Deleuze thought Bergson missed, however, was that the intermittence of the strip does nonetheless produce, in projection, images we can accept as cross sections of real temporality.

Indeed, in Deleuze's preliminary discussion of this issue (this issuance to motion) in *Cinema 1: The Movement-Image* (23–24), Epstein is adduced as chief authority on the point, yet from an earlier newspaper piece on Fernand Leger from 1923. No reference is made there, on Deleuze's part, to the more rigorous volume over a quarter of a century later that we've been concerned with, where the machine artifice of sequence is stressed in its intimate sync with "natural" vision (and its own abstracting idealities).[9] Instead, Deleuze is taken with Epstein's comparison not just of filmic camerawork in general, but of the single "shot" in particular, to a "cubist or simultaneist painting," an "open set" whose "surfaces are divided, trun-cated, decomposed, broken" (23), yet nonetheless cohering in a temporal gestalt where what is framed is instability itself—change compacted, time cross-sectioned and compressed. Deleuze, in effect, fuses Epstein and Bazin (the latter on the embalming and mummification, respectively, of time and change[10]) to counter Bergson's sense of a disintegrated continu-ity, with Deleuze stressing the way the spatial "mold" of the photogram undergoes transformative modulation on screen: the slice of frozen time having become, in the shot, a sample of unfurling duration.

This is just where Epstein's much later monograph on machinic intelli-gence might drive a clarifying wedge in this debate between the contested temporalities of Bergson and Deleuze. Epstein's claims for a machine-spurred thought on this score would, that is, intervene by insisting that embodied duration itself is only a stitched-together fiction not just in screen recognition but in everyday cognition: the product (because never other than a process) of molecular and even subatomic instabilities, psy-chic intermittences, and so forth. Even supposedly stable bodies are only constellations of invisible motion, while their duration, in movement or not, is constituted only by what we might call the invisible or cognitive-ly blurred gaps, the perpetual interruptions, overleapt by the fiction of presence in three-dimensional space. This is as much the case, there, as in the two-dimensional screen field—and in either case virtual through and through. Film itself, one level down from its imaged representation, is thus culture's ultimate mirror held up to nature. The discrete series of the image module on the film strip, spun past in material displacement and optical assimilation, is analogous to the whole cognized world, discontinuous at base, rather than concocting some suspicious falsification of that world. Only a continuing mystification can inoculate us against precisely this "venom." Put it that the cinematograph thinks for us the cellular, rather than just the celluloid, ensemble of perceptual experience. So it is that photogrammic shifts on the spun strip replay the firing of perceptual synapses in normal vision: evincing, thereby, screen motion's deep league with optical succession in the fitful subjective gestalt of any "world viewing." One result, as we'll find in turning shortly to Cavell on just that wording of the issue, is that any skepticism that the filmic mirage, together with the confidently beheld world, may each separately induce is indeed philosophically conjoined in the art(ifice) of cinema.[11]

The Vertical Mosaics of Photogram/mar

Concerning the collage model he summons, Epstein verges on a point he doesn't quite make, but that his own metaphor suggests—anticipating Rushdie's about the "dancing grain" of lost resolution. Each frame, we saw Epstein insist, is a variegated "mosaic" of light and shadow: a point all the clearer in the digital era, less figurative, about the composite pixel tiles of the image (rather than its emulsive filmic composite). But in his day, film was a linear mosaic as well, each unique field of light and dark in the single frame giving way to the recursive pure black of the frame line before yielding in turn to the next mottled image in automatized sequence. The optical collage of light and shadow in any still image becomes (as Deleuze quoted Epstein elsewhere to suggest) the quasi-cubist montage of succession itself, segment by differential segment, regardless of editing strategies the next level up. *Mosaic units in racing adjacency* thus underlie the prosaics of film movement before being adjusted for the visual poetics of tampered, amplified, and transmogrified vision in Epstein's own early practice—which on his account, as we know, only underscores the underlying: only confirms discontinuity in its oddest visible twists and blends.

It is no accident—in making a merely orthographic (rather than cinematographic) move from "truquage" to "trucage"—that all of this is just what Metz sums up as succinctly as possible in his description of the complex "tapestry" (674, rather than "mosaic") of such montage "connections." For only into the overall tricked weave of world representation—and precisely because of the technical options of its spatio-temporal illusionism—can the individual "special effect" be saliently (or invisibly) inserted. The base line is both the measure and the means of extravagance. Metz: "Each photogram is a photograph, but succeeds the preceding one only through the intervention of a 'blackness,' the duration of which is material for decision (and today has changed from the silent film). These photograms are themselves grouped into bundles (the 'shots'), whose concatenation creates a choice every time (straight cut, optical effect, etc.)" (674). And that "straight cut" is permitted (and figured as such in the material associations of its very name) only by the possibility of a discrete image slice between single frames. As is an "optical effect" like the cross-fade available only because of the laboratory occasion of superimposed frames. From the strip itself all innovation must be ripped.

As with the case of Metz after him, then, we may say that Epstein's is, in short, a theory of the photogram—yet ultimately a prescient theory of digital VFX as well. If film is a machine at large, it also depends on its derivative visual schemings and machinations. And if all film is a special effect, this exposed cause to any subsequent visual lyricism or optic subterfuge is at times made immanent and definitive. There is a kind of latent medium specification in Epstein's work, visual and critical alike, from which there is no reason to avert one's attention in order to rescue his more pungent body talk in the heady realm of *photogenie*. Nor is there reason not to come open-eyed and receptive, rather than metafilmically straitjacketed, to his own visual experiments. For it isn't just that Epstein, in his exploratory poetic filmmaking, graces the cinematographic plane with a new and layered strangeness, along with a set of specular and spectral new velocities and reversals. More important for philosophical uptake, as previous citations have meant to stress, he probes the cinematograph itself, the apparatus: bearing down on the wavering fabric of its own inherent phantasmagoria of loosened and fluid frames, no longer rocketed past as invariant sprocket speed.

As I hope this opening chapter has made plain by now, Epstein's partisan critical work in support of such experiment isn't some self-serving rhetoric to undergird his ingenuities. Rather, it points us to the underpinning fact of film on which this legendary practitioner knows, hands-on, his own visual investigations depend. At the editing table—at work, for instance, on his landmark *Usher* film—the essential mosaics of cinema, both rectangular and serial (the latter affording the possibility of the "cut" so integrally dependent, in Metz above, on the "bundled" photograms), take their sequential as well as in-frame shape: becoming, by turns, a palimpsest through superimposition; a moving framed portrait by trick insert; the haunting fall not of the titular House, in its sense of family lineage as well as architecture, but of its representative in Madeline Usher herself, through a slow-motion collapse reprised at different speeds. And so on. The "truquage" on which the cinematograph relies is the intrinsic linkage of discrete snapshot clarities whose laboratory manipulation could alone generate the optical dreamscape of Epstein's projection. In short, his theory isn't there to justify his practice; his practice requires just those constitutive filmic elements to which his philosophical writing thus justly attends—and by which it can be found widening out to the inferences of a far broader media archaeology, as well as human epistemology. Namely: an archaeology of sampled signals, compressive optic data, an intrinsically abridged continuum.

Compressive Vision

Where a writer like Hugo Munsterberg saw film operating in something like a partial power play of mind over matter, with the functions of attention, memory, imagination, and the like "impressed" on a concretely recorded world, Epstein, quite differently, and nearly half a century later, follows the express tenets of modern physics in taking filmic flicker and frameline elision as an evidentiary model for—rather than an exception to—the material operations of the waking mind as well as of the physical world whose phenomena it works to sort. This is the mind, or more accurately the brain, when understood as an inbuilt circuitry for the aggregation and synthesis of discontinuous impulses. Hence, a system of trigger mechanisms that are essentially binary at base.

We leapt ahead, early on, to the close of Epstein's volume, where his retrospective generalization bears with it an uncanny forecast as well; looking back to the Greeks and forward to unforeseen electronics, he signed on to the idea that "reality is but the harmony of Ideas and Numbers." If film has the intelligence of a machine, that is only because intelligence, human world processing, constitutes just such a machine to begin with, a protocomputer—or, in his late cryptic formulation, a network of "logarithmes sensoriels."[12] Evoked there is an organic calculus of cognition timed to the world's own intermittent infrastructure, including all the elisions and compressions of mental process—or, in terms closer to Munsterberg's psychology, its condensations and displacements. Such, then, are the measures rather than the mere means of perception in the cinemachines of motion capture. In Epstein's sense, the photo-genius of the screen—in its correlation with an embodied human mind, and emphasized thereby as computational as well as commutational—has two curious marginal dimensions as well. These carry us back, by one route, to the origins of photochemically generated images in photography—where in the evolution of camera technology, as it happens, the so-called binary logarithm does in fact equilibrate differences between focal lengths and exposure times at the algebraic basis of camera settings. The logarithmic trope also speeds us ahead, of course, to what we might well call the sensorial math of digital imaging, including the crucial "compression logarithm," otherwise known as the "logarithm operator" in "data range compression." A computational template thus emerges from precisely the voids and dead spots, true to the world's own, that are stitched over by the suturing in of consciousness to projected image. Just as one might choose to follow Friedrich Kittler in seeing the principle of intermittence rendering even the photographic film track—with its discrete toggle between on and off, here and gone—as a kind of differential operation well in advance of electronic binarity,[13] so one can see the kind of data compression enabled by the photogrammic track, with its compensatory perceptual infill, as an elemental procedure crucial to mediation in general across the evolution of its technical means.

This takes a minute to compass in its full historical sweep. Descended both from the optical toys of intermittence (the alternating flip of the thaumatrope, the spun slatted glimpses of the zoetrope) and from the subsequent microstaging of motion in chronophotography, cinema made—and smoothed—its flickering mark. The subsequent genealogical shift from the discontinuous serial image track to the bitmap transformations of digital image and editing only helps italicize how the history of the medium is the evolution of gaps, elisions, ellipses, compressions—all the way from backlit gram to LED-ignited granule, from cellular unit to digital fragment, picture cell to pixel (pic[ture] el[ement]). The mechanics of frame advance have given way to the dynamisms of frame refresh, alternation replaced by internal alteration. Attesting across all cases to a deep commonality in the primal binarism of on/off—visible, then gone—the abiding factor of *now here/now there* in the (logo/algo)rhythmic beat of sensation is phased across the optic limbo, the vanishing *now/here*, of the advancing in-between. As such, this phasing (in and out) is as true to photomechanical cinema as to the pixel morphs of digital image—with their microsecond switchings within (rather than between) image frames. And just as true, again via Epstein, as such ultimately compressive functions are to the human apprehension of duration itself in the lived world: always a synthesis keyed to the overriding of gaps.

Epstein may have in fact conjured for us a trajectory he never fully charts. Under his conceptual impetus, we may end up seeing the whole history of temporal media (at least of time-approximating plastic and now computerized art) as, in its truest shape, the history of compression per se: again, the generative illusion at the base of a "continuity" that remains, in fact, intermittent and elliptical. Even writing must typically discount the lacunae between lexemes that make possible its sematic continuum. Generative, yes, any such smoothing out of disjuncture, but one needs to be more specific in tracking the historical transformation, for screen media, from the photogram composite to the more literal "mosaic" of the pixel.[14] As Deleuze will be heard to insist in our next chapter, any account of image production needs its "genetic" determination. Or say: a recognition of the apparatus before the apparition. In filmic cinema, we can, of course, by an occasional distortion of normal screen pace, be made to see the increment itself (the photogram) in its directly projected trace function, be made to glimpse its transitional difference from an immediate precursor—a difference highlighted by negation, for instance, in the iterative freeze. Epstein capitalized on just such effects. When this mode of disclosure is translated to digital cinema, however, the sensorial "logarithms" are made manifest not (usually) at the binary level of the pixel sequence, still less at that of the algorithmic code that drives it, but in the more strictly associational epiphenomena of exactly that pic-celled (pic-elemented) shimmer—often remaining only tacit behind both the general artifice and the specific fracture of the CGI image—upon which the last two chapters will concentrate.

Historically contextualized, Epstein gives us a unique sneak preview of this in the whole circuit of his posited machinations for cinema and mind alike: a prescience all but unwitting. More than any other writer—in the mix of his own countermetaphysical thinking, with sensorial measures and metaphors for film drawn from math and physics—Epstein finds the intuitive terms for a medial revolution otherwise unforeseen in his day (and still only partially arrived, in ours, with the comparable thinking of a contemporary media theorist like Vilém Flusser). Tethered in Epstein's work, as we've seen, is a line of thought that bridges the filmic and the digital even from within his own monolithic concept of the screen machine, electric rather than electronic. On this note the coming chapters can bear one more postponed and embedded epigraph from literature, not this time from a magic realist like Rushdie, about the illusory cognitive magic that constitutes the real itself, but from a Romantic poem's penultimate line, evoking (here in translation) the whole audiovisual sensorium of human perception, or in other words:

The mind [l'esprit], that watchman made of ears and eyes, . . .

—Victor Hugo, "Written on the Pane of a Flemish Window" (1837)

In a famous clash between gifted literary theorists, Paul de Man chides Michael Riffaterre for missing what's really going on in—or, rather, emptied out from—that phrase's climactic distillation of the perceptual apparatus.[15] The poem's characterization (literally) of the mind, in this final personification, sets in after a fifteen-line series of discrepant audial and visual tropes, synesthetically cross-wired, each in description of a Flemish carillon tolling the passage of time, each administered in a transport of rhapsody by the first-person persona. All is focused by—and let's say (de) centered on—the mental idea of mind, or human spirit, experiencing the ringing signifiers of its own duration.

In this explicit phrasal interface between the mutual indetermination of mind and time, speaker and the belling of the hour, a philosophical thinker like Epstein (not just as poet but as audiovisual screen artist, and especially as media theorist) might have been quick to pick up on the way in which the metaphoric impact of the "watchman" trope is hardly self-contained. Indeed, its reverberation resembles the "venom" released by filmic artifice into the very concept of perception. In the figurative contamination at work in Hugo's densely metaphoric text, poetic language serves to realize, to materialize, the fact that mind (or "spirit" in French) is itself, according to de Man, a catachresis (that rare subclass of metaphor, like the "face" of a clock, or its "hands" for that matter): a figure of speech for which there is conventionally no literal alternative or anchor. The strained nature of the "watchman" trope, gender aside, for an audial as well as optical vigilance only exaggerates this ontological instability in figuring the mental apparatus of perception. As Epstein could later show on good evidence from theoretical physics, mind doesn't organize the cognitive signals of external stimuli by reconstructing the outer world's supposed integral coherence in an uninterrupted wedding of consciousness with duration, including time's perceived events and their entities. Instead, mind—like the so-called world, another sheer figure of speech, in turn, for the human being's perceptual field—is manifest, as film's revolutionary mechanism instructively enacts for us, only through an intermittence (both ontological and perceptual) that undermines all solidity in our "watchful" receipt of sense data, whether by "eyes" or "ears." Such is the "world viewed" that, for Epstein, is always and avowedly "subjective" on screen, "ideal," its pictured motion an accepted bridging of discontinuous frames: in short, a wholesale special effect. By analogy with which, as Epstein so dramatically implies back in that first epigraph, we are better ready to recognize all of sensorial reality as a kind of extracinematic trick.

Including time itself, in its interlock with mind. And if time can only be figured, not experienced, cinema offers its own fund of optic metaphors for any such effort. A striking contemporary turn in this circuit of technical association, though recovered and volatilized from the recreated scene of nineteenth-century photographic practice, comes into view at this pass in a prolonged transitional episode from Terence Davies's film *A Quiet Passion* (2016). Yet it is a fact less anomalous than it may at first seem, in recent narrative cinema, that the most concerted single screen attempt to mediate, however obliquely, the transition between photochemical and digital process appears in this "heritage film" context: not in some movie-about-moviemaking or some knowing sci-fi episode, but in an elegiac return to the predecessor of each medium alike in the fixed frames of photography. And marginalized there, at that, in its graphic emphasis, by the philosophically freighted scene of writing and recitation in a film of literary biography, where inscription is more urgently verbal than visual.

Compressed Time

The iterated transmedial moment whose tampered-with and internally laminated apparatus we're about to "read" offers an impacted node of disclosure in regard not just to a single poet's obsession with time and mortality, but to the metahistory of an automatic imaging lifted from time. With an unexpected twist, this instance of such arrest is accomplished as follows—operating as much by elided transition as does the present subhead in phonetic process: "Compress(ed)Time." At an early turning point in Davies's typically unconventional "biopic" of Emily Dickinson, the ongoing narrative is suspended—just after a sound-bridge recitation (in voiceover) of a poem in which the gravesite of a precipitous death is approached more quickly than it can be returned from by the shaken mourner. In the wake of this funerary note, plot developments are halted for what we expect to be a fixed visual record of the story's main participants: a fourfold set of family photographs taken from rigid poses, one after the other, by a photographer ducking behind his black-out curtain as the screen gives way, by reverse shot, to the stiff principles standing against a larger black drop cloth across the room. But the figures are initially framed, as if through the photographer's lens, from too great a distance for the logic of composition. It is at this point (anachronistically enough) that one smooth and patient tracking shot after another—four times over, and of approximately fifteen seconds each in duration—serves to close in on these stationed bodies until the still camera's frame can exclude everything of the far wall but the neutral background of hung cloth. At which point we cut to the next photo subject—not on the familiar magnesium flash of a recorded daguerreotype pose, but simply by the cue of halted and stabilized camera action. It isn't a case of cinema animating a photograph, but, in reverse, of gradual cinematic motion studying the previous historical condition of photography: long before any allowable movement in, let alone of, the frame.

But that is the least of it—in this hypertrophic registration—where spatial traverse is merely the armature of an overarching *trucage*. The "inward" movement imposed by the mobile cinematic, rather than photographic, camera is in the other sense a motion *forward*: temporal more than spatial. For in the midst of this very trajectory of approach by the weightless tracking shot, zeroing in on one present body after another, a subtle but decisive digital morphing—almost hallucinatory at first— zeroes out the present image and ages each face in fading stages before our eyes. Being photographed isn't just dying away from one present moment, but fading off into the serial vanishing of a life to come—as if each and every portrait anticipated the contemporaneous nineteenth century craze, especially in America, for an eventual mortuary imaging of the beloved dead. These four transfiguring "shots," then, are each a memento mori not just by default—a past never again to be recaptured— but by the visible corporeal inscription of an always ephemeral and here optically elided future.

Until a new plateau has been reached with the completion of the four portraits. At which point, as the viewer soon learns, the unearthly effect is implicitly returned to narrative sequence. For it is only as plot starts up again that we realize how these photos have translated the young Emily and her family to the point, in relative middle age, when they can be replaced by new actors for their subsequent roles in the main storyline, at least two thirds of it remaining. But until that rebooting of plot after this interlude of temporal adjustment, there is only the isolated mystery— and intelligence—of optical transmediation. Exposed thereby—when ballasted again by narrative (and here calling up that initial citation from Epstein on the cinematic "special effect")—is the logic of cinema's a priori conditions on their necessarily less-than-solid footing. Evinced in this way is the intellective machine's role in "providing the product of space and time variables," with the result (again) that the tricked nature of "cinematographic reality is therefore essentially the idea of a complete mode of location" (Epstein, 104). Put it that film opens a photographed object to twin coordinates: *placing* it in narrative time. Screen bodies, and never more obviously than in Davies's overt manipulation, find their unrooted presence mapped as a shifting locus on the double axes of time and space—and accelerated in Davies's case for a tunnel vision not just biographical but media-archaeological.

The drive of cinema as postphotographic technology—in "projecting" beyond the apparatus (and the moment) of mere chemical arrest—serves in this case, by high-tech digital finesse, to orchestrate the techniques of film's own outmoding in a tacit rehearsal of certain abiding figures for media evolution. If photography offers the death of change, and cinema unfolds the past in its own becoming-again, in this third case of electronic remodeling—rather than, respectively, time embalmed or change mummified, in either of those famous figurations from Bazin—we find, instead, *duration distilled*: the fast-forward of the body itself under both temporal duress and its serial impress. This is the body, not its actions or gestures, in computerized mutation—but true to itself nevertheless, at least in Epstein's subversive (venomous) sense: a body never as molecularly stabilized as it looks. Here, we may say, is one more philosophical event of machine thought, of cinema thinking, brought to view in the shot's threefold lamination of captured mechanical image, spatial qua temporal advance, and metanarrative compression in both narrative and digital terms. Before plot is reengaged—and beyond one's potential sense of the sequence as offering, in precis, the generic *biopic* in a strictly optical epitome (the *life-image*, so to say)—the cinemachine, in extending beyond its photographic origins, has at the same time borne in on its own technological foreclosure. The tracking shot has left the image track behind for the image file, offering, within its accelerated somatic depiction, an unmistakably digitized version of *time framed*. And this, we note, in all its Epsteinian ontological implications: the body as much mutated from within by cellular replacement over lived time as is the electronic image field refashioned from microsecond to microsecond. In its engineering of the postfilmic image, computerized cinematic intelligence thus continues to execute its own visual ruminations—where exemplary narrative ruptures, in a mode of the technological uncanny, are uniquely prone to help analyze in action what they evoke.[16] Certainly, from amidst the current era of rampant digital VFX, the radically backdated machinic alchemy at this turn of Davies's 2016 film about the mid-1800s—extrapolating from the first automated image to the latest in trick electronics—can be seen, in its operational intelligence, to be *thinking out* the manifested temporal substrate of the human body, and its imaging, for and before us as we watch.

So let me sum up, as succinctly as possible, what it is about Epstein's central and titular insight, made available in its new translation, that has served in part to sponsor and orient this essay on cinemachines. At bottom, at base, the essential intelligence of the machine as he educes it, indeed its genius, is to outwit the intrinsic falsity of its own kinesis. It accomplishes this not by the unimpeded conveyance of figures in motion but by inventing new figurations for motion itself: slow, fast, suspended, overlapped, reversed, and otherwise warped, torqued, and contorted. Or, now, electronically morphed. And above all—because below or beneath any one velocity or direction—definitively intermittent. Figures for motion itself, yes—and, in turn, for the time it takes. Or even, as just seen, for the abstracted speed of time itself. In such eccentric effects as superimposition or altered motion, "special" to the medium, the cinematograph's disguised constituents in Epstein's day (literally masked in jagged series by the blinkering rotation of the Maltese cross) stand revealed in deviation—as well as derivation—from their illusory serial norm. As does obtruded pixelation since then, vis-à-vis the supposed holistic image. Apparatus reading plugs as directly as possible into any and all such materialized "intelligence" briefings.

Our latest exemplum one more time, then. For what we see in Davies's eerie transitional effect can *only* be read—in its legible break from all visual or dramatic setting, if not from themes of time and death. It is in this way, alone, that the episode's preternatural reflex of "motion-picture" technology pries open in its gliding train a broad path of media archaeology. Filmic cinema moves pictures; digital pictures move themselves around from within. Change in frame, at the level of the substrate, supplants mere interchange. And the illusion of somatic transformation offers a unique test case in the matter of screen presence. The blur of superimposition—film is, after all, essentially filmy—finds a classic instance of exposed bodily transparency in the screen figuration, with its depthless surface, by which Dr. Jekyll becomes Mr. Hyde through a serial palimpsest of overlays in Rouben Mamoulian's 1931 version of the story. No more than those moving horses three decades before at the kinetoscope display in the Norris novel, it all remains "nothun but a drick." Coming to the fore half a century later than Mamoulian's film, however, and mobilized over three decades later yet by Davies, the process of computer morphing is instead internal to the image plane: a pic-cellular reconstitution. Linked all

the way back in Davies's episode to the fixed frame of precinematic photography, the scene's smooth double shift of camera distance and image
plane in tandem thus traces a gradual medial transformation deeper, in
technological cause, than any perceptible *effect*.

This sense of what cinema runs on, in the phases of its evolution,
will continue to give us plenty to go on as we close in for such readings
of individual narrative moments in the move from filmic to digital mediation. As the earlier epigraph from Rushdie makes plain by inference,
turning as it does on the issue of molecular integration in screen fidelity,
there persists a kind of scalar difference in mediation—one that will be
tracked in the pages to come—that helps distinguish the technological
from the ontological, even within the effort of a broad existential analogy
like Rushdie's for the illusory underlay of the real. For him, the "dancing
grain" of light and shadow on screen, rather than the entrainment of its
flickering single frames on the strip, exposes illusion's false bottom. This
difference locates those interwoven scales of image distribution—the mosaic luster of the single speckled frame, the mosaic clustering of one frame
after another in their rolling (even when no longer spooling) aggregate—
that cross between platforms and substrates at various pressure points of
optic resolution and coherence in the history of motorized screen motion.
With this chapter's subtitle in mind again, there is, theorizations aside,
no getting past the apparatus. Nor, when registered, does it speak only for
itself. This is the engrained double valence of apparatus reading. One can
not only read *it*, the machinic source, but read *with it*. One enters, thereby,
an implied narrative zone through the parameters of exactly such medial
support: as, just now, in our optical access to the force field of mortal eva-
nescence in Dickinson's life and verse—emblemized by Davies's elliptical
trucage of aging itself. Especially in the mode of certain sci-fi terms that
will come to preoccupy the latter half of this essay, we may well say, after
Epstein, that cinema continues to show forth, not just as all trick, all
"special effect" (in the world's true image), but as the artificial intelligence
that helps conceptualize the fabrications of our own "watchman" mind:
that cognition "made of ears and eyes"—whose apparatus is often invited
to meet the screen's halfway.

2 *Production Notes*

TECH SPECS

IN THE ROUTINE SENSE OF A SCREEN PROGRAM OR BROCHURE, PRODUCTION NOTES OFTEN include, of course, various details (and credit lines) regarding the component properties of screen technique. But how to note, to assess, the productivity of this technology, of the medium itself, in the narratives thus generated? That's the real question behind this book's *essaying* of an analytic method. Chapter titles are phrased to evoke, in shadow or counterpoint, the so-called publicity machine of marketing and exhibition in the dissemination of cinema's commercial products: advance media buzz, sneak previews, online or DVD featurettes, retro billings, festivals, press reviews, and the like. The intent is not so much ironic as icono*graphic* and media-archaeological. It concerns the machine legacy of the cinematograph down through its computerized remaking. Discussion thus looks beneath the "industry" sense of such mainstream lingo to what is in fact streamed as cinematic in the first place by the shifting means of industrial projection. This involves an apparatus variably geared for everything from an original 16 photo-frames per second through a standard 24 to the digital breakthrough of 120 fps (this last phenomenon explored shortly), including both 2- and 3-D formats in uneven phases of experimentation along the way. And the scrutiny called up involves, in turn, the narrative potential maximized by these conditions of the apparatus when made not just manifest but pointed.

Such emphases are the medium's technical "assertions" (Cavell's term, to follow) rather than mere assumptions. On the occasion of their emergence, we find cinematic artifacts annotating from within their own manufacture—glossing, amid the often high-gloss sheen and shimmer, the whole *trick* (Epstein, later Metz) of screen's virtual spaces and agents. Analytic stress in this chapter, and deliberately by contrast with its narrower publicity sense, falls not on the spotlighted selling points featured in the boasted "production values" of press kits—or so-called media kits—but, instead, on pressure points of the medium itself in its own productive functions. Within the spectacle, its technical specifications—and these at one with their narrative implementations. To be sure, that's what the 1946 Epstein argument has already previewed for us in light of the director's experimental screen work. In practice as well as proposition, Epstein's is a genuine *hypo*thesis: looking beneath the moving image to unearth the technics of the medium—and to speculate on, by activating, its definitive specular manifestations. Definitive because deviant: slowed, liquefied, overlain, unraveled. In all this, his own "scientific" orientation might also have looked back before midcentury physics to the modern science of signs as well. It's clear enough how his book summons higher mathematics, in addition to biophysics, in closing the gap between machinic intelligence and the very sensorium of human cognition that the cinematograph can seem at times to anatomize. To complement this extrafilmic perspective in certain unexpected ways, he could have returned to the ontological semiotics of Charles Saunders Peirce as well as, which he did, to the phenomenology of Henri Bergson. We'll make that return to Peirce for him.

Epstein, as we know, stresses the synthesizing work of the mind in its assimilation of discrete signals as no more than the representation (or interpretation) of coherent objects, and thus as subjective composites rather than freestanding entities and presences. Within their processing by the sensorium, these are "ideal" objects maintained in varying relationships from moment to moment. To exaggerate only slightly: the world comes to us, as projected by us, from stilled data animated in, over, and *as* time. For Epstein's emphasis on mathematically determined physical laws that condition the surmise of existent objects and the intervals of their notice—in other words, the mere *probability* of their image in front of us—one may begin to substitute the dimension of "potentiality" in Peirce. This is the inherent possibility of any "perceptual hypothesis" (termed *firstness*) in any categorical understanding or "interpretation" (*thirdness*) by which, in between, the "actual" (*secondness*) is manifest to the mind as sign.

Yet if there are "uneven developments," as mentioned above, in screen as well as broader industrial technologies, so are there in image theory. It may seem odd, in an essay on medium and method, that we need to take two steps back (to Peircean philosophy and classic film theory, Epstein through Metz) to make the necessary step forward into a pertinent New Media framework for cinematic effects on the narrative screen. Back to predigital production altogether, that is, fully apprehended in its determining base—so as to go forward, via the techniques of experimental video developed long since the initial computer revolution, to their own latest incorporation into cinematic process. Back to the likes of Stanley Cavell's film-philosophy here, in other words, in order to mitigate the rigorously postcinematic emphasis represented by the approach (via Peirce) of a media theorist like Mark B. N. Hansen. For it does seem, in Hansen's polemic, that the technical perspective best disposed to register the deep impact of digital New Media on narrative cinema parts company too fully with the long tradition of fabricated screen motion from which pixelation itself descends. That is what an archaeology of screen production needs first of all to note: the productivity of imaged motion itself from the always-intermittent ground up. Here is where archaeology can intercept a more obvious technological genealogy down through game imagery and avant-garde digital video.

As applied by Hansen to digital imaging, not at its advent but in its latest experimental instances, Peirce's approach helps to locate the "postperceptual image" that Hansen identifies as a kind of subliminal pixel activity detached from all perceived screen "phenomena" other than imaging itself in process.[1] In the broadest terms, for Hansen, Peirce serves to dismantle the difference between presence and representation, ontology and phenomenology, by insisting that nothing comes to us except as an index (or sign) of itself. Shades of Bergson here: the world constituted as image. And, in fact, the rescinded distinction involved in this line of thought, as Hansen shows, would complicate, if not raze at a single stroke, Bergson's objection to duration on screen as being only a manufactured rather than a lived continuum. We might think of it—and be helped to do so by the "intelligence" of cinemachinery—this way: time emerging in its own right as never anything but a function of thirdness, an abstraction. In the projection of a motion picture strip, speeding over its own discrete fixed stills, differential impressions come first, whatever object in motion may be impressing this sense of change upon us (secondness). But just here one might wish to stand back from Hansen's New Media orientation for the long view of firstness in the thrown light of the twentieth century's evolving cinemachines. One effect of this would be to fill in a certain blank between the Bergson-Deleuze lineage and Hansen's own move to twenty-first century digital mediation in its nonnarrative form: a blank that is also a transition in materiality and its platforms capable of shedding light, from within the sea changes of narrative cinema, on the eclipse of the filmic by the digital—as well as on recent subordinations of image study at large to the domain of pixel counterplay.

Though Hansen chooses the contemporary glitch aesthetic of "datamoshing" in experimental video to illustrate not just the postcinematic but the "post-perceptual" image, it is also the typical subperceptible stratum of the cinematic medium, whether filmic or digital, that is capable at times of the same foregrounded if elusive firstness. This is made most obvious, perhaps, in the narrative bewitching of the glitch, its preternatural narrativization, in the coming VFX curation of the last two chapters.[2] Normed into general imperceptibility, but sometimes bursting forth, what comes through in such optic episodes—related to the fact of stasis itself as basis in filmic cinema—is the motoring pixel binarism of its digital successor: each a variant of the on/off dialectic. For well short of glitch video, it is nevertheless often the case that the very fabric of attention in narrative cinema, together with its sensory resonance in the viewer's body, can be snagged by a sudden fraying of either the photogram train or the digital interlace. Everyone can think of examples—if not quite what to think of them from one case to the next.

Ground Zero?

So a question remains that might help probe a vexed common denominator between celluloid and digital cinema. It is this: what can be salvaged from Hansen's charge of "catastrophic reduction" in the uptake of Peirce by Deleuze? In this essay on "Algorithmic Sensibility," Hansen's objection is clear: "Deleuze's erroneous accusation regarding the limit of Peirce's thought ... results in Deleuze's postulation of a fourth category—Zeroness—that would lie beneath the three Peircean categories and, in particular, would come before Firstness." But isn't the postulation empirically (or say intuitively) justified, even if not logically necessary? Quoting Deleuze, in building on the point about the cubist accumulation of the image we saw him borrow from Epstein in chapter 2: "The perception-image will thus be like a degree zero in the deduction which is carried out as a function of the movement-image: there will be a 'zeroness' before Peirce's firstness" (*The Time-Image*, 32). This is only to say that there will be the conditions of perception on screen before perceived movement. Hansen may rightly object, on fundamental semiotic grounds, that firstness isn't an image at all, a perception, but rather a "perceptual hypothesis" that includes its own possibility, and that this vanquishes any need for "zeroness." But not the need for its recognized material constituents. The latter is what Deleuze elsewhere calls, in regard to differential frame cells on the celluloid strip, the "gaseous state" of a sensory-motor imaging not yet divided into action, reaction, and the rest. This, in the next paragraph from the one Hansen has quoted, is the realm of the "engramme"—or "photogramme," a constituent, as Deleuze clarifies by appositive in the glossary to volume 1: "not to be confused with a photo" (*The Movement-Image*, 217). Named there, in alternating fashion, is the substrate of firstness in both its inherent zeroing out of movement in discrete seriality and as the condition of all such perceived screen motion in latent fluctuation.

Not "zeroness," then, but perception minus one: "the genetic sign or the gaseous state of perception" (32), as amplified for the glossary in terms almost identical to Epstein's. For Deleuze stresses there "the genetic element of the perception-image"—and does indeed mean elemental unit, not just feature—"inseparable as such from certain dynamisms (immobilization, vibration, flickering, sweep, repetition, acceleration, deceleration, etc.)" Movement and its figuration of time depend on a perception that depends in turn on the machinic strip and its spun plasticity, but this is a medial first cause that is forgotten on screen, and by Deleuze himself for the most part, in the generated movement of bodies in action. It is thus a theoretical irony of Deleuze's focus in the two-volume commentary on cinema that its premise is so seldom invoked, and that its bearing on Bergson's critique of cinema so dismissively minimized. What Deleuze thinks has gone missing in Peirce, over Hansen's studied objections, goes mostly missing in Deleuze's own subsequent explorations. In his later narrative readings, that is, Deleuze downplays the very substrate that his philosophy had insisted on. He settles instead for what is "materialized," made "immanent"—in what we might call his neo-Peircean *semioptics*.

This avoidance will here be avoided. The need to distill what we can take as given about the apparatus, at the machinic level of its "specialized" projective effect, has indeed been the motive for bringing Epstein's cinephilia into confrontation with New Media theory across the vexed terrain of film-philosophy, where the hyphen may mark an internal tug-of-war between broad ontological claims and the pushback, or uprush, of filmic materiality. Whatever Deleuze got wrong, then, about firstness in Peirce, he got briefly right about first causes concerning his particular semiosis of choice in the screen image (as did Bergson too): movement-minus-one in its dynamized particles, whether engram or algorithmic blip, flickering cell or reticulated pixel. The fact that in either case you don't see, but only see *with*, this cinema-particular (and optically particulate) facet of manifestation is precisely what lets the firstness of potentialized perception come through as the initiatory work of semiosis, of signification. The engram (photogram) isn't a functional signifier all by itself, any more than is a phoneme in language. But, in another terminology famous from Peirce, the iconicity of the screen image is at the same time an index, a foregrounded material trace, not of the recorded world so much as of the unseen separate frames that compose its image in compacted series.[3] So that when Hansen as New Media theorist generalizes about firstness as offering "nothing more nor less than a means for liberating the image—the cinematic image included—from its overdetermination by the institution of cinema" (and this by its "extrusion . . . from the domain of the phenomenal") he is referencing an "extruded" pixelation that is functionally expelled from the bounds, and manifest labors, of representation. Digital process is banished, in this sense, from any resolved image. He has thus marked off a terrain quite separate from the purpose of this essay, which has set itself to study, instead, the differentiae of the image, its bits and pieces, precisely as determined by a narrative cinema that cannot at the same time deny or elide entirely their contributory rhythms and irruptions. Whereas Hansen sees experimental video as the "liberation" of digital mediality at the "post-perceptual" level, I find such medial inferences already freed to make their roughening mark on the phenomenal image of screen fictions. Here is an "extrusion" of the substrate in exactly the other sense from Hansen's—not an exclusion but an irruption—to be called "assertion" as we turn next to Cavell.

The foregoing theoretical divide should explain what I meant at the start, in reviewing provocations for this essay, in suggesting that the philosophical excitement and technological precision of New Media theory often minimize any incitement to a comparable reading of digitized narrative cinema. Yet wedding attention to the mutations of pixel vision, when called for in response to a given video artifact, requires no summary divorce from cinematic narrative, nor any immediate recourse to the category of "postcinema." In this sense, well this side of any "post-perceptual image," the so-called postcinematic image even within narrative cinema—as manifest, for instance, in the "expressed" pixel fritz that variously reappears in the screenings of the coming VFX roster—takes us to a *level of mediality* comparable to the precinematic (that is, subcinematic) molecularization of the photogram chain, its gaseous "genetic" base (in Deleuze's metaphor again). In the terms of a machinic "intelligence," proposed thereby is an *understanding* of the manifest image only by the recognition of what is *standing under* it in manufacture. In advance of all image, and in the very advancing of it, there is the generative process of *imaging*. This is where the primary intelligence of the machine must first of all "interpret" the continuum from its fundamental disjunctions, frame per (and contra) frame. And this is the case whether that vanishing frame is unified and photochemical—or already in composite motion, as a digital mosaic, from within its electronic patterning. Here, in short, to speak almost paradoxically, is where mediality, then or now, must stand its shifting ground in narrative representation.

"Assertions in Technique": Between Medium and Means

It is time, then, to bring the author of *New Philosophy for New Media* (Hansen) into conversation with some previous philosophy for the older screen medium.[4] To this approach, Cavell's work is sometimes resistant at one level, that of the material support, but not always—and sometimes seriously intriguing, especially in that chapter of *The World Viewed* called "Assertions in Technique." But the technical anomalies that interest Cavell there, as they and other such deviances were engaged by Epstein before him, come into rhetorical "assertion" for Cavell only against the backdrop of a cinematographic norm—whereas, for Epstein, these aberrations isolate and define the medium's essence from within the typically rationalized flow of world pictures. It is in this respect that the sketchily evoked "sensorial logarithms" of Epstein—encountered in the full compressive logic of their model, turning as it does on the artificial bridging of intermittence—could be brought into useful comparison with Cavell's abiding problematic of skepticism. For it is there that suspended disbelief about screen illusion might be thought to train us in the readier acceptance of the lurking fractures and voids that characterize, off-screen too, the discontinuous and potentially unnerving nature of the perceived world. And of our "subjection" to and before it as cognitive agents.

At the University of Chicago's Center for Teaching in 2017, a symposium on the conjoint teaching of film and philosophy included a circulated paper by philosopher James Conant, a onetime student of Cavell's, that is, despite the "Ontology" in its title, actually less insistent than Bazin on the material valence of the indexical imprint.[5] Now, and fair enough, Conant's understandable purpose, as preceded in print by Victor Perkins (a writer also important for Cavell), is the effort to separate—within what Conant calls "photographic narrative film"—the medium as such, or more to the point the medium qua aesthetic vehicle, from its sheer "material substrate."[6] Here, Conant is certainly right to stress how, photographic though it is, a movie, "in order for it to become a movie," must employ "further means for defeating this default ontology of the photographic image, in order to introduce the requisite ontological divide between the world of the viewer of the movie and the world of the movie." The essential means of "defeat," however, begin in precisely the transfer of photographic imprint to transparent backlit photogram in the underlying plastic matter at work in any transmission of the projected image: the serial infrastructure of motion itself. The defeat of this is crucial, but not total, I would add, not invulnerable to resurgence: always liable, varying Cavell, to reassertion—as if by way, again, of a return of the optical suppressed. We may say that such machinic functions come to recognition as something like the ontological unconscious of machinic "intelligence."

When Cavell famously defines the movies as a "succession of automatic world projections,"[7] his main claim, in the play between automatism and world, is clear enough. Call it manifestation via machination. But "succession," the more vexed term, happens at two levels: the first minimized by Cavell (as by Deleuze at this same period, though in neither case excluded) but stressed, of course, in Epstein before them. On the material level, there is the tracked path by which mere stills *succeed in making motion pictures*. Gone but not always forgotten on screen, their service is brought by design to the surface of narrative in certain filmic moments that, at the phenomenal level, can thus be found to philosophize their own process, whether, just for example, by overt freeze-frame disclosure or, in an analogous stasis, by frame-filling lockdown on a single diegetic photo.[8]

Freeze frames (triumphant in Truffaut), along with slow motion (legendary in Kurosawa), come in for the bulk of comment in "Assertions in Technique," splendidly discriminated in their aesthetic force from film to film. For Cavell, though, neither strip nor its activation as image track locates the "automatism," still less the "succession," at the relevant level indicated by his subtitle, *Reflections on the Ontology of Film*, where that benchmark philosophical term suggests, in its usual doubleness, both the being of film and the study thereof, say its technology and its science. In Cavell's usage, neither sense of strictly plastic succession points back to the moment of traced capture rather than its potential captivation for the viewer of its displayed world. In "More of the World Viewed," appended a decade later to the enlarged edition of his 1971 philosophical meditation, Cavell wants to make it further clear that cinema (he could still call it film), though based in photography, is not a projected record but rather a projection from the ground up, wherein "any role reality has played is not that of having been recorded" (183)—but rather of having been evoked by the configuration of camera angles and montage. Film does not record a space or event in the world whose site you can revisit, and thereby trust in that way, take on faith; it doesn't capture a segment of *the* world in space or time, but rather projects *a* world (itself sliced up, constitutively piecemeal) whose nature, to put it crudely, you take on faith.

Since Cavell wrote, and long since the films that counted for him, the fact that cinema is not a recording but a projection may seem all the clearer when it is no longer film at all, especially (and markedly) when infiltrated by so-called computer-generated imaging (CGI): in one subset of Pierce's semiotic terms, the irruption of pure icon without indexed objective record. This is just what the neo-Peircean Deleuze neared the end of his life by explicitly querying in his second film book: wondering, as noted earlier, whether what the French call the "numeric" image of computerization might do to change cinema fundamentally. If, according to Cavell's deepest logic, this digital turn might be said only to enhance cinema's antiskeptical exercise in conviction for the invested viewer, it doesn't at the same time remove—as a good deal of recent writing might otherwise suggest—precisely those ontological questions about automatism and projection so powerfully knotted up in Cavell's proper insistence on cinema's (former) photographic basis.

But does this "basis" constitute film's onetime *medium*, and if not, why not? Are the cinemachines—what he calls the "machines of magic" (145), and precisely in connection with their "technique"—not rightly the place to anchor any definition of the medium? In unpacking his idea of cinema as "world viewed," Cavell does allow that "succession" is a factor that "includes the various degrees of motion in moving pictures: both "the motion depicted" and "the current of successive frames in depicting it" (72–73)—the "current," as it were, that makes for the screen present. By contrast, in clarification of "automatic," he has gone back to photochemical origins, since this term for him "emphasizes the mechanical fact of photography, in particular the absence of the human hand in forming these objects." But it is the second-degree automatism of succession itself, first on the strip, then as edited track, that is the crux of "world projections" (plural) on screen. Cavell is scarcely inclined to deny this, but the question remains whether this crux is medial or just mechanical: "One necessity of movies is that the thread of film itself be drawn across light" (142). But, in regard to this plastic "thread," a question of Cavell's immediately follows, and ours from it: "Is this a possibility of some medium of film?" Of *some* medium? One among several? Or, rather, of something we might right want to call *the* medium of film? Cavell actually thinks the latter, at least in certain cases, or seems to, as when shots of immobility in the "epilogue" of Antonioni's *Eclipse*, for instance, put us in mind of the "patience" required of succession itself on the strip, frame after frame, to automatize such fixity. This is a striking moment in Cavell's account, where the narrative thread sends us directly back to the "thread of film" (142) in its felt alternative (such is his point) to the sheer iterations of a freeze frame. For "depicted motionlessness feels and looks different from motionless depiction" (142). This gravitation to fixity in Antonioni, a stalling of camera and actor alike, is very much in the spirit of Epstein's thinking: a negative realization for one of film's more assertive technical options (the freeze) that, even when the overt technical tampering is avoided, actually returns us to the paradoxical shifting bedrock of its own possibility in the photogram chain.

And returns us, therefore, to something like medial "acknowledgment," one of Cavell's key terms across many philosophical registers, from Shake-speare to screwball comedy. Like much else in this engrossing chapter on "Assertions in Technique," however, its title powerfully (whether or not in-tentionally) equivocates. With its choice of preposition, it seems to evoke what might be asserted *about* the filmic medium by such exertions (and expressions) of its technical basis—as opposed, say, to mere "assertions *of* technique" for their own signifying sake, or sense. Yet it's no accident that six chapters separate this late one from "The Medium and Media of Film." Nothing about mediation can finally, for Cavell, be reduced, whether "assertive" or not, to the technological substrate of spooled celluloid and its edited "succession." To vary the intervening chapter title, "The Camera's Implication," with its own double sense of inference and complicity, there is no notion in Cavell that the medium should depend necessarily on the strip's implication, whether passively entailed or by active intimation.

In Cavell's claim about the nature of mediation behind the screen's "world view," he is responding initially to Panofsky's isolation, for the art of cinema, of certain "unique and specific possibilities of the new medium" (31). These "possibilities" are not necessarily technical ingredients, in their gradient linear form as celluloid frames, and in any case are summed too quickly, according to Cavell's paraphrase, "as the dynamization of space and the spatialization of time" (31). Realizing that more "specificity" will be required, Cavell concentrates at this point on Panofsky's plural noun instead. Such "possibilities" are factored in only if they *count* aesthetically, from case to case. And what would "give significance" in a particular nar-rative case is not a given. So "possibilities" cannot be known in advance, but only glimpsed in emergence from film to film.[9] Indeed, insisting that the full "possibilities" of a medium cannot be known ahead of its local achievements may seem to suggest that the medium is realized, or actual-ized, differently from film to film, rather than just manipulated differently.

Again the slippery logic of the genitive seems pertinent. The "possibilities of the medium" is a concept as well as a phrase that can take medium as its object, waiting for various potentiations (as in a grammar like "the elements of film"). Alternatively, the suggestion may be that the medium can be defined (the so-called equative genitive) only by its own possibilities (as in the "powers of film") whenever a technical condition is made to signify, given significance. This isn't circular reasoning, but it separates the issue of "unique and specific" not just from the category of manifest properties but from that of underlying components, present to representation even when not visibly implemented by it. Or have it that that sticking point of "possibilities" (the full range of their potential, say, in a neo-Peircean hypothetical firstness) remains detached from what one tends to call "conditions of possibility" (and for which Deleuze felt the need for identifying a zero degree). In an expanded and necessarily wordy paraphrase, this seems the gist of Cavell's logic, at least up to a point: medial conditions, however defined, make possible whatever potential assertions of specific properties can be made significant as technique. But Cavell's terminological point is ultimately narrower and more surprising yet. Rather than media creating possibilities, possibilities create media. This is a truly extreme claim: "The discovery of a new possibility is the discovery of a new medium" (32)—by which he must mean a specific means of communication. Luckily, helpfully, his insights mostly tack well this side of a position so hard to implement in any material terms. It is the counterpremise of this essay, then, that there must be something short of the open standard of "possibility"—in locating mediality—that would have to do with the inbred potential of the filmic system.[10] Or call it the difference between aesthetic possibility and medial (because technical) *provision*. Where two of Cavell's key terms—"automatism" and "succession"—have achieved, as if in the etymological sense, an *ostentatious* recent enhancement.

Halftime at High Speed

When Cavell departs from Panofsky's overgeneralized sense of cinematic possibilities as comprised by "the dynamization of space and the spatialization of time," there is no explicit thought given to the space/time ratios of millimeters and microseconds on speeding strip or "thread"—and none implicit in respect to the subsequent (unforeseen by him in 1971) speeds of computerized pixel array. Staying with Cavell's original terms for a moment longer, we discover ourselves on untrodden, though not necessarily entirely uncharted, ground. A certain byplay in Cavell's thought between material property and medial technique, elsewhere between actualized possibility and significance, should still apply. We need to find out.

So far, compression as a fact of mediation: a point established in the "Sneak Preview" and pursued further in regard to the "assertion" of its available deviances at the level of technical disclosure. But how, in other contexts, to read the *lack* of any obvious assertion in the very throes of innovation (via even more rapid and subliminal compressions)? I ask in anticipation of a neo-Cavellian reading of the most compressed, elision-smooth, flicker-fused, and vividly virtual-presence film in the annals of cinema—barely enshrined at all in contemporary media history and lost (at least so far) to any chance of a recovered first-hand experience. The question again, then, rephrased: how to read a cinemachinic experiment, if in a seamlessly new digital mode, that asserts nothing in particular about camera or lab work except the astonishing luminous clarity of its own self-successive chain of accelerated "world projections"? If not thereby "asserted," what is nonetheless averred about the process of technical mediation in such a film?—namely, Ang Lee's *Billy Lynn's Long Halftime Walk* (2016), a little-seen box-office disaster that, worse yet, was almost never seen as intended. For it was available in the year of its US release only in two public venues, in LA and New York, that were equipped to project it in its intended 4K ultra-high-definition 3-D—with its "succession of world pictures" whipping past at five times the normal frame rate, 120 fps, and thus more closely approximating the way the compressive structures of human optics sample the world itself in normal vision. To my eye, there in Manhattan at the AMC Lincoln Square Theater, the film was in every sense an event: a technical revelation and an adventure of eerie presence, of things happening before one's eyes at a new level of unimpeded interface—even while incorporating in a definitive fashion, as we'll see, that other and more particular version of this planar designation in Slavoj Žižek's sense of the "interface effect." With no optical allusion to an electronic matrix until halfway through its Super Bowl halftime centerpiece, Ang Lee's privatized psychological extravaganza of the image per se, rather than its spectacle, stuns us from the first frames forward with the power of the unprecedented, which never lets up.

If *Billy Lynn* was massively underseen, it has also been quite systematically underappreciated in the spotty press as well. In the context of the present discussion, we might say that its notices were heavy on "production notes" (the film making it to the cover, for instance, of the *American*

Cinematographer magazine), but that it garnered little serious attention otherwise. Dismissive critics repeatedly found it an ill-matched wedding between low-keyed psychological drama and a hypertechnology whose capacity for spectacle was by turns wasted on a raft of talky close-ups, undersold in routine Iraq War flashbacks, and squandered in a pyrotechnical Super Bowl show whose own digital grandstanding was beneath the film's pay grade. But this threefold division of labor was precisely the nub of its experimental venture, which unfolds as its own metacommentary on the epitomizing cinematic affect of the close-up (newly effected at super high-speed "attention"), on the suspended distinction between present (presence) and past in the traumatic flashback, and on the electronic gimmickry and showmanship of arena pageants against which this screen breakthrough is in fact meant to avow its own more engrossing technology as counterdisplay. On all three fronts, the ungodly clarity of the image—or is godly more like the right idiom here?—reaches to unprecedented levels of medial immersion. Which is to say that, in its entirely realist scenography of mostly bland interior locations or familiar bleacher seats, the film nonetheless takes us, as cliché might have it, to places—by bringing their details so vehemently forward—where cinema has never before been. And emplaces us there. In ways impossible finally to describe unless you've in fact "been there" (may the technology take hold again somewhere!), suffice it to say that the viewer sits face to face with a peopled world seen with the clarity one associates with a very clean mirror.

In just these ways, *Billy Lynn* induces a rare experience in either photogrammic or digital cinema: a completely knowing participation in projection's more than ever invisible basis. Where possible, one sought out the movie precisely to see the retooled cinemachine at work: recorded bodies standing and moving before the viewer with a nonetheless preternatural im-mediacy. This essay's resistance to hypostatizing the quasi-haptic dimension of screen viewing as an encounter between spectator and screen "body" might seem sorely tested by this film. Might. But I would say, rather, that the incomparable sense of presence instilled by technique here is never separable, even in this case, from the felt *trucage* of the technology that induces it. In terms of Deleuze's departure from Peirce: zeroness and virtuality, machination and mirage, are rendered inextricable as we look.

Certainly no "academic" viewer lucky enough to have caught the film on either coast could have ignored its rather complete, almost asymptotic, convergence of apparatus and body theory: a more-than snapshot sharpness in rapid-fire visceral multiplication, a case of *photogenie* in extremis, and so on. Defying the routines of screen spectacle in its normal panoramic ambitions, the eerie hyperrealist—and thus less naturalistic than preternatural—immediacy of the image in Ang Lee's approach is focused repeatedly on the human close-up. This venture in specular intimacy, including its risky commercial wager, comes across as an implicitly media-historical gloss on the prominence of the close-up as cinematic touchstone: from Bela Balázs (represented in the coming "Featurette") through Eisenstein to Epstein and later Deleuze. And in the maximal sharpness of the image, in all its riveting perspicuity, the avowed cinema-specificity of the canonical close-up seems at the same time to dissolve, across the crispness of its own resolution, into a quasi-direct somatic engagement with the viewer as well. What results is the further sensorial quotient of actually being there—and often too close for comfort at that. Activated by such means are all the tributary affects this is likely to trigger, both in prolonged scenes of tearful intimacy and their occasional punctuation by assaulting memory flashes from Iraq firefights. Much of the time, to put it in a corporeal paradox, we find ourselves as if staring into the eyes of subjectivity itself. Which is why the introvert performance of the hero, together with the film's frequent lack of any notable dynamism in camerawork, is both so marked and so cogently motivated. In the immediacy of the image per se, the enhanced medial apparatus—though its optical innovation is never far from mind—goes into suspension as such. At this interface of an almost inhabited fidelity, you are *there* because it is here before you.

In the process—which is to say in this high-velocity procession of separately indecipherable frames, digital now rather than photogrammic—we may well be reminded that there was, after all, something centrally underspecified in Cavell's definition of film as a "succession of automatic world projections"—rather than just world *pictures*. At least from the vantage of Ang Lee's cinematographic upgrade, Cavell's formulation may seem latent with a Bazinian teleology that would take us, within the ambit of "projections" (in the sense of participatory investment as well as thrown light) from standard screen formats through 3-D to virtual reality—with the World Viewed being less and less comprised of mere pictures of itself in succession, and more and more its tangible (photogenic, now electrogenetic) approximation. Here, then, in *Billy Lynn*, is automaticity disappearing into ontology on the cusp of full illusionism, rather than just the normative effects of framed representation. Or in Epstein's terms, full "irrealism." If, according again to Conant's Cavellian emphasis, standard film must, in a war of optical wills, "defeat" photography's documentary offices (as well as its stasis) in order to bridge the gap between our world, faithfully recorded, and the screen's cinematic fiction, then Ang Lee's extraordinary initiative has—more decisively than ever before—served to defeat the single resolved image cell altogether, sweeping the field by whisking the individual digital frame (and its own thousandfold composite) into a faster-than-ever effacement of itself. This is the case even while, for the informed viewer, motion is rendered only by seeming more *mysteriously* rooted than ever in the image's transitional disappearance. In the line of descent from photograph to pixel array, we are responding yet again, as Epstein would have seen it—as he in fact all but foresaw it in his dialectic of impulse and number, percept and concept, input and abstraction—to the intermittence and compression of corporeal sight, not just its screen sightings. So the imaged and the imaging body, screen and spectator, owe their interface in this case to more than normal spectatorship. Viewing approaches to an unmediated looking that only serves further to reflect, intensively, on the technology that has simulated it. It is not enough to say, then, that *Billy Lynn* achieves an almost embodied visuality in a unique fulfillment of *photogenie*. By any account, Ang Lee's experiment also delivers the electronically refurbished cinemachine in a new apotheosis.

The seamless hyperlucidity of this experiment operates at an opposite pole from a pivotal moment in the director's previous film—a movie whose elegiac turning point, given its VFX execution, might seem to have heralded a very different tendency in sci-fi films over the intervening half decade. Elegiac, and metacinematic as well. In *Life of Pi* (2012), we've marveled all along at special effects that could allow a Bengal tiger to cohabit with a castaway boy in shot after seaborne shot, until realizing finally, and famously, that this has all been a cover story for more traumatic human predation. So that the tricks were part of a first-degree fake as well: all montage in this special case operating as explicit *trucage*, a radical "irrealism" confessed ex post facto: again, echoing *McTeague*, "nothun but a drick" that the brutalized mind has played on itself. And if, like the interviewer in the closing scene, we prefer the "story with the tiger" to the gruesome truth, this is only to say that we sign on, in retroactive acceptance, to the impossible movie we've just watched.

A movie whose first open hint of the eventual reveal comes in its flamboyant underwater fantasy sequence: the film's VFX bonanza, in which we see through the eyes of the tiger what the boy alone could be projecting through him into undersea visions. This we recognize, after all the stunning anatomical coherence of *trucage* up to this point, when a submerged image of the boy's dead mother, amid swarms of more fabulous undersea creatures, surfaces toward the camera. Already splotchy and composite, as if at first evoking an Indian temple mosaic, the image then splinters into the kind of quasi-pixelation made possible by the so-called particle system, used in CGI for such effects as fog and meteor trails and explosions (as if named for the particulate matter it often simulates).[11] But with a difference here, where no atmospheric effect is represented—and where it is instead a bodily image that is dissipated, in ways we've elsewhere become inured to lately in the decimation of real flesh (see especially Luc Besson's *Lucy* in chapter 6). Applied to the approaching face of the dead mother as the POV burrows through its disintegrated plane, the technique—anticipating its near kin in much subsequent sci-fi—operates in this case as a trope, rather than a locus, of *dissolution* per se: of life, presence, even the stability of memory. The mourned maternal image is thereby an illusion as transitory as the whole digitally *effected* fantasy of the film turns out to have been.

The fluid hallucination of this shot is not a manifestly digitized image, but rather an optical allusion to pixelation itself as the computer-engineered truth beneath it, more deeply submerged than the undersea face. Like dust motes or cinders elsewhere, snowflakes or exploded glass slivers, the fissured globules of such an effect cannot help but summon by metonymy the miniscule bitmap clusters that generate it. In transferring Deleuze's terms for the photogram or engram in filmic cinema (understood above as the "gaseous" state of a screen projection, its serial molecules not yet bound into image), we might say that this post-filmic "particle effect" of the VFX arsenal—devised for the simulation of real-world gaseous phenomena, their spray and vapor, their efferv- and evan-escence—is here returned toward the new engrammatic state of the pixel array that composites it. What results is a potential reading of its disintegration as the fractalized sign of its own piecemeal constitution.

The work of optical allusion six years later in *Billy Lynn's Long Halftime Walk* is of a different order altogether, as we will find. But what about the plot itself of that later film, in its widely assumed mismatch with technique? Or ask: how does the new cinematography achieve—or abort—its narratographic potential? To answer, even tentatively, requires addressing again, in more detail, those leading and blanket objections to the film, mentioned above: the matter of the close-up first; then the backing off in time rather than space to underdeveloped memory inserts; then the tacky splendors of the halftime extravaganza and its computerized stadium backdrop. Building on canonical thinking about the close-up in Balázs, its place in Deleuze's "affection-image" is only one conceptual pressure point in the Deleuzian system that *Billy Lynn's* hypertrophic vividness can serve to highlight. Deleuze derives his entire system from Bergson, of course, only by first forgiving him his resistance to film, which Bergson distrusted, so we've seen, as the mechanical simulation of the world as image, one discrete capture after another, split second by split second. For Bergson, this abets the mistaken way in which the mind betrays memory, as well as perception itself, by conceiving of it as separate slices of time rather than as inseparable moments in the continuous medium of duration (the illusory continuum, of course, that Epstein's machinic intelligence thinks differently, differentially).[12]

While the camera is scrutinizing Billy Lynn's watery-eyed features with such determination (and definition) that it seems to screen even his tear ducts, not just the occasional welling up of tears, the halftime hiatus of the plot pulls the protagonist two ways from center. Its titular duration sketches, at twin levels, not just the interregnum between quasi-gladiatorial gridiron encounters at the Super Bowl, where Billy's heroic squad from Iraq is literally paraded in a turn of political theater and patriotic dazzle, but also the entire length of the film between "tours of duty" in the Iraq "theater" of war: between, that is, Billy's furlough and his planned redeployment, an interregnum in this more literal, martial sense. In this middle space of plot, the whole sense of an ongoing narrative is almost forestalled by a Las Vegas money man bidding for film rights on the heroic saga of Billy and his squad, as if their story were a closed one, ready for Hollywood repackaging. With Billy already on show at the stadium for his heroics, this backstage bid for a further narrativization strikes him as a bridge too far. So back he goes into the militarized fray, as if for a reality check.

In the mounting (and middling) meantime, the logic of suspended action is sustained across all those uncanny close-ups on the faces of his crew, lined up in stadium seats for whole low-keyed scenes at a time. And this premium on faciality is further thrown into relief when, as part of the halftime "walk," they take their assigned, stagey places—Billy front and center—before a digitally generated LED display of their own features magnified to stadium scale in the pop graphics that conclude the halftime extravaganza. With the "grounding" image (rather than its background) sharper than any filmic or digital moving image has ever been—jutting out in 3-D in front of a 2-D blur of oversized and pulsing bulb-like digital blips clustering in pointillist exaggeration of Billy's battle-tested stature—here is an "assertion in technique" at two scales of digital presentation, where 4K hi-def comes into further definition by immanent contrast.

The result is a computerized version, as well, of Slavoj Žižek's "interface effect," as described in his punning commentary "Back to the Suture," where he considers the facial image and its own doubling in the same frame—not by cutting, say, between body and mirror image, but by secondary representation (Citizen Kane dwarfed by his own campaign poster, for instance).[13] Putting the very concept of editing and montage under analysis by suspension, such a conflation by interface can seem to suggest that the screen's own technological plane of duplication is absorbing its original into the same optic field.

With Billy standing at fragile patriotic attention before his own broadcast real-time publicity image, with its inflated and frail approximation of seen reality, it is here, as fireworks go off (in particle system effects, for all we know), that sonic free association triggers the first flashback from playing field to the gun bursts of the Iraq killing fields. In a second iteration of the interface, and against a thematized limit case of digital HD and 3-D alike, the parched earth and its distant sniper targets are dramatically reflected in the battle goggles of Billy and his squad leader. In Žižek's terms again, it is as if shot and its reverse shot are held in focus in the elided distance of imminent firing lines: the very ground of carnage made present to their vision—and, by reflection, ours as well—across the immediacy both of technical close-up and transferred adrenaline rush. As plot then reverts to the halftime hoopla breached by this narrative return of the repressed, the vapid and humiliating parade of star heroics is soon over. But in the backstage subplot, in Billy's final rejection of the movie deal—and its metacinematic dealing out of the film's own overarching ontological irony—Billy explodes at the would-be producer after being patronized and lowballed in the offer: "You can't make a movie of this . . . It's our life." But of course Ang Lee has done just that, in a mode of machination whose lifelikeness, in the final spiraling of an implied technological paradox, is the exception that proves Billy's rule.

In the process, *Billy Lynn's Long Halftime Walk* reads almost like the self-conscious tailing off of the Mideast war film after its many commercial disappointments—in all their metafilmic re-mediations through helmet cams, infrared gunsights, and drone transmits. In this halftime as interregnum, the plot (despite flashbacks and a pending stop-loss return to the war) leaves all that wired violence behind in an aesthetic of the upfront (albeit hypermedial) 3-D close-up. What is here "asserted in technique" (to follow Cavell)—if only appreciated technologically after consultation with the "production notes," though lambent and unmistakable in every superrealist frame—is a radical fivefold increase in (to vary Cavell) the automaticities of "succession," together with a resulting new depth of "projection" into a credibly dimensioned 3-D space. This (to vary Epstein) is a very smart movie; what the "intelligence" of its machine cogitates for us at the almost palpable level of perception is a deep cinematic affect well before any emotional identification, where (to vary Peirce) the virtual is all but actualized by the machinic "interpretant" as real. Perhaps Epstein's term for film's fit with the physical world, the "irreal" (an alternative to "unreal" that comes into usage for the first time in the early 1940s, just before he wrote), has never been more apt. With that term offering a more closely matched contrast with the "surreal" as well, we may be helped to recognize how film's is an unnerving and *ir*rational "intelligence" operating to an/atomize perception itself from within its own "mosaic" fields—and speeds—of view.

Ang Lee's newly engineered shift rate, of course, disappears the optic subunits (encoded digital frames rather than indexed photograms) faster than ever before—in the history of "world projections"—into the all the more nearly "realized" scene. We don't see this increased pixel differentiation "phenomenally," but we sense the result as a new phenomenon: metacinematic as well as technical. Here is a streamlined "defeat" of the fixed frame that Conant would recognize, one assumes, as all the more quintessentially Cavellian. In this way we are affected by the conditioning genius (intelligence) of this one film's unique approximation to nothing less than the synaptic rate of human perception itself. A neo-Bazinian teleology of realism has brought us to the brink not of a reproduced world, but of a surrogate human vision. At this level, *Billy Lynn*'s uncanny counterpart to—or interlock with—the brain's own perceptual engineering offers itself, at the narrative level, as yet another subliminal parable of time (on screen as well as off) as no more than the abstract "interpretant" of subliminal change per se, graphed in the now-reigning apparatus by pixel shifts.

Beyond its pervasive aura of the virtual in our everyday sense, *Billy Lynn* explicitly tips its hand (and its digital iceberg) only in that halftime computerized backdrop: vast representational duplicate (and crude "mosaic") as simultaneous interface of the "living image" in Žižek's desutured sense. One level of grandiose and static digitization valorizes by contrast the subperceptual race of pixels whose magic transparency records it. How other "tips" (at once hints and crests) at this level of medial disclosure may help plumb the zero-degree substrate of imaging's conditioning potential in the films to come, what other technical "assertions" (sometimes, yes, "extrusions") are likely to be educed by narrative detail itself, we'll have to see—even when we're not always sure quite what we're looking at. But the main thrust so far should, in its forward momentum, be clear. In recognizing the value (and potential valences) of mediality as an analytic complement to ontological semiotics—when, as it were, signs of life are projected on screen—we are making space for further apparatus reading to come, operating time and again at the threshold of the phenomenal.

Once more, then, the dovetailing of media and method in this essay's approach, whose assumptions have accumulated to the point of a further generalization in light of solidifying cross-disciplinary paradigms. If one suspects that film-philosophy has come of age as the posterity of Theory's premature death (not just rumors of it), such a guess puts extra pressure on the nature of its hyphenated disciplinary latch. Yet the very typography of this conjoint field—interpretive force field rather than just academic collaboration—visualizes a bridged gap that can only be forded by a philosophy of production itself, rather than just of selected narrative artifacts. Some cinematic narratives raise philosophical issues, to be sure. But others, and not necessarily fewer, raise from latency a medial condition that itself invites philosophical scrutiny, if only by particular encounter from movie to movie.

This is to say that in determining the "being" of the image, there is also the making of it—as Cavell himself does mean to acknowledge in the categorical interplay between "succession" and its primary photo-chemical "automatism." This is also what Deleuze, for instance, knew he needed to stress, at the start, regarding film's molecular impetus at the level of the engram. In film-philosophical terms, the very least one can say is this: how soon one puts this definitive condition of the moving image behind one in viewing movies—as Deleuze immediately does in his allegiance to Bergsonian *durée*, and as Cavell mostly does—is itself a media-philosophical question, not just an opening up to more certified modes of philosophy. And on this question, more than we might have known without the recent textual gathering and translation next up for discussion, history has weighed in. Recovered there is just what the tech specs inherent to the produced image will continue to annotate about their own narrative productivity.

3 *Featurette*

THE MAKING OF A MEDIUM

MEDIUMS ARE MADE RATHER THAN BORN, AND NOT JUST, IN THE CASE OF SCREEN MEDIA, by being technically conceived and manufactured instead of organically gestated—but made as well by the discourse that grows up around, and with, them into a settled maturity. Such a discourse, in the case of "the film medium," was so eventually settled, both entrenched and vernacularly cemented, that, despite its century-long institutionalization as "the cinema," the material epithet "film" survived its own mode of production. As slow as it was to elevate the cinematographic process to *a* medium, let alone to an art, the work of commentary, by the end of the century, was just as slow to give up on the description "film"—and its further academic institutionalization in "film studies"—even after there was no film left, no celluloid cells, in generating the play of image on the reflective silver screen or its LED progeny. That laggard terminological moment aside, it is easy enough to see the complexities that earlier writers were trying to compass in singling out what was most urgently new about screen pictures, rather than in theorizing some indisputable unitary basis for their machination.

For Panofsky in his 1936 lecture "Style and Medium in the Motion Pictures"—much later pursued and nuanced by Cavell, as we've seen—the distinguished art historian, in his preoccupation with "the unique and specific possibilities of the new medium," was openly partial to the true newness he remembered in the era of silent film (still preferring Garbo, for instance, before the "talkies," and Garbo silent even in her own sound films).[1] The nearness to the new is even more pronounced, of course, in Weimar (and earlier German) writing from the preceding three decades of screen imaging—beginning before the term "medium" enjoyed any international circulation in categorizing this new machine display. That close to the source, there was certainly more "promise" than existing archive—as our turn to the title and contents of a recent archival anthology of the period is about to make abundantly clear.

Determinations of mediality aside, the motion picture's most influential early designation, in the form of a trademark, was born of etymology, christened in French, identified by international cognates, and figured in discourse by synecdoche. The whole was a thing of parts—and inter-linked phases. A machine at once for recording, printing, and projecting images, the *cinématographe*—before its machinic aspects were segregated and refined—had staying power as a name by reason, no doubt, of just this combinatory operation. Though principally indicating the ingenious object or tool as engine of spectacle, the name seemed to capture by associ-ation the whole kinetic operation, even with little necessary connection to its intended etymological sense of *motion-writing* in the patented coinage. Any parallel with the light-writing of the photo-graph is instructive in pre-cisely its limits, since what Henry Fox Talbot famously called "the pencil of nature" has already made its mark, in photography, at the imprint stage. After which, the resultant "writing" only becomes visible once the stain has reached, through whatever negative stages, the glass plate or treated sheet—affixed there for all later viewing. By contrast, the kineto-graph's writing in mobile light is recursive, taking place once in recording, and then again, time and again, in the retraced "graphing"—the scrawl and crawl and rush—of the projected image. The broad technical, subjective, and ideological circuit of "apparatus theory" decades later might have found early license for its encompassing terminological bracket (including not just strip and motored reels but the viewer's conscription by suture's ocular "discourse") in both the process and the nomenclature of all things *cinématographique*. In any case, for the early European press, the name—including its linguistic cousins across the Continent—stuck.

For German commentary at the time, it is not hard to appreciate why the "kine" of the eventual nickname *kino* was taken up first and foremost as a composite phenomenon of kinetic generation, rather than a single transmissive means understood as "medium." Its operation, we might say, was *too mediated* for distillation as one aesthetic format—operating across time as well as space. Indeed, many of the later debates about film's medium specificity (phenomenological versus material, for instance) can be thought to derive from the original, if soon superseded, threefold nature of its founding apparatus as camera, lab, and projector all in one: a machine for capture, storage, transfer, and release alike. Though not approached strictly as a new rotary machine, the cinematograph's op-tical effects weren't yet granted, in sum, either the essentialized plastic materiality, on the one hand, or the communicative transmit, on the oth-er, associated with medium status in standard aesthetic vocabularies.[2] The cinemachine entered commentary in its aspect as *invention* instead:

technological marvel, attraction, event. A source of wonder, it was also a spur to impressive speculation as well as spectation. So it is important to note that, if the "prestige" term medium was slow in coming, as a kind of aesthetic given and imprimatur, there was no lack of seriousness attending the phenomenon of the projected serial imprint—all the more so, perhaps, since the process was still under definition. And it was just this international commentary—especially perceptive in certain sectors of the European press, German as well as French—that, in its eventual discursive momentum, *made the medium* as such: understood from writer to writer in whatever mode of sociological notice, technical scrutiny, or cultural premonition (or, as below, world-historical "promise").

The Weimar colloquy around the new popular spectacle took shape in a searching if short-form journalism, by no means limited to "reviewing," concerned not just with immediate vistas on screen but with the wider horizon of potential in the workings of the *kinematographen*—as glimpsed quite often in the most salient functions of its new powers. As was later the case for Epstein next door in France, uniqueness was at a premium; the unprecedented seemed definitive. The means, that is, elicited attention before the documentary or narrative content. And there was as much to catch the analytic imagination as even the eye. This is why one finds in much early German writing about the "film-writing" of the "kineto-graph"—with its close commentary on film's textures, material tropes, and ocular rhythms—a model for the present essay on what is special to cinema as special effect. And in the broader terms of a philosophized apparatus, this archival material serves to backdate precisely the nuanced but sometimes elusive play between epistemology and medial ontology that the conversation between Epstein and both Deleuze and Cavell, among others, has been arranged to audit.

Kinovation

The anthology that collects this newly translated journalistic material under the title *The Promise of Cinema* is a riveting documentary trove.[3] The curious reader can start anywhere, dip in at random. Begin with name recognition if the temptation can't be resisted. From 1925, from *Der Tag*, this, for instance, from Béla Balázs ("Reel Consciousness") on the autodocumentary impulse of the new medium, including the record of a filmmaker's own death in certain celluloid cases. Balázs's comments offer a reaction to motion capture extraordinary for its time and proleptic of ours: "This is a new form of self-reflection. These people reflect themselves by filming themselves. The inner process of accounting for oneself has been externalized" (59). This isn't just Munsterberg's sense of film as mental state, as dream, as unconscious projection, but film as a prosthetic self-image: "This self-perception . . . is mechanically fixed. The film of self-control, which consciousness used to run within the brain, is now transposed onto the reel of a camera, and consciousness, which has mirrored itself *for itself alone* in internal division until now, delegates this function to a machine that records the mirror image *for others to see as well*" (59) Though this is not Balázs's point, the issue comes up in other articles—for sown here, of course, are the very seeds of surveillance that is elsewhere an issue for the German press: "In this way, subjective consciousness becomes social consciousness" (59): the self seen from without. Despite technological rupture and medial breakthrough, the underlying continuum suggested at this point between self-consciousness and external image, the brain's own reflexive witness and the flickering bodily image in projection, is one about whose common denominator, in intermittence per se, we can imagine— we have in fact already, in effect, read—Epstein's further gloss on. For the crux here is precisely the crossing between epistemology and ontology, perceptual apparatus and the discontinuous structure of existence.

Moreover, beyond anything we might term film theory or postmetaphysical philosophy, a whole ambient field of psychoanalytic criticism is anticipated in those remarks by Balázs. The internal circuit of "consciousness" per se, to repeat, "has mirrored itself *for itself alone* in internal division until now." From now on, however, the split is externalized, projected— not as "screen memory" but as indexical trace, not psychoanalytically but psychotechnically. Merely shift the italics—and the metafilmic point on which we'll be closing in is comparably refracted: "which has *mirrored itself* for itself alone in internal division until now." The figurative mirror of self-image has been technologically extroverted as the reflective mechanics of screen optics—on the way to being refigured again within film plots from Keaton (and before) to the latest sci-fi (the tellingly named *Self/Less* below). But perhaps the most arresting stress here is the thought that "self-control" amounts to an "inner film" (of imagistic self-monitoring) to begin with. From Balázs to Bernard Stiegler: a path not often traced or travelled.[4] Many such untrodden and often astonishing routes forward are sketched—and cleared—in the pages of *The Promise*.

It is impossible to overstate the number of fronts on which these journalist pieces are both prescient and philosophically rich—and how rigorously, even if economically, they grapple with the ontological quandaries of space and time posed by the newly viewed motion of the human body on screen. Dominant throughout, as perhaps the main strand of reaction, is an emphasis on the recorded somatic gesture, in all its difference from both theater and photography. But few if any of the writers, sampled so extensively in the Weimar anthology, fail to engage such effects in at least tacitly mechanistic terms, a matter of ocular science and technology—and directed not just at a new phenomenon of exhibition but aimed at times toward latent convergences between cinema's disclosures and modern paradigms for the signal systems of human cognition itself. Impossible then, as well, to overstate the connections with Epstein's psychomechanics of the medium—especially when, as noted, no sooner does he insist on the subjective nature of all motion on screen, coproduced by the eye in collaboration with the speeding discontinuous images of the strip, than his commentary radically "naturalizes" this by reminding us, as do several of the German cultural commentators before him, that the mind itself operates on comparable electromagnetic principles developed over evolutionary time. Even a set designer for UFA, one Leo Witlin, theorizes the eye's function apart from the narrative camera's by stressing, in a piece called "On the Psychomechanics of the Spectators," the nature of the human eye as a "wireless sort of sensor" (137): a device for the telepresencing, one might say, of the world viewed.

A Berlin-based doctor, Eduard Baumer, weighs in on "Cinematography and Epistemology" (79–81). Writing in unmentioned parallel to Bergson, though without the critique of mechanization, Baumer returns to Heraclitus in stressing cinema's new participation in "the flow of time"—and sees the scientific potential of cinematography, through time-lapse technology, as the speeding of time into its own mode of visibility as an otherwise imperceptible motion. Similar arguments are later on file in the anthology by Siegfried Kracauer, from *Frankfurter Zeitung* in 1925. In a short article called "Mountains, Clouds, People," Kracauer's point is that a motion "faster than reality" allows certain "objects" to "rush by and dissipate" under the effects of the "kinematographen"—and thus to be seen as never before, *in their change*, through being "cheated of their duration by the time lapse" (97). Again, as in Epstein: Bergson's complaint turned on its head: the cheat redeemed as epistemological bonus. Across several of the collected articles, none as dubious as Bergson about the new cinemachine, it is clear that in this mechanical disruption of time-space ratios, with the accelerated dis-placement of objects that results, the swindle perpetrated by frame advance, the very deceit of succession, is a fraudulence true enough to the eye's normal working to deserve the name of analysis rather than mere illusion. In this context, the time lapse between frames themselves in even normal projection, anathema to Bergson, is isolated as definitional by many of Epstein's German predecessors: the uniqueness of the medium foregrounded at times in overdrive.

With the earliest chronological clusterings of these pieces helpfully partitioned by the editors, including over a dozen brief essays in each category, the theoretical originality of response comes clear at a glance. Rubrics like "A New Sensorium" (rather than a fresh appeal to established senses), "The World in Motion" (rather than the moving world), "The Time Machine" (rather than the mechanics of recorded time), "The Magic of the Body" (the transformative alchemy that film exerts upon the recorded body as well as freshly discovers there): all these subdivided arenas of comment serve to register, by digesting, the distinct conceptual weight of these occasional pieces—and the depth of their deliberations.[5] In the aptly titled *The Promise of Cinema*, we are repeatedly looking forward, in these often clairvoyant prognostications, to the vicissitudes of technological history. Promises, promises, yes. Some kept, some voided, some exceeded, some betrayed. Cinema history, like history at large, is likely to fulfill certain sectors of expectation while "going back on" other seeming assurances. And cinema historians, returning here to what German commentary saw portended by the new medium—what it foresaw as the future of vision and record both, in everything from new focalizations of human consciousness to enhancements in forensic science—are offered by this archive a genuinely new purchase on once-assumed vectors of potential, on truncated dead ends, and on many a bent trajectory in between. What *The Promise of Cinema* witnesses to, that is, by sheer force of evidence and on one technical, social, or psychological front after another, is a tacit pledge of developmental energy either borne out, reneged on, or technologically recalibrated.

From piece to piece, the medium—without commentary ever using that term—is quite exhaustively parsed. One reads not just certain documents of response within the context of a vibrant national cinema like Weimar's but, more grippingly yet, a prehistory of film theory in its rise and eclipse since. To characterize just some preoccupations of these early texts—and to do so in a German variation on that baseline keynote query of André Bazin (whose ontology these writers so often anticipate)—the underlying issue throughout, as later for Epstein, too: *Was ist Kino*? What is its essential constitution as well as its promise? A structure of "illusion" in itself (several pieces with that term in their title), as well as the cause of hallucination in others (Albert Hellwig, "Illusions and Hallucinations during Cinematographic Projections," 45–47, stressing the imagined sonic equivalents sprung from silent screen images), cinema is also understood as a tool of epistemology readied for surveillance (Wilhelm Von Ledebur, "Cinematography in the Service of the Police," 535–37). And there are related forecasts of broadcast systems, including the "telecinema" that will eventuate not just in "home cinema" but in CCTV (Arthur Korn, "Why We Still Do Not Have Television: Possibilities of Electric Television," 590–92; Ernst Steffen, "Telecinema in the Home," 595–97).[6]

Beyond forecasts of broadcast, and elsewhere of 3-D, these writers didn't stop short of imaging our own horizon for optical technology in the various manifestations of what we now call virtual reality—at least in the form of the remote and weaponized image of drone warfare in its proleptic form as a gunnery game. One essay is quite intriguing in this regard. It operates as if to upend (or at any rate to complement) the considerable number of pieces in *The Promise* claiming cinema as a machine of immortality—an overcoming of death, of oblivion, by retained image. This outlier is the anonymous essay from 1914 titled "The Cinematograph as Shooting Gallery" (259–60) that stands out not just for the care of its reporting (some of these articles do read, in fact, like the tech-nerd blogs of their day) but for the ingenuity of the paracinematographic technology under description. Characterized in lucid if complex detail is a "living target" display in Leipzig, where two vertically rotating paper scrolls (mobile screens)—one behind the other, and the latter intensely backlit—allow for aerial gunnery practice at a new level of rapidly trained mastery. Guided by an exacting journalistic prose rather than a fleeting image, still it takes an intense concentration all its own in order to "see" what is being described. With moving images of fighter planes projected on the foremost mobile sheet or screen, this "war movie," when penetrated by a bullet that rips a hole in both surfaces, allows the player-marksman to gauge his accuracy and try again almost immediately in perfecting his aim. This is possible because the bright hole of light, spoiling the image for a split second in pinpointing the attempted "kill"—like some contemporary laser targeting device—is quickly repaired in the continuous scrolling of the background paper, occluding the light again as soon as its puncture wound is registered. Beyond the celluloid source, two further film "strips" are thus at play. Whereas the second, background scroll is rotated beyond any one bullet hole, thus blocking the backlight, the first vertical sheet of projected aerial imagery, display plane of the "movie" itself, is only rolled away when its perforations are too numerous to sustain the image field.

What is so extraordinary about this whole sideshow apparatus is the displaced logic of the image track it instruments, whereby the on/off of the representational image on the strip has been redoubled by the flickering intermittence of a second light source. Not only is the basic transparent reel of serialized image (on the projected photogram track) transferred to its opaque counterpart in those spooling surfaces, only the first of which is reflective, but, in the process, the beam of visibility is also aggressively reversed by the "rear projection" of sheer illumination. Here, then, the normal discontinuity of frame advance, as elided on the single screen of standard projection, is maximized instead in the service of erasure rather than pictured motion—sheer disappearance—in the racing forward of the background's perforated surface. The bite-sized light flare from behind, as if snuffed out at once, constitutes a disappeared piercing that amounts to an editing device achieved in tandem by two parallel planes of projection. In coordinated operation, we might see those two paper scrims offering a first layered interface in the long march toward computerized virtuality and the commerce of video gaming. In their own right, they offer a rare case of the "special effect" displaced from camera or lab to the participatory conditions of exhibition itself.

The normal manifestation of optic ingenuity, prominent on screen apart from any such cases of anomalous interaction, was also much on the mind of those early German commentators, even when not quite in determinate view—as evidenced by their frequent allusions to the "mirrors" used in filming, as well as in specific references to the legendary Schüfftan process. Central to the thinking of the early press, these machinations offered a synecdoche for the illusory nature of the medium at large: the whole apparatus manifested as an outsize magic mirror. At times, the mirror trope is casual and passing in this journalistic prose, especially if the medium's supposed passive realism as documentary footage is the point being pressed, as in the notion that on screen "everything is real, a mirror image of nature" (Johannes Gaulke, "Art and Cinema in War," 271–73). But a figuration of film as retentive mirror can be given a more skeptical spin as well. Singling out the simulated image within the broad category of illusory presence on screen, one critic wonders at the suspension of disbelief induced even when the audience knows that a particular set or vista, a given scenography of action, is "just magnifications of toysized models? Or, according to the most recent information, they are often just cleverly photographed mirror images?" (signed K. W., "What is Film Illusion," 335–37), with an editorial footnote that directs us to the Schüfftan device and the inventor's own celebration of it (Eugen Schüfftan, "My Process," 589–90)—a note whose lead one is naturally eager to follow.

It is a complicated "process" indeed—hard to sum-up without dia-

grams, but easy enough to apprehend, regardless of the images it manip-
ulates, as emblematic of the medium tout court—in all the ingenuity of its
potentially artificial framings.[7] Derived from a history of optical illusion
on stage and in visual toys, the semitransparent Schüfftan mirror captures
by reflection (at a 45-degree angle), though only on part of its surface, an
architectural model or transparency positioned just behind the camera.
The remainder of the thinly reflective surface has been peeled clean, and
thus made transparent, so that real human motion can be introduced
into the frame by a trick of inset perspective.[8] Fritz Lang's cinema provides a classic example: the giant maw of Moloch devouring its victims in
Metropolis (1926) only by the cinematographer's having filmed them at a
sufficient distance so that, within the surrounding field of the gargantuan
(reflected) image of the looming factory gargoyle, they would seem to be
the monster's dwarfed pawns. Or, earlier in the same film, look again at the
racing athletes in the vast modernist stadium inset in longshot within a
mirrored model designed to evoke their subordination to an architecture
conceived at an imposing grander scale.[9]

In sampling *The Promise*, one soon sees how the idea of a world in realist
reflection on screen came into conflict with the widely recognized "tricks
of the trade." Mirror, mirror on the wall: early re/viewers of the new film
sets, seeing anything but "nature" held up to view, were not registering the
scopic ingenuities of undetectable mirrors as merely part and parcel of the
assembled mise-en-scène—let alone restricting such tricks to simulated
mirrors that become spatial thresholds within certain fantastic turns of
narrative (below). They often felt themselves to be looking directly into a
partial mirror plane, suppressed as such, as the defining optic field of the
entire projected spectacle, with human motion just a proportional subset
of the deceptive frame's rectangular expanse. However readily smoothed
over by suspended disbelief, such fakery came straight to mind as repre-
senting the virtuality of screen space all told, even when no effects more
special than the mere apparition of projected motion were entailed. Well
before Epstein and Metz, film commentary was thus grappling with the
very idea, if not of montage as *trucage*, at least of image as mirage.

Yet this is only part of the illusionist picture, so to say: its encompassing paradigm. Aside from profilmic mirrors on the set, there are, in fact,
those mirror *simulations* induced in the lab as overt "special effects." It
is here, too, that the magic mirror becomes, in journalistic response, an
implied pars pro toto for the framed image plane of the screen. Among
recorded enthusiasms for early Expressionist cinema, there is this effu-
sive mention of *The Student of Prague*, for instance, pitting the wondrous

against the awful within the new sublimities of machinic vision. Along
with "magical views of old Prague," in the form of historical fabrications,
"there are images that make our eyes widen in horror: as when the mys-
terious Dr. Scapinelli releases the reflection of the student Balduin from
the mirror…" (Henrik Galeen, "Fantastic Film," 447–49). If the particular
special effects of mirror trickery in the Schüfftan process, because of its
German inventor and its frequent use in Weimar production, may seem
to haunt the German discourse regarding cinema's complex plane(s) of
image, both by metaphors of reflection and by namesake technical allusion, certainly the inference of the synecdochic mirror plane is by no
means restricted to German film. Yet this is not to deny that, when looking
back in American production, three years before *The Student of Prague*, to
Edison's short film on *Frankenstein* (1910), with its double mirror *trucage*,
we aren't likely to appreciate even more fully the trope of the mental mirror
of self-consciousness, in its full psychological reach, that is brought out
in Balázs's commentary a decade and a half later, quite apart from any
special effects of the German fantastic.

So consider, in this light, the fable of "self-projected" moral deformity
into which Edison turned his "liberal adaptation of Mrs. Shelley's story"
(as the first intertitle has it). Very liberal: an entirely free riff, as a matter of
fact. The avenging Creature disappears from the wedding night chambers
of Dr. Frankenstein when, horrified by his fiendish image in a full-length
mirror, he covers his eyes in the foreground space and—out of sight, out
of embodied mind—is removed by jump cut (bested, disappeared from
the world) into the displaced vestige of his mirror form. This horrified
moment of autorecognition is wholly and terminally reified, his corporal
form implicitly dead on arrival at mere self-image in an allegorical turn of
confronted monstrosity. This first phase of the mirror episode has been
achieved by a match cut on the mirror's standing frame (now secret portal)
opening back into a real space, at one remove from the main set, to which
the Creature's presumed reflection has been transferred. He exists now
only in reflection, not in front of its surface. But the next, and immediately rhyming, effect is arranged , in lab rather than mise-en-scène, by a
shuffled inlay of secondary optic planes in matte projection, a subsidiary
movie-within-the-movie. When Frankenstein, that is, returns to discover
his attempted nemesis locked away in the realm of the virtual, his final
anathematizing gesture—pointing in accusation and contempt straight
at the rebuffed Creature in the uncanny depth of the mirror—serves to
trigger a second trick shift, caught here in mid lap dissolve (note the right
leg of monster and maker together in the almost jump-cut image).

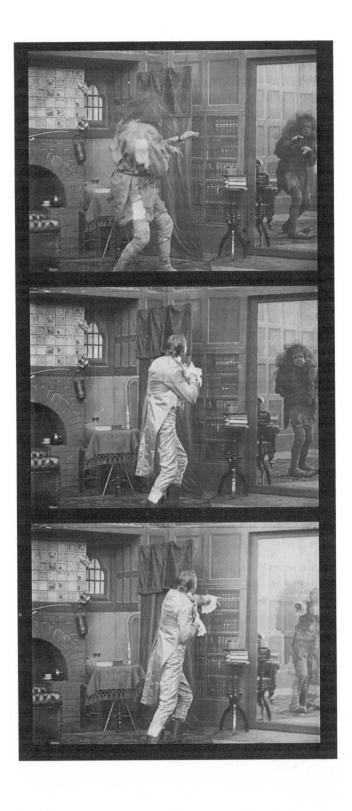

Substituted thereby, in the ellipsis permitted by a brief flash of light (dawning!), is a real mirror again: a normalized reflecting plane confirmed when Frankenstein throws himself against his own image in a gesture of impulsive contact—for the first and last time—with the moral deformation he has spawned. He is at last, as allegory would obviously have it, looking his own megalomania squarely in the face. In Edison's *Frankenstein*, that is, the magically imputed deep space of otherness and supernal displacement brings extirpation to the monstrous along the direct line of sight from abjected subject to usurping reflection. If the aura of mirror artifice infuses the rhetoric of illusion for the Weimar journalists of the *kinematographen*, one might have suspected it, and rightly, to be—perhaps all the more intimately—a reflexive scopic trope as well for the inventor of the so-called kinetoscope and the magic of its spectral framed views.

And back across the Atlantic, the German press was no less alert to the screen's kinetic magic in general. Graphic or optic, plastic or specular, serial or mutational, screen motion is scoped out by contemporaneous German writing as the fabrication it is—and the philosophical provocation. The artificial space and displacement of time-elapsed change in a compressional technology, the tricked visual surface of "truc(q)age" in all its forms: these—so we keep seeing in the contemporaneous press of the time, and as we began with in Epstein's summa on this point years later—represent cinema in embryo and in essence. And, yet again, cinema in postfilmic prospect as well—with the legacy of such effects being legion in digital movie making. The pixelated terrain of CGI, along with the magic landscapes it manifests, is one undeniable telos of a once indexical registration in what becomes, on screen, a wholly illusory space. If the "promise" of cinema is cast forward to the medium's postfilmic phase, the spotty but representative evidence of the coming "Festival," as anticipated with a particular mirror instance next in this section, shows *trucage* achieving its several destinies with an often quite lethal vengeance.

Mirror and Smoke

This is certainly the case with digital trickery that calls out for inclusion here, before the coming roundup of similar sci-fi spectacles, in connection not just with Balázs's mirror trope for the externalization of self-consciousness but also with his greater renown as the cinema's leading theorist of the facial close-up. The mirror close-up I have in mind comes from a thinly veiled remake of a minor masterpiece of Lang-like neo-noir by John Frankenheimer, *Seconds* (1966). The loose and uninvolving update by cult director Tarsem Singh, called *Self/less* (2015), finds its thematic as well as its technological matrix in a flashpoint of manifold mirror imaging reminiscent, as well, of Lang's optical ironies. And it does so, moreover, in a way that tacitly rehearses many of the intuitions of German writing about the montage logic and "third dimensional" future of the medium.

In service to the dying body now, rather than just the alienated psyche (as in the "rebirths" of *Seconds*), the electronic process of "shedding" names the technological metempsychosis by which the consciousness of a dying self can be expensively computer-transplanted into a younger, abler body—no one else's really this time, no worries, just cloned from a healthy specimen. That's what we're told, the client hero along with us. This cover story is sustained until the plot twist reveals that these proxy bodies (not in the form of disfigured corpses, as in *Seconds*, of the sort necessary to explain away the subject's disappearance) do, nonetheless, turn out to be (as in *Seconds* after all) murder victims done in when needed in the corporate scheme of things. Nor, beyond this considerable moral glitch, is the system itself quite perfect. Even after electronic brain transplant, identity traces of the formerly incarnate subjects threaten to erupt into the newly implanted consciousness, causing psychotic breakdown if medication isn't routinely administered. The lower-tech paradigm of the criminal brain transmigrated into the receptacle of Dr. Baum's remote-controlled agency, from Lang's *Testament of Dr. Mabuse* (1933), comes readily to mind as archetype.

The evil genius behind the corporate scheme of Singh's plot—who, we discover, has had his own psyche nefariously "rebooted" in this way—is at the last minute cornered by the hero in the surveillance chamber of his own laboratory, where, once before, he had trapped his patient and patsy. This is a foursquare space enclosed by two-way mirrors whose bulletproof glass he has high-handedly demonstrated, for their repelled firepower, in an earlier scene. The tables are now turned on Dr. Frankenstein. That's the plot twist so far, as the film's whole mise-en-scène is about to implode in a magic mirror of confounded suture. Spatial orientation plays between two and three dimensions in a way that inverts the entire depth of field into the shallowest form of self-replication—and this in a final metacinematic irony of special effects. Here's the way the scene breaks down, in two senses (and registers): narrative and optic.

In this ironic staging of their final face-off, the slick reincarnated villain can persist in languorously threatening the hero only by narcissistically staring at his own mirror image while merely imagining his furious interlocutor in the miked space beyond. With the biotech entrepreneur's enraged antagonist looking back through the irreversible glass interface, unseen, the protocols of suture in the shot/countershot pattern are deactivated on the spot. But we haven't seen anything yet. In snide conversation with his own image, behind which waits, invisibly, the potential nemesis of his whole criminal empire, the suavely suited mad scientist notices that his wavering sight must be distorting his image in the mirror. This is a fact silently conveyed to us, through his eyes, by way of the presumed digital warping of his mirrored face (stopping just short of pixel breakup): exactly the effect we've associated earlier in the film with unbidden flashbacks from a co-opted body's former psychic tenant, when the proper medication is wearing off.

No problem, thinks the villain, with a confident smirk. A pill will normalize. Here, then, in a play of reverse shots alternating between already reborn subject and his undulating mirror double, the reembodied mastermind is, we presume, only *seeing things*. Yet that presumption survives no longer than the villain himself. And not even that long, since in a sudden medium shot we see the deformation of his mirrored body as in fact there (by poetic license?) in the mirror in front of his actual standing form, corrective medication in hand.

But what we've taken, if noticed at all, for a slight liberty is actually a fuller cheat. For what we assumed to be the entirely subjective POV shot of the buckling self-image isn't subjective at all, but rather—as it gradually comes clear to us, by literally coming through to us—the objectively glimpsed result of a flamethrower wielded by the invisible hero and melting through the otherwise impenetrable reflective pane from its far side.

The effect is almost blackly comedic. After such suture, a nonvirtual countershot at last: the immediate incineration of the no-longer-reflected villain. In the longer perspectival view of cinema technique: the carefully aligned transparent zone of the Schüfftan mirror, letting the actor(s) show through, is converted here, in this version of looking glass as rabbit hole, to the gap(e) of a negated—and annihilating—line of sight.

Yet the scopic parable is even more technologically ingrown and baroque than it may at first seem. The Schüfftan mirror that once allowed for in-camera scalar adjustments and their subterfuges has been supplanted in this case, of course, by the postindexical plane of VFX cinema in its electronic manifestations, but only then to be laid bare in a way that operates, in the upshot, as an interface for dismantling the seemingly high tech *trucage* into a slowly perceived one of old-fashioned machine ingenuity in weaponizing the image plane itself. In terms of an imagined teleology of realism leading from sound synchronization through color to stereoptic deep focus, as codified by Bazin and anticipated by the early German press, this sudden and instantaneously obliterated illusionism, as presumed subjective hallucination, is in fact a kind of perversely "lived"—and died— 3-D penetration of an optic rectangle. So it is that the mistaken plane of image, from within a misjudged subjective shot, ends up decimating the space of mere looking. Though at first interpreted as a biomedical setback from the villain's literalized point of view, the shock for the supposedly knowing viewer—sharing that line of vision—amounts to one kind of low-keyed CGI simulation (of melting glass) mistaken for another sort of digital trope (the electronic return, so to speak, of the cortical repressed).

As explored early on by divergent assumptions of the German press, such cross-purposes of the screen medium's evidentiary potential, in the pull between epistemology and reflexive ontology, find something like their ironized, digitally manipulated vanishing point in the two-way surveillance chamber of *Self/less* and its material meltdown. As so often in genre history, the narrativized VFX logic of dystopian sci-fi can stand forth as an encoded version of cinematic optics gone wrong, the imageering of the medium extrapolated to a violent diegetic realization—or call it, again, a technological "promise" hypertrophically betrayed in fulfilment. What if the screen's magic mirror could actually disgorge into spectatorial space the often lethal force otherwise cordoned off by its own image plane? As more than one German writer glimpsed, techniques like the Schüfftan mirror, however much under erasure on screen, camouflaging their own process, still spoke to the grounding (and groundless) fact of all cinema as an uncertain field of virtuality and illusion, including the horrors of the Weimar fantastic. Moreover, what can't help but intrigue even a cursory reader of *The Promise* is how so much of that early German intuition about scopic force fields, as reshaped by the new motion picture medium, can come bearing down on the most circumscribed, however showy, effects of postfilmic cinema. Tarsem Singh wasn't reading German film theory before some storyboard session devoted to this climactic scene. German film theory had read his options in advance, without the least glimpse of the simulated electronic image to come.

In just this respect, there is another enfolded irony of screen history lodged at the climax of *Self/less*—an almost literal wrinkle—that might also recall early German film and its optically alert commentary. In the single, high-profile film most often adduced for instances of the special effects mirror of the Schüfftan process—no surprise, given the game-changing status of the sci-fi mise-en-scène in Lang's *Metropolis*—there is also the associated effect of the "ripple wipe" that suggests the clearing phobic vision of Freder, allowing the figural revelation of the devouring Moloch to return to ethical clarity as none other than the recognized factory engines of his father's predatory exploitation. Nine decades (and a new medial substrate) later, it is as if that ripple effect has found perverse new life in the cinemachine of Singh's narrative. It has done so through the digitally simulated dissolution of an actual glass plane: not just the coruscating mind's-eye image we take it to be at first, but a true buckling of the surface. A once purely discursive effect has turned murderous here as the optic waver turns—through that blistering meltdown pictured above—to open flame. The virtual has been captured again by the real, though of course still at the narrative remove of CGI production. All that early German wonder at the play between illusion and hallucination, trompe l'oeil and willing further involvement, can help in realizing the fully anomalous nature of that mirror effect in *Self/less*—as if its double disintegration were the film's both effacing and e-facing title shot.

The force of the medial flip-flop here is as hard to exaggerate as it is to sum up in any simple fashion. The familiar ruse of digital manipulation that the viewer has assumed is being paraded up to this point—yet another welcome finesse of computerized illusion in sci-fi cinema, helping us see through the eyes of biomorphic aberration—is instead *turned* upon us in a kind of techno-rhetorical irony. This happens at the very moment when we realize that the passively accepted digital morph of the villain's mirrored face is in fact, in media-historical terms, reverse engineered so as to disclose its optical evidence as the simplest mechanical action of burn and melt across a vulnerable material surface. He thinks his eyes are playing tricks on him when, instead, the film has been—on our own vision. As a misread symptom of somatic disintegration, whether objective or subjective in its focalization, this is not only the scene's epistemological swivel but its archaeological crux. Once the beam of presumed CGI projection is realized to have been routed only through the deceptive free indirect discourse of the victim's eyeline match, the game—and the trick—is up. The two-way ocular contrivance of the surveillance pane becomes, in just this fashion, a rearview mirror on the whole techne and ontology of a long-evolving special effects aesthetic. In this montage of *trucage* reversed, detricked, VFX cinema stares into the face of its own prehistory. As if in an ingrown allegory of sutured illusionism, cinema's ordinary fantasy of a two-way mirror on a world elsewhere (in Stanley Cavell's sense, a world, like that of a photography, present to me in my absence from it) summarily implodes. For all the sophisticated opacities of illusionist digital figments lately implemented in the VFX arsenal, the wavering image reverts here from something like the enforced narcissistic closed circuit of self-scrutiny (Balázs) to the sudden countershot of thrown light (and heat) per se in what amounts to the cone of vision in fatal parody. In Singh's extended figuration, we may even sense a deep pun not on smoke and mirrors plural (nor on a false pronunciation of his own last name, for that matter) but on a single incinerated mirror and the resultant human smoke—reserved for the cremation of an already once-reanimated villain, ashes to ashes.

One decade short of a full century, as well as an epochal shift in cinemachines, separates *Sherlock Jr.*—and Keaton's step-through of a mirror that isn't (chapter 4)—from the mordant trope of autoimage in *Self/less*. In between, there are few double turns of *fake* trickery, or in other words falsified *trucage*, mirror ironies or not, to compare with these emblematic moments: the special effect exposed in its own right as a second-order ploy, the subterfuge of a mere ocular misrecognition. In *Sherlock Jr.*, the fantasized screen sleuth walks through a mirror that never was one. In

Self/less, the architect of identity sees his image distorted by a biochemical disturbance that isn't. Melting in this latter case, not some subjective figuration via technological anamorphosis, is for once just what it looks like—just as, in the former comic moment, the only thing in, rather than on, a wall that you can walk through is a portal, not a looking glass. With each inset rectangle only troping the screen in its strange two-way psychodynamics of focal length and ocular recess, neither can be trusted. Where one offers magic access, the other is the momentary cover story of self-annihilation. Each a parable of subjectivity rerouted through the coils of the apparatus, once plastic, now pixelated? Why not? How otherwise?

Chronologically, we've come a long way in screen history, as well as in these pages. Taking brief stock, in transition, can help register certain developing plateaus in the argument so far. Epstein, in looking back from the 1940s on his engagements with surrealist cinema as early as the 1920s—when brought together with the German writings of Balázs and a whole squadron of other Weimar first responders—invites a potentially revised view of our current disciplinary terrain, as the last chapter began to suggest. In the aftermath of High Theory, whether mourned or eagerly surmounted, elegized or purged—and in the aftermath, as it has simultaneously happened, of the film medium in its entirety—the broad upsurge in early cinema studies may well seem more than merely coterminous with this phasing out (regarding the apparatus) not just of ideological abstraction but of the material substrate itself. This disciplinary uptick may seem, in fact, at least in its drift toward earlier film writing as well, compensatory. Nearer to the onset of the "new" screen technology, such Weimar commentary, in all its scrupulous wonder, was also closer—in focus as well as historical proximity (as so notable in the astute journalism of the period)—to that technology's palpable technical bearings. In the niche specializations of the later screen academy, what we may be living through in the last couple of decades—still working through—isn't necessarily just a glance back to a nostalgic bastion of incipient cinephilia, so thoroughly dissipated now by digital imaging and its multiplicity of platforms. Instead, the now long-established trend of early film historicism—so notably marked by its adjunct attachment to "classic" commentary—could well be taken as, in its own way, a hankering after theory itself in an epoch of mere *studies*. Be this as it may, time and again the evidence makes plain that all truly perceptive screen observation in the early years of the medium, always with mechanics in view and in mind, tends indeed to be *media-theoretical*. So that, by looking back, all the way back, we are always looking forward—and most immediately, to the silent films next called up for "rerun": films that so unabashedly plug-in to the celebrated magic of the recently new and still experimental medium. From this reversible historicism, if one may call it that, we have much, by extrapolation, still to learn in contemplating the transformative "intelligence" of the cinemachine. In the evidence that remains for testing here, two genre tendencies economically divide up the field of play between filmic farce and cautionary digital debacle, ranging from the pranks of slapstick to the grandiose optic implosions of apocalyptic sci-fi.

4 *Rerun Triple Bill*

KINKS OF COMEDY

Vernacular exaggeration (and paradox) can come to discussion's aid at a transitional point like this. What philosopher of time Henri Bergson resisted—found, we may idiomatically presume, *laughably sad*—about the turn-of-the-century cinematograph does not stop there. This is because film's way of spewing forth, for screen display, what one now calls a time-based medium—to Bergson's eye, merely an optic sputter of misrepresented duration—can take us straight to his influential essay "Laughter."[1] And from there to the effects I would identify as the *comedial* disruptions of mechanized motion in certain filmic turns: the machinic kinks of their risible hijinks. All too selectively screened, of course, in this rerun theater of investigation, exemplary cases nonetheless default to *cinemechanics* in instructive ways. And therefore connect directly with Epstein's template for engineered sequence—operating still-by-still in a frame-advance rhythm clarified by the very possibility of its own altered tempos. This is for him the undeniable core of cinema's world-historical advance in both visual imaging and its poetry, to say nothing of its implied philosophy of an intertwined time and space.

In the opening chapter on "Signs" in *The Intelligence of a Machine*, a section revealingly called "Bewitched Wheels" is followed by Epstein's treatment of "The Reversability of Time." He stresses there the link between "avant-garde film" and "burlesque comedy" (thinking of a single unnamed instance of both together) in their shared instinct—because their technical potential—for reversing the "vectors" of time and thereby moving back from "effect to cause" (4). What the "cinematograph" thus "describes, with clear precision" ("describes" as if in the sense of inscribes or sketches as well as more neutrally depicts)—and here, the crux of Epstein's whole counterintuitive argument about the thinking machine—is therefore a conception of temporality that "humanity could scarcely represent to itself" (4). Backward time has to be thought for us in machinic images. And from that previous formulation of Epstein's, a broader suggestion yet. The intelligence of cinema—though described always by its mechanical status as "cinematograph" as well as its screen result in motion picturing—may serve ultimately to posit the very idea of thought, of human cognition, as a "representation to itself." This is exactly the founding notion that yet again aligns Epstein with the logic of Peircean semiotics—perceptual stimulus as cognitive sign—discussed in "Production Notes." Even aside from any such implied definition of consciousness-as-image in its own discontinuous segmental generation, however, we could be content at this stage simply to settle such questions, for cinema in particular, as raised by Epstein in his passing link between the quintessential and the burlesque. What is it that aligns cases where the apparatus is pressed to its aesthetic limits, on the one hand, with, on the other, the accidents of slapstick? What links emerge between programmatic intensities and zany contingencies? Between the probing avant-garde gesture and the goof? Each, of course, has its genius. And both depend on conditions only implicitly visible on the image surface.

Even broader terms of comparison, however, come into play at this juncture. Apart from the slapstick of pantomime, its mugging, pratfalls, and the rest, there is often something verging on the seriocomic in the deadpan unearthing of cause from the superficial ground of effect, of technicity from opticality, even in noncomic film: an irruption so complete that its double take can seem almost giddy. This is all the more likely to be the case, then, in explicit comedies near to the founding moment of cinema—not least those by directors arriving from stage careers to film's fresh possibilities (Keaton, Chaplin). For these are artists in whose work such instances of machinic upset often seem fixated with keen delight on the disparity between tool and illusion in the not wholly familiarized new medium. This wry surprise over what may thus be pried loose from conveyance—for exposure at the level of haphazard event—can be found even, in a similar cross-mapping of performance modes, when explicitly replaying the shift from stage to screen in a later Hollywood remake of a Broadway production: from hit "show" to sheer visual display. Hence the common denominator, in the forthcoming discussion, aligning Keaton and Chaplin with the early 1940s screwball romp of Olsen and Johnson in translating their own *Hellzapoppin!* from stage musical to the impossibly botched metafilmic screening of its own reflexive theatrical plot.

This was part of my topic—in light of Bergsonian paradigms for both comedy at large and for film as a medium of its execution—at the Berlin conference on comedy at the Institute for Cultural Inquiry in 2016. As a kind of epigraph, the program brochure featured this joke from Ernst Lubitsch's 1939 *Ninotchka*, a comic turn verbal of course rather than visual—and quite rigorously so in its conjuring of the categorically absent, the invisible referent under negation: "A man goes into a cafe and asks the waiter for a cup of coffee, without cream. The waiter goes away, but returns again within a couple of minutes. 'I'm so sorry sir,' he says. 'We don't have any cream. We have milk though. Would you like your coffee without milk instead?'" Under the title "The Positive Negative," the conference had thus set out to explore the cognitive logistics of just such logical contradictions, visual as well as verbal, in the "stubborn obstinacy" of screen comedy, which becomes an "inexhaustible laboratory of such a strange surplus negativity." In anticipating an agenda devoted to this brand of paradox, the conference mission statement summed it this way: "Film comedy adheres to a logic of nonsense in which coffee without cream is precisely non-identical to coffee without milk: the positive negative."[2] My own contribution was intended to pursue this rule of the counterpositive all the way back to the processed negativity of the celluloid photogram in its constitutive disavowal, its negation, by screen motion—whenever, that is, this fact of filmic mediation is found rising to a level of disclosure so blatant, so risible, as to constitute a joke—or, in other words, whenever the intelligence of the machine seems, in every sense, knowingly at play.

By my concentrating, here as well, on Keaton from the early 1920s and Olsen and Johnson from the early 1940s, the paradoxical flip-flops of metamedial comedy thus drawn out are meant to show how, long before the TV laugh track, screen farce can work to turn the fact of the track itself into one long laugh. Such comedy delivers the ridiculous as merely the flip side of the potentially sublime, the screen's sublimated "view." In their reach back to the stratum of photochemical "exposure," such pranks of the apparatus do in their own way, then, and precisely in their knack for exposing the subliminal norm to ridicule, turn the positive negative. Between Keaton's *Sherlock Jr.* and its madcap homage in *Hellzapoppin!*, in connection with Bergson's theory of verbal comedy, the fuller rerun roster here will return us to certain ironies of technological mediation attendant on Chaplin's interim wrestle with sound cinema in *Modern Times* (1936): a semitalkie, as it were, poised halfway between Keaton's silence and screwball's yammer.

Factoring the Filmic

Entering from the middle of this slapstick sequence may well help clarify the poles. So, with Keaton on hold, we start with a famous episode about modern industrial technology comprising the first third of Chaplin's feature-length *Modern Times* (1936), whose factory setting grows inseparable, if not quite indistinguishable, from the workings of film's own industrial production and, in the case of voice recording, its suspect innovations. As the most technologically conflicted, so to say, of Chaplin's late and recalcitrantly "silent" films—after the passing satiric experiment with miked vocal static in *City Lights* five years before—*Modern Times* includes, first and foremost among its apparatus ironies, the fact that it is "a talkie" merely by proxy. Voice is carried only through the vinyl whine of a recorded sales pitch or, in present emission, through the raspy aggression of the corporate President in closed-circuit and one-way broadcast to the factory floor—and from there to the invaded privacy of the time-clocked privy, where the voice of authority further demands more speed and efficiency. When Chaplin's own voice is finally heard in the last scene, it is only a sing-song gibberish: music, not speech. Across the main factory episode that begins the film, certainly, Chaplin sustains his international essence as the seen but not heard—and does so against blatant alternatives in audial technique.

As restricted at first to an entirely inimical audiovisual frame in that one-way telescreen—the image of authority appearing alongside Charlie without ever containing him in its reproduced field of vision—all noise is limited to *its* hectoring voice transmission, never our hero's. Following from this double-pronged satire of corporate *command* and *oversight*, once Charlie has gone "nuts" by being expected to tighten a countless series of them at high speed on the assembly line's conveyer belt, he is sucked into the bowels of the factory apparatus as if it were a composite of gargantuan film spools rather than turbine wheels. In default of any mediated surveillance relay from the President's POV, we have until now seen only the hero full-screen, not his secondary image. We have watched Charlie only as our star, that is, not in power's line of sight as a managerial pawn. And now, one literalized level down, we see *how*. As the film cuts from the factory floor to a medium shot of those mechanical innards—this previously off-frame (and subframe) space—we encounter one of the great iconic sets in the history of film. It is as if it were the *inset* stage, one stratum beneath the President's screens-within-the-screen, for laying bare a sophisticated engineering equivalent to that which makes the whole film possible. Round and round goes the serially propelled human figure, his wrenches flailing as he goes, bolting himself as character to his own laborious treadmill, servicing his own mechanism, ultimately cause to his own star effect.

But with a resistant difference, even so, because Chaplin is still fending off the "talking picture" and its two-track rotary mechanics, still holding out for the purism of the soundless moving body choreographed in its usual comic dips and slips—many of them quasi-mechanistic themselves, of course, for all their antic dance of gesture. By this point in film history, Chaplin's silence has become deafening—and obliquely alluded to here in association with the dehumanized phonographic sales pitch as well as the grating address of the industrial overlord. With Charlie submitted at bodily (rather than aesthetic) risk, headfirst, to the spinning motors of corporate production, this exposure of the works is no doubt also to be correlated, at least in part, with the new burdens of synchronization brought on by sound technology. Certainly, the importunate sound of the President's image on the giant control screen compounds the "mechanical salesman" whose recorded voice touts a robotic feeding machine (mechanical intake rather than phonic output) designed to Taylorize one of life's most organic functions—and where steel lug nuts, misplaced in the course of emergency repair, are automatically fed to Charlie as a guinea pig, in a deflected punning travesty, no doubt, of "bolting food." These tandem indignities of industrialized sound and its dehumanizing consequences offer the clearest twofold satire of an aggressive cacophony at one with technical efficiency. And the satire is then more pointedly allegorized on the literal underside of factory production, where the inexorable new submission to a reeling sound track (other than the musical motifs composed by Chaplin himself) can be inferred as well from the carefully geared and sprocket-tightened cinemachine that the "talking film" also requires, and to which the pure image of the star body is always at peril of being sacrificed.

This gets us to what accounts, via the exquisite precision of its famous set, for the true probative brilliance of this "underworld" episode in the context of the film's layered techno-critique. For when the gears go into reverse, and spew their victim back out of their churning innards onto the factory floor again, the process is achieved by an all but indistinguishable trick of plastic and material resource: a strictly optical, rather than embodied, *rewind*. All the director needed to do—in lab rather than factory, and as if coached by Epstein in his early allegiance to cinema's unique properties in the picturing (and refiguring) of motion—is to rewind the photo strip that has produced the image in the first place, while leaving the ironic calliope music on the sound track for its contrapuntal comedy in association with this mirthless merry-go-round. Isolated here is exactly the machinic option that, as it happens, the one-way nature of sound recording could never tolerate. It isn't that Chaplin the director has troubled to have the giant wh/r/eels of the set geared so that they could reverse direction, with Charlie lifted improbably up and back into the initial aperture through which he initially slid face-first and straight down. Any Hollywood-factory cost efficiency would rule that out. You tell me, here, whether Charlie is coming or going.

Right. A full decade before Epstein made his suggestive link between burlesque and the avant-garde, between slapstick and the tricks of the medium per se, between screen lyricism and filmic "special effects"—and this on the very score of the reverse action that is only made possible by the nature of film's serial increments—Chaplin has rendered up a comparable disclosure of the medium's calibrated microlinkages in a parable of the apparatus as serial gearbox.

The incremental plasticity of the strip, the Epsteinian modulation of the photogram's separate fixed-frame molds, couldn't be more succinctly rehearsed. In ways hard for the naked eye to perceive in the grips of spectacle, we thus come upon what, fusing Epstein with Metz, one might call illusionism squared: the metafilmic specification of an inherent special effect. Motoring this reversal of time's curved arrow via the rotary vectors of industrial machination, that is, what we apprehend here, at least under repeated scrutiny, is the simple reverse enchainment of the photogram sequence—for which the rotarized Charlie, Chaplin's screen double, is both emblem and scapegoat at once, international poster boy and celluloid figment. Burst on-screen from the realm of the constitutively off-limits, there can't have been many greater tropes of motion picturing in the whole history of cinema—and certainly not in so knowing a reflex of its medium as a cinemachine.

Body/Language: "Reciprocal Interference of Series"

In plot-long fantasy rather than local trope, the question of such technological doubling has been raised more explicitly, by dream parable, in Keaton's *Sherlock Jr.* a dozen years before—and in ways equally available for illustrating Bergson's theory of "laughter" as the rendering mechanistic of human action. In his broad category of "transposition," such is comedy's signal displacement from norm to deviance, whether the comedy is physical or linguistic, cinematic or verbal.[3] Like the human form, human speech becomes, in wordplay, when saying other than it seems, a mechanical as much as a discursive function—and thus matches the routines of slapstick in taking on a life of its own, radically linguistic rather than technological. As a putative human tool, that is, speech is suddenly acting on its own behalf, acting *up*. Mechanical, this backfire of wording, because something in the nature, or rather the works, of language itself has taken over from the locus of expressive intent. As Bergson sees it, language is operating on its own behalf, taking charge, taking liberties. No episode could more readily distill Bergson's sense of mechanization than Chaplin spun on the revolving rack of his own medium. But Keaton's greater reliance on silent intertitles, and his readier way with verbal and ocular puns, makes clearer than ever the link between Bergson's theory of verbal as well as visual comedy and the philosopher's rejection on similar grounds—a rarely noted bridge between phases of his thought—of film's own bodily "mechanization," its engineering rather than inhabitation of *durée*.

With the category of mechanical "transposition" broken down by examples in Bergson's "Laughter," the three hallmarks of verbal as well as physical comedy are repetition, inversion, and interference. We might think of them, respectively, as the rut, the upending, and the static disruption of natural motion—or communication. The last disturbance is more fully characterized by Bergson as "reciprocal interference of series" (123), when one train of association is double-crossed by an alternative through a "transposition" from one received register to its anomalous counterpart. We think we are reading along idiomatically enough, when the phrasing is suddenly blindsided by a completely different sense of its wording. Blindsided—or more like mechanically overturned in a two-way collision. And there is a further mechanistic reciprocity as well, for it is by way of response, by our own reactions in the automatic belly laugh, that we too are mechanized. Here, then, is yet another and early version of an ethics of affect easily attached to screen viewing as well as theatrical and literary comedy. Attempting to align examples of verbal and visual jokes in Bergson's mechanistic terms, one might turn to examples in Dickens where the engineering of lexical options gets out ahead of syntactic coherence in the trope of syllepsis ("taking-together," alternately known as zeugma). And find support for this in the latent cinematic analogs for it in a notable earlier comparison of Dickensian syntax and screen editing. In his canonical essay "Dickens, Griffith, and the Film Today," Eisenstein singled out *Dombey and Son* (1848) less for its comic verve, certainly, than—published, as it happens, though unmentioned by Eisenstein, in the same year as *The Communist Manifesto*—for its pervasive motif of a bourgeois chill emanating from the capitalist frigidity of its title figure.[4] Though not adducing this description of Mr. Dombey as the vessel of a capitalist ego, Eisenstein would certainly have seen "stiff with starch and arrogance" as a symptom of that condition in the very first chapter—if not a Bergsonian logical "interference" of descriptive sequence in a mechanical "transposition" from couture to deportment.

And mechanized in a quite specific way. When the comic rudiment of staggered "repetition" extends, in the case of an "equivocal" linguistic "situation," to verbal "puns" and other dualisms, this is part of exactly what Bergson means by that specialized subset of "transposition" known as a "reciprocal interference of series" (123). Each convergent referential element undoes the stability of the other—as in the case of "stiff with starch and arrogance," with its short circuit between wardrobe and psychology. Yet how, beyond capitalist critique, might this align with Eisenstein on Dickensian "editing" technique? A ready example comes to hand in the form of a full compound predicate, not a just prepositional pairing (as *with* a and b). It happens that the first instance of such a sylleptic trope in Dickens's own first novel, *Pickwick Papers*, appears in a compound (if elliptical) verb phrase that double-tracks Mr. Pickwick as he "fell into the barrow and fast asleep, simultaneously" (chap. 19). This discrepant effect matches the stiff grammatical linkage in a stilted inversion given by Eisenstein, apart from his focus on Dickens, as the verbal equivalent of a forced and flaccid montage: "Came the rain and two students" (253). In prose rather than edited image, such an internal montage of actions—

rendered in nonparallel grammar, but "simultaneously"—is Dickens's own version of something between a jump cut and a match cut, straining at the continuity that its own conjunction posits. Neither strictly repetitive (the difference marked by *and* prevents that) nor inverted (since a commonality rather than a flipped sense is posited), "reciprocal interference of series" seems indeed, in this case, a name for the tempered jarring of this cut on action.

Just this kind of *syntactic* pun finds its redoubtable screen update when Groucho Marx, in dismissing Mrs. Teasedale in *Duck Soup* (Leo McCarey, 1933), plays between three (not just two) divergent senses of the preposition "in," regarding both mood and mode of exit, for a sylleptic brush-off capped by a homophonic pun on *huff* for *half*: "If you can't get a taxi you can leave in a huff. If that's too soon, you can leave in a minute and a huff." More than one colloquial series, to be sure, is "interfered" with in those dovetailed alternatives. As is the case in Howard Hawks's film of *His Girl Friday*, in a grammatical quick cut not there in the theatrical source (the 1928 play *The Front Page*). Its transposed seriality is as fast in syntactic overrun as is the ricochet of reverse shots in this same newsroom sequence. This is the moment when the exclamatory grammar of confirmation (in an announced proper noun) turns adjectival on the spot to somatize nomenclature into anatomical euphemism. "What was the name of the mayor's first wife?" / "The one with the wart on her?" / "Right." / "Fanny." Again Bergson: two lines of apperception intercepting and almost discommoding each other, here in a verbal pratfall regarding the phantom blemish of a derrière.

This fillip of overlapping dialogue, this match-cut superimposition of separate semantic streams—choose your preferred cinematic metaphor—manifests another version of the Bergsonian "reciprocal interference" that buckles convergent sequences out of shape, foiling serial continuity along its own dialogue channels. However felt or analogized, such a mechanical hiccup in sense renders obtrusive the comic equivalent of those overridden breaches in the forced rather than organic continuum, according to Bergson, that make the cinematographic effect a mockery of lived duration. Low comedy thus waxes philosophical by default, from within its own nonsensical, if punningly recuperated, fault lines. In the rapidly elided space between preposition and its object (turned subject) in this Hawksian banter—"on her... Fanny"—flickers, that is, the grammatical equivalent of some jammed frame advance giving the lie to all sense of the seamless on screen: here in an open disjunctive counterpoint across the slipstream of syntax itself.

Certainly the kind of verbal dexterity, sampled from Dickens through Groucho to Howard Hawks, models the investigative slippage that makes visual slapstick tick—and stick: a conceptual traction behind the manifest frolic. Analysis is thus able to move rather directly from Dickensian sylleptic comedy to the comparable optic splits and forkings in Keaton. If one takes the Bergsonian format of a "reciprocal interference of series" in a spatial rather than temporal sense for screen gags, especially if the series lays itself out along an actual visible axis traversed by narrative action, then one model for the comedy in the central dream sequence of Keaton's 1924 masterwork, *Sherlock Jr.*, is prepared in the waking time plot of *Our Hospitality* the year before: and not just with the tricked perception of its wardrobe jokes but in optical regard to the camera-managed sight lines that facilitate them. Indeed, much of Keaton's double-take humor turns on the difference, in metafilmic comedy, within the turn—or wrench— between an orthogonal axis of spectation, as channeled further by point of view within frame, and the alternate vectors of lateral action. Such, within the diegesis, is Keaton's deep instinct for thematizing precisely the difference between screen plane and the vectored gestures it isolates and frames. Sight gags in his films turn with striking frequency on the ironic twist of sight lines, which is one of the main ways in Keaton that the comic is rendered reflexive, *comedial*. In the mode of apparatus reading invited here, the work of the *dispositif* can thus tacitly be read as its own kind of wry "frame-up," bracketing actions that redraw their own lines of sight, and alike of motion, before our eyes.

Abetted by the comedy of camera angles, certainly, are the deft costume shifts across gender (and species!) in *Our Hospitality*. Within the feuding and murderous world of its plot, for instance, we see Buster, in a tight spot, finding that the door behind him is to a closet rather than any possible escape route. Except, except. . . . He spies a dress hanging there. Scene change, then another, and across an elided transformation he leaves the house of his lethal enemies in full-body disguise, soon crossing paths with an armed villain. Reverse shot, and one kind of centaur-like paradox (another pending) is exposed: frocked female above, presumptive trousered man showing through below, panted and panting. But that top/bottom division, in plane, is now dynamized for a genuine camera comedy, rather than just a visible disjuncture and joke. Off goes Keaton on horseback, with his camouflage now masking his whole face in the wind, and further encumbered by an umbrella that was no part of the original disguise. *We* see this, but the villains *don't*, and as they prepare to put a bullet in his back in the next shot, it turns out, in the swivel of the screen's own syntax, that their target—actually his deceptively garmented ride, without its rider, eventually turning sideways to expose the mistake—is even more literally the horse's ass than they had supposed him to be. The axis of apperception, that is, has shifted 90 degrees: the orthogonal become horizontal. Serial motion has not just been interfered with, but intercepted at right angles—with the transferred disguise of parasol, gingham, and bonnet, now adorning the horse's behind, being either the accidental result of Buster's flight on foot or a set of deliberate decoys, as of course they are on Keaton the director's part. Either way, the categorical abstractions of Bergsonian analysis still certainly pertain. With the horse suddenly discovered frocked in ladylike getup on its nether end, we are thrown momentarily by the transposed interference of two previously coextensive "series": the once simultaneous vectors of the hero's female disguise and his animal conveyance, in lateral flight—positioned now, in his absence, both at a 90-degree angle to, and at cognitive odds with, each other in a weaponized line of sight.

Projective Vision: Asleep at the Reel

It is, however, a fuller-scale structure of comic right angles that organizes the unforgettable inspiration of next year's *Sherlock Jr.*, where axial crisscrossing in the syntax of serial action torques directionality itself in a primal filmic manner. Once the dreaming Buster as truant projectionist has jumped into the world of his own screening, to become its detective hero, this transgression triggers the symbolic permeability of all obstacles, framed screen-like shapes or otherwise, in the ensuing fantasy plot. But what this freak dream option also does is to spotlight, by the projector's beam itself, the normally uninhabited point of intersection between the straight-ahead gaze of the film spectator and the lateral motions that dynamize the projected world thus viewed.

Before this dream logic takes hold, with its barrage of visual double entendres among other interferences, it has been up to the title cards, with their repeated word play, to match or anticipate the visual tricks— including tricks on visibility itself—with a running set of puns all their own. When the wannabe detective Sherlock, inundated by untold gallons of water from a storage tank at railside, is called (in the title card) "all wet as a detective," the joke operates as if in answer to the first flat-footed phrasal straddle by his movie-theater boss: "Before you clean up any mysteries— clean up this theater," a lax variant of syllepsis. Buster is here reprimanded, in a prioritizing of literal over figurative "cleanup," for having taken a study break, where he has mistakenly assumed that merely licking his thumb will allow a legible fingerprinting. The real nature of visual imprint, however, is about to be disclosed in the projection booth. It is there that Buster's falling asleep in propria persona, after starting the reel, allows his *trucage* double, by obtrusively filmic superimposition, to study his way into the detective film in progress after trying to wake his originary self to the thievery underway. In an unabashed send-up, this oneiric turn accompanies a film brought to us, in an early version of corporate diversification, from the conglomerate known here as Veronal Productions: named, no less, for the period's sleeping pill of choice.

Perhaps our first clue to the vestigial vaudeville logic of Keaton's cinematic stunts comes in an oddly residual gimmick next. So that he can turn the screen characters into the identificatory circuit of figures from his waking life that our detective manqué wishes to *project* onto the screen's genre plot, the prerecorded principles oddly turn their backs, as if about to apply a theatrical disguise, and only turn round again, after superimposition, when ready to reveal their new avatars. Even this, though, invites axial reflection as a metafilmic gesture, for in looking away they are also, and in fact, looking along the same sightline as our projecting hero, settling themselves into alignment with his fantasy before returning to the work of suture by which he will eventually learn from them how to come on romantically to his girlfriend.

What follows first, however, is his famous trial by editorial ordeal— often a literal (upending) crash course in jump-cut editing—transacted across the fissures of a pointless montage-for-montage's-sake that slows his access to the screen plot he has both slept and leapt his way into. In a frenetic discontinuity more implausible than any finessed duration repudiated by Bergson concerning the medium's intermittent basis, this rapid-fire editing tosses the hero from one scenography to another across visual puns inferred from the discrepant locales—like being thrown to the lions in one case, as metaphor for submission to the violence of screen syntax, and then no sooner finding himself out to sea (on a tiny ocean atoll) than high and dry (on a cliffhanger-like mountain's edge). With no coherent narrative yet in sight, these are the figments—the latent figures—of its very incipience, where, in an extreme case of silent cinema, the reverberations of the unworded quite literally *call the shots*. And if no other logic of thirdness (in Peirce's terms again) has supervened in order to interpret this raced and incoherent shot plan, that is also to suggest that even its firstness as image chain as well as its secondness as di/visible sites, has reverted to some kind of arbitrary exercise in serial juxtaposition—one level up from the unitary engram. It is as if montage has been reduced, beneath all organic flow, toward the arbitrary "genetic" units (Deleuze's initial stress on a zero-value basis in motion picturing) of the photogram chain per se. What Buster must *put himself through*, in two axes at once, is not just the perpendicular barrier of the screen but its own parallel montage within frame, its inherent optic seriality. In order not to be outsmarted by the "intelligence of a machine" in his unconscious access to it, the dreaming Buster must thus leap two barriers at once: no sooner diving across projection's facilitating material surface than, as a result, divining the very fissures (Epstein) of intermittence from there out.

Accompanying all this in its wordplay, both text-based and inferential, it is almost as if *Sherlock Jr.* saw *Modern Times* coming in respect to the latter's derivations from a silent verbal matrix. Factory *oversight*, the worker *overwrought*, the character *wound too tight* on his own automated belt, the *nuts* that silently pun on his labor and its breakdown alike, as if to suggest further, for all the frenzied grip and tension, *a screw loose* somewhere, and then the indirect *bolting* of food that ensues by accident with the feeding machine before, by inversion, he is fed to another like it as icon of the cinemachine: these are the same sort of twisted idioms that, in *Sherlock Jr.*, go unsaid at the start of the film-within-the-film but have already, in the frame tale, been translated to such intertitles as Buster's obligation to "clean up" the theater rather than the mystery, before his washed-up status as sleuth is punned on by the "all wet" of his trainyard dousing. Idiom after idiom gets flipped to the duplicate of its normal intent, the literal turned figurative. Verbal norms and adages are *displaced*, yes, or in Bergson's sense, interfered with reciprocally: unsettling the positive/ negative poles of literalization itself.

Only after our being initially slapped silly, along with Buster, by that unruly and illogical montage do we finally, in a kind of optical syllepsis of focus, both dolly- and iris-in on the immersive and frame-filling diegesis of the screened melodrama. And from there out, permeability is to be had for the asking, with walls and bodies penetrated at will. But one discomfiture, one dramatically horizontal threat, stands out from that opening barrage of spatial (and often idiomatic) displacements. This happens when Buster, not yet Sherlock within the fantasized screen access, is intercepted at right angles—and nearly run down—by the flickering horizontal blur of train cars and framed windows whipping past. In the midst of an unmistakable cinematic hazing, here, by inference, is a fleeting apparition of the speeding celluloid track itself—cinemachine as primal locomotion.

In an example of Bergson's repetition and inversion as comic staples, to say nothing of fluctuant serial discontinuity at the basis of cinema's falsified motion, this speeding rotary mechanization—already a synecdochic threat within the editing blitz of Buster's own oneiric projection—also recurs to a suggestive transitional moment. It follows (from) the waking-life prelude, that is, in which Buster has been able to make the most of train locomotion, if only briefly, by leaping from car to speeding rectangular car (with the camera frame tightly envisioning, without following, his lateral progress). Though naturalized as a horizontal rather than vertical recurrence, it is as if, by retinal parable, he were running in place across separate photograms (the movement-image maintained in frame, as it were, by the many more similar shapes that speed beneath). The effect is stretched out until the whole length of the train has finally, his luck with it, *left the station*—and he is flooded by the water tank whose spout he uses to break his fall. Clearly "all wet" in his detective role, he returns to see "what he could to his other job," that aggressive preposition anticipating the transformation that his dreaming narrative libido is about to perform— as if in illustration of the punning condensations and displacements in Freud's theory of the unconscious and its jokes.

Having passed with our hero through the interface of the screen's reflective surface, we soon get another emblematic scene of a supposed image plane at right angles to bodily motion, again the lateral and the orthogonal both at odds and in oddball collaboration. For after Sherlock the detective is spruced by his Butler, presumed sight lines are reversed and collapsed in his move through the looking glass. What we took to be a beveled mirror frame, full-length and wall-wide, rather like the black border of the theatrical screen, is actually revealed to be a threshold into a second parallel room, not just an optical duplicate of the first: a room where wind is blowing identical curtains in little cognate billows.

In this "sylleptic" screen syntax, transliteration might have it that Sherlock no sooner got *through* with his primping than the looking glass as well. Yet the "mirror" was not even a filmic *trucage*, just an optical illusion of frame and reflected (rather than merely parallel) rug, chair, vase, and fabric motion. We never saw anything but the empty floor space of a decorated room. It was simply "reframed" for us perceptually as something else. Now, like the opaque interface of the framed screen beneath the theater's proscenium arch in the pivotal episode, this planar expanse is also, to our surprise, a second unrealized portal taken advantage of by Buster. Moreover, as if that faux mirror weren't enough to equivocate the very notion of spatial adjacency—penetrated where one expects only reflective optics—the subsequent shot ups the ante. It shows us a room where what is locked behind, not within, a bulking wall safe is a space that turns out, quite literally out—via the interference and reversal of any utilitarian logic—to be the whole supposedly outer world made safe for this invulnerable dream agent. In further positive/ negative reversal, what didn't seem a portal, but was, is answered now by a barrier turned narrative threshold. From the vantage of Epstein's stress on intermittence, looking either half a decade back from his Poe film or two decades from *The Intelligence of a Machine*, what Keaton's absurdist continuities between built spaces and framed second worlds serve to foreground, or at least to figure, is the wholesale figment of continuity on the normative screen plane.

And so a pause is in order for, yes, reflection. Mirrors real or tricked have been catching more light in separate phases of this essay than its author originally imagined. They've become a kind of motif, but only because they are so often installed, both in commentary and in screen imaging, as a master trope: figure for the apparatus in action. As Weimar journalism noted early on, the reflective screen often embeds *other* planar illusionism to just this end. Long before Shüfftan, whose differently "unseen" mirrors were stationed to invert and embed the "off-frame" miniature into the optic field of screen action, the special-effects mirror of Edison showed us something seemingly there, right there, that wasn't. By mirror inversion, as it were, Keaton's effect works, oppositely, to trick us into thinking that what seems right there before our eyes actually somehow isn't—as the phantom mirror negates itself as a positive door. As part of Keaton's wry way with right angles, and the physics of sightlines, we *presume* the object of his perpendicular gaze while settling for our own at right angles to it. The play between orthographic and horizontal vectors that pervades his stunts is brought forward here not just to surprise us but to confound our sense of surface itself in this reflection on the screen's own reflective plane. And not just that, but to remind us that Keaton as Sherlock is already a secondary reflection of Buster—the Undead incarnation of the apparatus per se—who thus, vampire-like, feeding however benignly on his own fantasies, deserves no further (tertiary) reflection. Or put the latent allegory more generally. Already, in Epstein's sense, a "truquage" of continuity as visible organic agency, this quintessential incarnation of the screen actor inherits, by machinic birthright, a mastery of all subsidiary discontinuities in his passage through demarcated and segmented space.

In short, if we pause over that mirror, Keaton certainly doesn't. Once again, he charges ahead—and in its iconographic terms for diegesis itself—straight into the *safe space* that is another metaphor for it. Fresh from two risky episodes of railroad locomotion—each of them obliquely figuring the filmic agent's transcendence of an underlying Epsteinian discontinuity—the new dream self, empowered now, can use the warning bar at an urban railroad crossing to intercept (at a right-angled "interference" again) the automotive track of his pursuers in their speeding convertible. Thinly disguised behind even this armature of physical comedy is the vernacular notion of *lowering the boom* on his enemies—one of those moments in which Bergson's "reciprocal interference of series" seems operating, wholesale, between the otherwise autonomous realms of verbal and visual articulation. In what follows next, certain physical stunts from Keaton's acrobatic vaudeville career are slyly imbricated with screen devices. This happens when a lap dissolve removes the nearest wall of the villains' hideout so as to turn it, wholly in frame, into a parody of cinema's fourth wall—just a few moments before, at a slightly canted right angle to it, Buster dives through the carefully prepared packaging of a woman's dress (gender transposition yet again) and pops out, this time no cut involved, fully cross-dressed. Having come out as a woman, by some weird chiastic logic, and once shedding the dress in pursuit by the thieves, he next goes into a woman, diving straight through both her open suitcase of odds and ends for sale and her abdomen behind it. This is accomplished by an old stage trick that forces us to imagine another shift in head-on angles: here from inside an adjacent barn, where we would see the accomplice's legs lifted high above the hidden trap door through which Keaton could leap onto, say, a mattress. On screen, however, the reciprocal interference of series verges on an eviscerating (if still comic) violence.

These two wardrobe stunts are then topped when a giant tractor looms from the side like a bulking disaster for the motorcycled hero on collision course with it. Tension mounts, until it turns 90 degrees to reveal its own mechanism on stills, granting easy passage beneath its engine and driver. And this is topped yet again, once the impending threat of one motorized contraption is overcome, when twin vehicles themselves come to the rescue next. Through the gap in a dilapidated trestle bridge, a pair of oncoming trucks make their implausible hairsbreadth way at right angles to the structure, only for this motorized instance of reciprocal interference—this dream-scenario serendipity—to be timed exactly, at right angles, to the hero's speeding over the chasm they have bridged for him. And finally, again at right angles to the downstream motion of his sinking convertible, the canvas top converts further to a sail—and, all washed up again in unspoken metaphor this time, Buster wakes at his projector to study in a direct eyeline match, now, the progress of an amorous demonstration on screen, modeling his every move, in shot/reverse shot, on the erotic gestures of the *Hearts and Pearls* denouement.

Yet after the final clinch and kiss, an elliptical cross-fade yields to the horizontal axis of the screen frame itself, with the doubled twins of the screen couple leaving the projectionist scratching his head in consternation about the precipitous nature of cause and effect, both in sexual coupling and in screen syntax. The dream overlay figured at the start by laboratory superimposition has become a diegetic, because genetic, doubling, technique folded back into action as a real world conundrum for the naïve hero. This, then, rounding out the dream logic, is the ur-perpendicular from which all the others derive: the right angle by which the beam from a fixed camera in the booth intersects the lateral action on screen that its play of light and shadow in fact generates. And it is just this establishing right angle, between an apparent optic source in the booth and the resulting appearance of motion in thrown shadows, that awaits send-up in *Hellzapoppin!* So, too, in that same later film, with the screen that disappears (though this time from inside the plot looking out) to give the players visual access to their own audience. Ocular (not bodily) penetrability, and even before that, perpendicularity: these are the ground rules of reflection, as well as of "automatic world projections" (Cavell), that are allegorized by Keaton and pursued by Olsen and Johnson as, in each case, the positive/negative of impossible audience participation.

At every stage in the optical metaplot of Keaton's film, things have been transposed and reversed, turned inside out—offering, if you will, the counterpositive of what they picture. Screen vs. aperture, mirror vs. portal, warning boom vs. catapult, wall vs. skewed trap door, hole vs. bridge, euphemistic sexual ellipsis vs. time-lapse explanatory dissolve: things aren't just commutable; they call up the opposite or negative inversion of what they seem. That Paris waiter in *Ninotchka* must have taken a night class or two with Bergson at the Sorbonne on the theory of comic inversion. You can't not have cream in any decisive way; you can only not have the milk we do have. Slapstick at the level of Keaton's geometrical sophistication—so keenly aware of point of view and its depictions, and deceptions, and of the risible precisions that film allows in this regard in outstripping the limits of stage comedy—slapstick like this isn't just metafilmic in some general sense. It does indeed opt for the logic of the double negative. It offers a rhetoric of litotes made material. That retreating figure is *not not* a woman's outfit seen from the rear, if only a horse's rear. That second room is *not not* a mirror image of the first. That combination-lock safe door is *not not* a way out of the scene. That broken scaffolding will *not not* be an asset in transit. That automobile chassis is *not not* a ship's hull. That screen kiss is *not not* the proximate cause of reproductions other than filmic. Litotes, double negative, yes, but in the serial disclosure of such ironies, I would insist, this is film's delirious illustration of sylleptic syntax as well. A truant dream Buster overcomes by coming over and through not just boxcars and trestle gaps and windows and walls but gender difference itself, only in the end, his waking self still confused by its residue, to be back at work and at sea again.

Putting on a Movie

In both understandings of that phrase: mounting a movie's production while sending it up. A decade and a half after *Sherlock Jr.*, and making an even more direct transit from stage to screen farce across the seasoned genre formula of "Let's put on a show," 1941's *Hellzapoppin!* is pivoted around a set of no-doubt derivative (and markedly more erotic) complications in a metafilmic projection booth. The self-reflexive hijinks of this film's very low comedy operate, more broadly and blatantly, within the same two Keatonesque axes: screen-aimed focal point, on the one hand, and lateral action across it, on the other. With an absurd transposition from one ontological level to another, the tantalizing body of a woman on the filmed stage set causes our delegated POV to dawdle over her scantily clad make-up ritual until we realize, by jump cut to the booth, that it is the projectionist's supposedly empowered fixation that has slowed down the tracking shot by shifting the projector leftward. Libidinal investment momentarily—and farcically—confounds the drive of narrative, rather than being leashed to it as usual. This happens while the main actors are moving past her figure to the right, furious (as if they would realize it!) that the optic pace has been selfishly retarded by the projectionist—and demanding in supposedly discrete pantomime that the operator keep up with plot's horizontal movement. It is as if Metz's double articulation of cinematic desire, based on primary and secondary identification with recording lens and character, respectively, has been commandeered and deranged. The result is that camerawork can be rerouted by the desires of a characterized operator: the operator not of the recording camera itself, but only—and preposterously—of the fixed image's later relay system in the booth.[5]

Even before this, it is our line of sight only, or so we assume, that is occluded by a hand-scrawled transparency placed over the lens by the projectionist, relaying the message from an irate mother that one "Stinky Miller," if in the audience, should "go home at once." But in a Bergsonian repetition and inversion of this triggering joke, and a further reversal of sightlines, the diegetic characters on screen join in the harangue, the second time around, and help send Stinky on his silhouetted way out of the auditorium. Reversing the impossible line of sight and flight in *Sherlock Jr.*, where an overidentified spectator breaches the screen, the Olsen and Johnson film thus anticipates the alternate axis between diegetic characters and spectators in Woody Allen's *The Purple Rose of Cairo* (1985), where a screen hero interrupts his own plot by pausing to question a patron about her repeated viewing of his eponymous film-within-the-film.

In this respect, *Hellzapoppin!*, by sheer accident of nomenclature, installs a unique version of what cognitive narratology calls the pushing and *popping* of the deictic field (where, for instance, the variable "you" of direct address is located), shifting the level of indication from space of event to plane of discourse. Layered one more time here, between the *narrated* space of reception and a subsidiary screen narrative, the jolt of the joke still operates: pushing back from direct address *before* the screen (superimposed on it) to a disgruntled vocative *from* it. Concerning the diegetic scene of projection in the movie theater where the film we're watching is also being watched, the here and now of handwritten address to the truant boy in the time of exhibition (on a portable, if not mobile, transparency) would, needless to say, have no logical narrative connection with the prerecorded characters behind it on the internal screen. Instead, in this comic "inversion" (Bergson), or call it this negative/positive twist, the deictic of the vocative in the urgent address to Stinky—pushed back from spell-breaking superimposed scrawl to inner graphic disruption for the on-screen fictional characters—now oddly pops out again to refigure the screen as just such a transparency, rather than a reflective surface. For, right after the screen couple's disgruntled frame-breaking shout-out to Stinky, they turn back to painting the stage set within which they will star, and where the hero has previously been reflected in a false-front glass window. With no further preparation, a cut now takes us to the other side of that transparent p(l)ane in a tighter close-up (presumably from inside the house), no window edges visible, with the heroine now cheerfully painting—as if on the screen surface itself, in answer to the previous hand held transparency—a sketch of their prospective dream home accompanying the lyrics of a musical interlude.

We are a far cry here from just a scripted filter over the lens. Yet even if this whole episode went primarily to remind us of the projectionist's hand in exhibition, and its sudden disruptions, it would have earned its keep in the metafilmic comedy now building to its peak. More illogical momentum, however, has certainly been achieved—and is now made good on. Where Keaton's projected desire triggers the magic transformations on screen, here it is instead—following the projectionist's absurd, disruptive ogling of the actress—the aggressive desire of a caricatured female nemesis barging into the projection booth, like something out of the Marx brothers, that flummoxes the operator into botching everything from sprocket alignment to reel change. Writing five years later, though certainly without specific comment on this American farce, Epstein might have seen in it the *idiocy* of an otherwise intelligent machine when its sequencing goes out of whack, when intermittence gets an unpoliced upper hand. Yet what this accident still thinks for us, the spectators, about the underlying machination of the apparatus—and such is the upending force of this comedy—occurs to the characters themselves at one remarkable turn (or roll) of projection: occurs not just as idea but as event. It *happens* to them as they fall between the cracks in the normal slipstream of their own recorded ontology.

Unprecedented: that the frameline per se should be made present in this way to the characters it helps invisibly to propel. Except perhaps for Chaplin in *Modern Times*, and there only by industrial analogy: the star image inched forward at high speeds around the coiled innards of his own intelligent (if potentially malevolent) machine. Or by Keaton, again if only by optical analogy, sustaining his in-frame image before us only by moving from one tracked rectangle (one speeding boxcar) to another over their intermittent treacherous gaps. Such ingrown scenes of screen action—when not just realized but essentialized, figured by visual transposition to the diegesis, and, so to speak, made light of there—serve to delimit the very springs of *comediality*.

When the photogram chain is interrupted in *Hellzapoppin!*, the characters try taking action themselves, by pulling down the particularly bulky frame line—or pulling themselves up to another sprocket-aligned rectangle—giving a special vertical emphasis to any more general theory of off-frame space. The move is as ingenious as it is ludicrous. And useless— there being no edge to grab in that sense.

These characters, as if we didn't know it by now, are the epiphenomena of the machine, not its masters. The next effort to recover the norm is the projectionist's, but he ends up putting the film in upside down, again reminding us—in full-screen inversion—of its photogrammic materiality and verticality alike when operating, right side up or not, at right angles to the arc light's beam. Even more illogically, when he switches reels again, the film-within-the film becomes a kind of punning *double picture* where a shoot-'em-up Western has overlain, from behind, not just its image but its whole threatening diegesis upon the main characters, resulting in an actual gunshot from—and in—the rear. This happens when the frame ratio changes from an ominous close-up of the vengeful Indian to a medium shot (pun no doubt intended) that allows the rifle itself the focal length it needs.

The collapse of the cinemachine could scarcely be more complete. Misalignment versus inversion versus superposition: jammed adjacent frames popping us from the plot to its obtruded apparatus; flipped reel turning the whole thing upside down; overlaid frames inducing a cross-fire of both plot- and sight lines. This threefold optic farce is in a very particular way *definitive*. Instead of being jinxed by such disjunctures, of course, screen comedy turns them to optical puns, one image for the plot, one for the razzed if not downright unraveled medium. Irreverence runs deep. Through such kinks in the "thread" (Cavell) of reeled celluloid, filmic (rather than just film) comedy backflips to a wild realization of its

own underlay. In Bergson: repetition, inversion, reciprocal interference of series. In Olsen and Johnson: snagged differential iteration, upside-down spools, and the collisional nonsense of interfering projected worlds—with one transposed upon, sneaking up upon, the other from behind. Beyond any narratively assimilable "assertions in technique" (Cavell)—beyond any unique power of the photogram chain, like pause or acceleration, that might affiliate the hijinks of machinic comedy with the ingenuities of the avant-garde (Epstein)—here is the apparatus not appropriated for rhetoric but dismantled as coherent image system.

Antics/Mechanics/Ethics

A tempting plateau opens at this point on the very ground of theoretical reorientation. For we can retrack two of our previous film-philosophy intersections across some further and intriguing cross-mapped terrain. For Cavell, cinema is, uncontroversially, and throughout *The World Viewed*, an "automatism." But he coins his own far more deliberately alienating term in his major philosophical work, *The Claim of Reason*. It is a term for one's doubt of the Other as availably human: a suspicion, under skepticism, of "automatonity."[6] In such a withering mood of mind, disengaged from any interpersonal ethics, everything and everyone seems alien to humanizing recognition, to intimate acknowledgment: ultimately a false front, an artificial intelligence, emptied, robotic. Which invites us, or might, to triangulate the basic automatism of cinema with, on the one side, the particular automata to which slapstick screen figures are sometimes reduced, those ricocheting bodies of comic agency, and, on the other, the larger paradigm of skepticism's distancing of the world through a dubious response to its inhabitants as virtual automata: a universe merely *going through the motions* as real. Not immediately obvious, this triangulation, its effort can benefit from other theoretical conjunctures already on tap in these annotations.

In particular, a repeated touchstone of Cavell's thought centers on the way movies can offer a kind of screened-off test of one's credence in the world—as if to say, those endearing or enduring figures, those human shapes, are of course only "automatic ... projections," but we can feel for them anyway, acknowledge them as enough like us to care about their travails. To paraphrase the logic, in this overt a way, helps bring Cavell's frame of reference into relation with Bergson around a curious reversal from which, as Cavell himself suggestively says, "further paths beckon." For us, it is equally the case that earlier routes are harked back to and retraced. Cavell: "Picking up Bergson's idea of the comic as the encrusting or the obtruding of the mechanical or material onto or out of the living, we might conceive of laughter as the natural response to automatonity when we know the other to be human." Skepticism is, then, the reverse: "In that case it would follow from the absence of our laughter in the face of the impression or imagination of automatonity in others that we do not know others to be human." This is to say that Bergson's sense of laugher, as inducing an almost mechanical reaction to an already degraded human fullness, is symmetrically matched by skepticism's eroded confidence in the lived world.

But the question still hangs in the rarefied air between ontology and ethics: how does this reversal overlap with our separate effort to align Bergson on the rejected material discontinuity of film and Bergson on that mechanical reductivenes of comedy involved in the denaturalizing joke on page and stage well before screen? And how might this alignment be enhanced by putting Cavell on the dubieties of skepticism, with its automatonization of the other, together with Cavell on the undenied machinic basis of film? Only examples can, in the long run, negotiate. And an enforced if staggered continuity is often the weft of their sequencing. Chaplin in *Modern Times* is explicitly engorged by the industrial apparatus, to become not a cog in its wheeling engines, nor just grit in its machine, but spasmodic grist for the mill of its productive slapstick visualization. Keaton converts random things of the outer world to tools for his extravagant use, even while becoming a kind of instrumental body himself, a mere link in the mechanics of transit. Split from within screen manifestation like one of their own blatant verbal puns, together Olsen and Johnson get caught between frames not as people, with any credible agency to correct the automatism, but as mere aspects of a photogrammic snag in its serial aggregation.

And with Weimar responses behind us, we can look to melodrama rather than comedy as well. Think of one of the most renowned special effects in early German cinema, and let the "intelligence" of Fritz Lang's machine think it through for you as a parable of its own technical possibility. In *Metropolis*, the proletarian Maria operates as the robot version of herself several times over, "automatonity" gone rampant: the actress as screen automatism to begin with, as second-order product of the apparatus; then the faux heroine, the black-magic duplicate, undergoing mechanical superimposition in the special effect of her electrochemical machinic transfer from steel mannequin to refleshed deceptive seductress. And thereafter the persisting sense of living illusion associated with her false center of consciousness—all this as an exaggerated embodiment of skeptical paranoia, where no inwardness can be trusted. Cavell's film-philosophy seems distilled in such a node of multiple *trucage*. To undergo mechanical reproduction within plot, and thus to fuse with the automatism *of* plot, is for the robot to tell cinema's story as well as its own—and to raise by travesty the everyday anxieties associated with skepticism: the doubt of other minds behind the image of other bodies. Doubts which normal movies, free of temptress automata, and even in this same movie in regard to the ethical vulnerabilities of the "real Maria," can serve to work through—often, for Cavell, almost by allegory—in the visual pressure points of their own narrative trajectories.

That is, of course, where we have been looking in the work of apparatus reading: at nodes of narrative inference flagged by special effectuations of cinematographic technique. Whereas Keaton transported his stage tricks almost directly to film, yet found in camera placement their fullest dialectical refinement, the plot and in-joke of *Hellzapoppin!* is to translate a Broadway spectacle to the mode of a play-within-a-play, but then to render that embedding structure so frenetically filmic, not just cinematic, that transmedial tensions are wallowed in unabashedly. But at one late point (and *my* last point), they are indulged not just shamelessly but, though showily still, almost subtly. For here—in the metatheater of *Hellzapoppin!*—the most intriguing shot of all is a reciprocal interference between the axis of projection and the vertical axis not of the photogram chain per se, or at least only by association, but of an onstage curtain-raising. At the width of the entire proscenium, this shot holds on the slowly lifted representational scrim that, in a classic theatrical trope of framed display, is matched exactly to the *tableau vivante* of the poised dancers behind it—until, when the difference widens to clearer view, eventually bisecting the stage's vertical dimension, we are reminded not just of filmic as well as theatrical transparencies but again of the photogram series itself and its near duplicates in the choreography of differential motion.

In comic epiphany here is not primarily the similarity between real and pictured bodies. At the level of material support or substrate, what is unveiled is the veil itself, the curtain of imprinted image whose vertical motion alone inaugurates the artifice of depicted movement. And does so, in this case, by way of an unusual ambiguation of (Peircean) firstness—as we initially try to make out what the layered image is in fact an image of. Unlike in photochemical process, two negatives, interfering with each other reciprocally, can make not a positive, but something positively surprising. To speak sylleptically, what is being "sent up" at this point—both lifted and travestied—is the illusionist stage scrim and the film work at once. The very mode of transparency, at a metafilmic premium, interferes (Bergson again) with its own duplicate so as to lay bare what is always and already there.

Moreover, in the media-archaeological terms that may be brought to mind by this *comedial* gambit, one suspects that something from the prehistory of cinema has been reconstituted in the realm of the motion picture when understood as the mere moving of picture planes. It is as if the simultaneously positive and negative aspects of the daguerreotype's constitutive lamination, each bonded inextricably to the other in their function as two-dimensional countermolds, have been pried apart for a serial and more obviously two-ply disclosure. In this deeply mediacentric as well as comedic sense—pointing us back to the technics of projection, as Dickensian comedy does to the mechanics of wording and grammar— the only motion inherent to this or any cinematographic dance of action comes, at base, from a sheer vertical lift in the differential shuffle and shunt between frames. Speaking metagenerically, it's always no less than funny—with disavowal itself inverted—to be put not just in mind but in view of this. And even if everything else in this blatant movie-about-movies could be chalked up to straight self-referentiality, which I began by hiving off from the more pervasive domain of apparatus reading, this curtain-raising moment would operate otherwise. It engages, instead, with the frank materiality of plastic mediation. It does so in a manner— speaking *strictly* figuratively, and on both sides of the equation—that can seem to get under both the film's own skin and ours alike.

   Comedial—or, if you prefer, in an alternative imbrication of the *comedic* with its own means: *comediatic*. The deep-seated belly laugh (Bergson)—in somatic response not just to bodies in risible distress but to the unnerved materiality of the image track itself: that's what makes otherwise self-estranged bedfellows of burlesque turns and avant-garde ventures (Epstein), shtick and considered estrangement. The triple bill here—Keaton, Chaplin, Olsen and Johnson—does indeed send out such experimental shock waves across the comedic genre and its foregrounded technics. For any comparable probing of cinema's medial support in the era of computerized filmmaking, however, one wouldn't turn first to the kind of comedic techno fantasy mounted by the 2006 film *Click*, where the new electronic affordances of home video manipulation are rendered magic when gifted to the hero by a mad scientist in the form of a "universal remote" that fantastically allows him to vary the pace, and arrest the crisis points, of his whole private cosmos. One wants instances less palpably ludicrous, related more directly to the tissue of retinal impressions in movie viewing. One would look sooner and more closely, that is, beyond any direct thematics of computerized video powers, to the denser technological grain of blockbuster sci-fi: this for its reflex CGI figures of digital mediation in the stressed (in both senses) pixel texture of its optic basis.

5 *VFX Festival*

SF AND BEYOND

I DON'T KNOW WHETHER THERE'S EVER BEEN SUCH A FESTIVAL IN OFF-PAGE EXHIBITION space. Probably would have seemed too narrowly techie. Better, as a rule, to go with genre, and all its pyrotechnic violence, in luring the crowds. I can well imagine "Killer SF" as a college campus series. But the point here isn't to entertain *with*, but to entertain the technological issues—become narratival questions—raised *by* such popular fare. However improbable such a festival venue as the one conjured for these final two chapters, certain avenues to comparative disclosure are likely to be thrown open the harder we concentrate on such a cluster of recent SF (sci-fi) productions. Call the intensities and compressions they summon SFVFX for short— or simply SFX—before the long look their complexities elicit, especially in the image-dispersive violence in which they themselves specialize. Further, as with any good festival, some retro attention should aptly be paid: here in the Midnight Movie mode of 1950s low-budget sci-fi that might well be grouped under the rubric "Monster Bs"—including the landmark essay about this genre seedbed by Susan Sontag, quotations excerpted in the festival flyer, where her emphasis, we'll find, ignores the telltale image distortions of a violence that is for her merely narrated rather than fully *mediated*.

On this and related fronts, how far we've come. A once hot-button social issue like "graphic violence on film" has chilled of late. But not as fast as celluloid film itself has waned. The scare quotes around that loaded idea of "graphic violence," in respect to postfilmic screen narrative, would today flag something more like a pleonasm than a polemical rallying cry. Graphic violence is now almost entirely a matter of violent computer graphics. Almost two decades ago, Alejandro Amenábar's reflexive thriller *Tesis* (1996) portrayed a snuff-film ring inadvertently stumbled upon by a graduate student doing her doctoral thesis on screen violence. Long before their own retributive serial assassinations at the final turn of plot, the end was already in sight for these homicidal pornographers and their genre's morbid "realism"—and this by way of an oblique omen. For their ringleader was first detected by none other than electronic CCTV when prowling in the film archives of the university: digital imaging his undoing. Hence the media-historical irony, since in many ways the very traffic in "ultrareal" mayhem is now rendered moot by digital imaging of another sort, the flesh of any victim almost easier to simulate by CGI than to assault, to fabricate electronically than to violate in embodied form.[1]

What we were once warned against growing habituated to on screen, the rampant violation of human bodies, is now so fully virtualized and hyperbolic that the threat of inurement applies more to its aesthetics than to its ethics.[2] Destruction in CGI is mostly a game of digital bits and pixels, added, subtracted, morphed. The severing of limbs can seem less a medical emergency at the plot level than a Photoshop stunt. To "off" a blast victim is a rapid-fire function of the digital on/offs in the detonation not of some hidden bomb but of the covert chameleon binarities of an aggregated picture plane. In sum, the "aesthetic" at stake involves a certain level of retinal anesthesia. Screen spectacle generally needs us numbed these days not so much to what we *are shown* (a given mauling or extermination of the body, the extirpation of vehicles or built space) but to what we *actually see* (the overall computer duping of any such showy destruction). Numbed—or in passive wonderment at the high-tech fun of it. But when our computer-savviness is more actively called up in response to such vulnerable scenery and violent scenarios, it may sometimes be diverted along unexpected thematic (or, in response, "narratographic") channels in the process. Those diversions—within blockbuster cinema's overall distraction factory—are what lift the electronic medium to peculiar notice under the concentration of apparatus reading. The screen story's drama is one thing, its manifestation another: action versus manufacture. Pain thresholds are contained within the narrative; the thresholds of violence operate increasingly at the implied plane of representation instead. Bodies mutilated are only bitmaps manipulated. This is one reason why the longstanding phonetic rebus F/X (including Robert Mandell's 1986 film by that name)—for the kind of lab "eff/ects" more specialized than standard cinematography—has undergone a telltale change in the newer argot of VFX. Telltale, because so much of the entire V(isual) field of current filmmaking is now *effected* by computer generation—and more often on high-powered laptop than in lab. Here, then, the decisive reinvention of the cinemachine, from the algorithmic ground up.

Whether viewed eventually on portable computer, some other mobile device, or the still reflective "silver screen," the specialized sectors of the image given over to "effects" have their often violent work marked out for them—even if muted by the familiarities of pixelation. Their tendency to disintegrate the optically materialized coherence of human anatomy or built space—if only by the tacitly perceptible signals of computer rend(er)ing—can reduce even the most flamboyant damage to the inference of a mere digital figment. This doesn't have to be "visible" as such to be obvious, but occasionally it is. Such exemplary moments are the focus of annotation in these paired last chapters, where CGI protocols aspire to their own incipient poetics of violation at the very interface of display. Short of this, the norm is maintained. The digital aesthetic of Hollywood violence, if there is such a thing—or, say, the digital mimesis of violence—is inseparable from a general electronic prosthesis in screen spectacle, amounting at times to the wholesale supplanting of filmed (recorded) by fabricated (scribed, graphed) event. No longer photograms in racing process, the motion picture is often, in the new etymological sense noted previously, all picture cells (pic-elements: pixels). Watching movies lately without seeing this, or at least sensing it, would be a way of going blind to the digital operations that, in certain impacted instances, invite narrative to render the medium as part of the message. It would, in this essay's terms, be a refusal to let the latest modality of the cinemachine do some of your thinking for you as you watch.

With the kind of apparatus-keyed attention that is always implicitly media-historical, this chapter's scrutiny of CGI effects returns eventually to the thick of apparatus theory itself for Christian Metz's founding sense of camera identification within the constructedness of montage. It does so, in part, to sketch an unexplored aesthetico-philosophical lineage between the radical epistemology of Epstein's "truquage"—film's global specular trick—and the specified disclosures of the same in Metz's more detailed genealogy of *trucage* and its syntactic doubles. Within a broader range of illusionist devices and maneuvers—as we'll see so rigorously explored by Metz—what is lifted to prominence is exactly that technical field of laboratory effects gradually mastered for variable use by photogrammic cinema. In contrast, their computer counterparts may well seem under experimental investigation still, when not just exploited, by filmic cinema's digital successor. For such is the "intelligence" of the cinemachine 2.0, as before it the filmic apparatus, that—under thematic pressure—it does tend to think out its own conditions for us in their most striking visual renditions.

The Algorithmic Unconscious

On the big screen, the digital may operate as a kind of retinal latency. The technological levelings of electronic convergence do not, in other words, guarantee explicit cinematic recognition as such.[3] But sometimes the digital condition of narrative spectacle is hard to miss. For, now and then, computer rendering is allowed to show *through*, not just show, the rendered (the rent or obliterated) scene of violence it generates. This happens in certain surcharged moments of optical demolition directed at an electronically delineated space and its traversing objects or bodies. *Delineated*—because exposed as such through an aberrant warping or jamming in the otherwise uninterrupted digital scan and its acknowledged horizontal tracery. And there is another etymological resonance at work around the edges of this issue as well. Whereas "decimation," from *decimal*, first meant the lethal reduction of a Roman enemy by one-tenth of its combat manpower, it is now a term applied by video engineers to the compression of computer imaging (by binary, of course, rather than decimal calibration). Conceptualized rather than perceptible, think of such technical decimation as the generative function whose inferences are most often registered on the narrative screen in those scenes of violence perpetrated by—and at certain points *against*—the image plane itself. In those latter manifestations, so we'll see, mimesis is given over—even if unwittingly—to its own allegoresis.

But when I speak of narrative analysis as a way of not going blind to the medium, I speak so much in metaphor that the main point needs stressing again—along with some further specification of its inferences. The fact remains that the medium, whether digital now, or filmic before, is as a rule—the literal rule of aligned vertical track or pixel grid—invisible as such in its visual force. Against this neutral backdrop, or underlay, such is that specialness of effect in sci-fi that goes not just genre- but species-deep: this, by probing the evolutionary difference between filmic and digital *first causes*. In the *Post-Cinema* volume, Shane Denson looks in fact to the machinic ramification of cinema's surface spectacle in the mass-release *Transformers* series—based not on comic books (Marvel) but, as it happens, on trademark composite toys (Hasbro). Given the refusal of stable reference in the piecemeal composition and elusive robotic oscillation of these eponymous entities, Denson stresses their *"failure* to coalesce into coherent objects."[4] But given their effect in narrative space—operating in part as glimpsed cause of their own effect—why is this a "failure" of the image so much as its explicit default to its pixel existence in the first place, for which the flailing facets of the robotic surfaces are a kind of fractalized epiphany?

This alternative explanation seems so much the case that the very term *Transformer* would appear to name the algorithmic process itself that triggers their unstable materialization in the first place: a source within narrative, needless to say, not of their failure, but of their very power. In what thereby surfaces of the ordinarily "subperceptual," we find here the figure or emblem —or call it the very picture, from the midst of digital cinema— of the electronic image's own generativity. And the emblematic, in this sense, even manages to surface at one point within the actual dramatic scenario of a recent installment in this franchise. When, in *Transformers: The Age of Extinction* (Michael Bay, 2014), we get an explanation for the CGI metallurgy of the giant morphing bots, with their miraculous constitution by "molecularly unstable atoms," a sample is pictured in isolation as so malleable that it looks—when held in the hand and then self-levitated— like nothing so much as a swath of little pixel cubes, tiny dice in the game of transformative chance and its will to shape. The frame grab of this requires the split-second intersection of a self-illustrative malleability.

Caught only for a fleeting instant on screen in this discernible form, here is a structuring material discrete and coagulant by turns: flux itself. Tapping its own pixelated substrate, the very (algo)rhythm of spectacle often witnesses implicitly in this way, even when rerouted through an evoked nanoculture, to its algorithmic basis.

Explosive Blow-Ups

A point of comparison from a kindred medium: the exposed substrate of low-res compression in the enormously enlarged jpeg imagery of German conceptual photographer Thomas Ruff. In a 2014 show on violent images in contemporary art at the Hirshhorn Museum in Washington, DC, under the title "Damage Control," almost half a gallery's wall space is occupied by two of Ruff's outsize photoscapes from the middle years of the last decade and the rubble of its war on terror horizons, blurred in transmission by the pixelations of internet distance. The overweaning force of Ruff's gargantuan photo planes seems there to remind us that nothing comes clear in the real-time transmit they evoke, no matter how exaggerated the scale—nothing except disintegration itself and its figurative geopolitical murk. In these monumental (untitled) blowups of found web imagery—from a suite of works ranging, for instance, from the falling Twin Towers of 9/11 to bombed-out Mideast cityscapes and their smoke-laden traces—what gets troped by pixel breakup and its dispersed accuracy of registration is in part the underlying *fragmentation* of a globally networked culture of remote witness and its impoverished clarities, with no resolution available in any sense.

In cinema as well as conceptual web photography, and more obviously now than ever before, any putative aesthetics of captured violence is necessarily preceded by its technics. "On screen violence" as a discursive topic in contemporary media study could, so formulated, be almost entirely taken up by a hyphenated and medium-bound determination like "on-screen violence." And in two senses at that, since movies, in their most striking VFX displays, are now *made* on screen, in computer rendering, not just viewed there—so that the violent spectacle of any and all "decimation" is indeed, to vary the Hirshhorn rubric, a matter of "controlled" visual "damage" at the plane of the pixelated image field itself. What sufficient reminders of this, by way of recent film evidence in these last paired chapters, will both solicit and conceptually permit is a considered schematic reworking, and technological update, of the most deep-going account of screen illusionism: again, the theory of *trucage* (the cinematic "trick effect") by Christian Metz, which explores far more exhaustively (but no more intrinsically) than Epstein's equivalent "truquage" the medium-definitive properties of the motion picture in varying relays between represented world and its mere narration, between pictured action and technological syntax.[5]

Lethal Beaming

On this score, compare Steven Spielberg's *War of the Worlds* (2005) to George Pal's earlier production (1953) of the H. G. Wells story (directed by

Byron Haskin)—in particular, concerning the luminous "death ray." This is the ultimate weapon that, in each case, pictures the cinematic beam of projection in functional reverse (annihilating rather than animating)—yet in secret equivalence after all, narrative projection being the cause of all such effects. With the familiar postwar overtones of Hiroshima and Nagasaki in 1950s sci-fi, one dramatic consequence of the prelaser heat ray is to sear away bodies into their own photograph-like shadows: ghostly afterimages stretched across the ground where they once stood. Anticinematography: not the immortality of mummification but its parody as a strictly ashen index in a flattened planar remnant.

We find the same reflexive technological inversion in the Spielberg remake—but with the axis of contrast narrowed by CGI so that the constitutive and the violative seem more nearly two sides to the same coin of digital similitude. When Tom Cruise races forward in a tracking close-up in flight from the marauding alien "tripods" (once more an evoked camerawork apparatus in malign travesty), the death ray picks off one fleeing human body after another behind him. In this case, in contrast to the 1953 film, the killer beam leaves no singed trace but only, as part of the VFX spectacle, shreds of clothing to which the weapon's strictly organic targeting is indifferent. Again, by a tacit CGI logic: not just eviscerated but instantaneously disintegrated flesh. Here is a variant of optic trickery's missing limb: the entire body gone missing, a totalized mutilation of presence. Everyone is turned into that classic example in Metz of "invisible *trucage*": namely, the absent anatomy of the hero in another Wells story frequently brought to the screen, beginning with the original *Invisible Man* (James Whale, 1933). Manifest there, according to Metz, is a "perceived" sleight of sight that leaves nothing actually to "see" (664). Or, in Spielberg's digital case, nothing much—but at the same time all there is: disappearance incarnate.

This is to say that in the moment of effacing transition in Spielberg's *trucage* for *War of the Worlds*—like an arrested and truncated digital morph—we may well spot after all, in the blink of a pixel grid, the Hollywood technique behind the alien techne. The death-ray premise is trumped, in effect, by its own execution. Updated from primitive atomic extermination as phobic model, the lethal beam incinerates without flame like a neutron bomb—eradicating all organic matter. But it does so not just by a blatant special effect of the instantly (invisibly) pulverized human form but by a specific digital effect of computerized breakup before lightning-speed deletion. We are meant to *almost* see the human displacement taking place in this disappearance. But what we're also likely to discern is a figure for it:

a metaphor drawn from its own electronic configuration. This is because a split second's welting and melting away of the zapped body—too fast for legibility as organic violence—reads like just what it is: a splintering and erasure of one designated sector in the digital plane.

This is clearest when, in the middle distance behind Cruise, the camera cuts to the comparable headshot of a woman also running vainly from the random savagery of the death ray—whose face suddenly implodes in a microsecond's digital fissuring of the screen zone it occupies. The anatomical decimation comes across—decidedly if only subliminally (to vary Metz's "invisible but perceptible")—as the "avowed machination" (664) breaking through. Or in this postmachinic case, call it the momentarily blown cover of the movie's image engineering (its electronic *imageering*) obtruded under narrative stress. So that one may well think all the way back to the jump-cut eradication of extraterrestrials with the astronaut's magic umbrella in the first sci-fi film, *A Trip to the Moon* (Georges Méliès, 1902), with its blithe confession—indeed bald celebration—of the disjunctive powers of a new montage regime. Long after Méliès, together Pal and Spielberg, half a century apart, divide up—though of course far more mutedly (say more "trickily")—the remaining reflexive terrain of such filmic and postfilmic disclosure as the very figure of fantastic violence.

In Spielberg's case, too, there is deposited—literally dropped—a particularly plangent in-joke in the age of streaming small-screen video, linked here to the comparable scale of private camcorder transcription. For at one point his framing isolates *en abyme*—in a single (or actually redoubled) street-level shot of "posthumous videography"—the difference between "being there" and its safer big screen rendition.

Unmanned imaging, so to speak—like the premise of the projected spectacle that embeds it. This shot is a beautiful little visual idea that remains focused, in both senses, on the ongoing digital record of a looming digitized threat. Eloquent in the clarity of its scalar recess, it offers an update of the eyewitness screen-within-the-screen of broadcast disasters across the postwar history of the genre—as well as of all those evidentiary photographs in its 1950s phase adduced in equivocal proof of mutant or alien sightings.

Spaces Zeroed Out

Shortly after Spielberg's remake, as it happens, the eponymous hero of *Iron Man* (Jon Favreau, 2008), at the computer keypad of his private high-tech machine shop, uses voice-recognition software to activate the assembly line for his magic metal armor. As the robot tools go into motion, he says partly to the artificial intelligence linked up with his computer microphone, partly to himself (and of course to the rest of us): "Not bad for ones and zeros." But the scene was cut before release, appearing only on the DVD supplement. It is too much an in-joke, perhaps, about the computerized special effects that "operate" this spectacular equipment in the first place, let alone about the CGI techniques that follow. For it is mere binary numeration, too, that animates the superhero's morphed, iron-plated incarnation in the ensuing VFX extravaganza and its retributive violence. Though audiences may care less about the ones and zeros of it all than about the ABC of genre thrills, the distinction is increasingly difficult to make in the era of the cinemachine 2.0. And especially because the toggling of the 1s and 0s in CGI is just as often run through its permutations to zero out as to instantiate some image, some electronic figment: put differently, some special VFX of the X-ed out.

   With the upgraded fatal electronics of *War of the Worlds* in mind—and for a comparable time span between original and remake, as if technologically chronicled in its transformed optics—look to the 1951 admonitory fable of *The Day the Earth Stood Still* in its later incarnation (Scott Derrickson, 2008), where Biblicized swarms of locusts, in the form of flying metallic insectiles (under generation from the likes, again, of the particle system deployed in *The Life of Pi*), devour nonliving forms—including whole public buildings and arenas—like a million tiny "bytes" taken out of out of earth's built reality by its alien deconstruction.

The predatory ravenous erosion of a public structure by a negative blitz (a vacuuming up) of its graphic constituents is merely the retinal obverse of VFX cinema's far more common internal disintegration and dispersion. Whether the millionfold pixelated entities are coming or going, that's the narrative—but not the mediatic—question. For what needs notice in all this, not least, is the unsaid idiom by which this digital chipping away at the bedrock of human reality often seems immediately derived from its unspoken source in the so-called computer *chip*, shivering things to bits in diffused fragments and shavings. Suffice it to say, in overview, that time and again in the CGI moment, the seethe and shiver of pixel-like forms—not necessarily "moshed," as in an experimental video, but tossed up in more discrete form from the digital matrix—can roughen the image plane as lesions in representation as well as corrosions of the narrative's pictured bodies, buildings, and machines: a damage at the very surface of mirage. As witness to this pixel craze of recent screen effects—craze also in the sense of a splintered screen sheen, a VFX glaze shattered into minute fractures—one is barely surprised to find on website offer, as a tie-in to the *Day the Earth* remake, various displays of digital "wallpaper." In hyperdefinition, these include a shot of the iconic London skyline, for instance, with Big Ben and environs nibbled away at from within their own digital composites by the alien pixel storm cloud, updated from the death ray of the 1950s original. If the 2008 film, a decade back now, couldn't be said to have struck any new cultural nerve, it did seem to open a vein of pixel infestation and pestilence ever since.

Film history isn't left behind by digital projection at such moments but instead, to borrow sci-fi's own lingo, beamed up in review. Hence, in the spotty Festival of this chapter, the suitable midnight venue for some of the least known and literally juiciest of alien threats in the early days of postwar sci-fi: pustulant mutational organisms, either in black and white or in color, sucking dry their human victims—and sharing many a double bill with atomically resurgent dinosaurs or invasive alien creatures, occasionally even in experimental 3-D. Marked thereby is one stage in a VFX teleology from black-and-white through widescreen color toward the potential VR destiny of entertainment imaging—and its recent halfway house in theaters equipped for so-called 4DX3D. One might think of the hard-wired mechanical (as well as projected) thrills of this limited-venue exhibition format for *Avengers: Infinity War* (Anthony and Joe Russo, 2018), for instance—with its motorized vibrations, jolting seat backs, lurching chair arms, controlled water spray, and the restless rest—as not just up-grading the shimmering optic embrace of IMAX 3-D but competing in the zone of direct anatomical engagement with the visceral kick, if not the interactivity, of gamer thrills. Yet the innovation could just as well be seen as a travesty in advance of fully VR "cinema." Stopping short of any such turn to surrogate "presence" rather than engrossing presentation, the recent history of VFX has its own story to tell on the way there, one to which the next chapter returns. And with a critical backstory we can profit from revisiting in the meantime.

The Imageering of Disaster

In tracing the cinematics of a genre's postfilmic phase, the results are, of course, best tested against classic paradigms—this, in order to elicit a sense of the filmic residual when operating at a clarifying depth beneath obvious technical and thematic transformations. And, given the evidence constellated here and in the coming chapter, there is a ready canonical touchstone in the critical literature. Many are the mortal threats found posed, and thus ideologically propounded, in the 1950s heyday of the sci-fi genre diagnosed in Susan Sontag's famous "Imagination of Disaster" essay from 1966.[6] While noting the generous budgeting of special effects as central both to the genre's "charm" and to its realist conviction (though not in any particular way, for her, to its thematic purchase), Sontag identifies figurative threats in the individual as much as apocalyptic vein, metaphoric crises biological as well as interplanetary in the weight of their radical "alienations." One is struck in retrospect, however, with the medial valence of certain imagined disasters—certain, say, disaster imaging—amid her rolodex of examples, films listed by her as sociological litmus tests rather than enlisted for visual analysis. For the image plane is sometimes powerfully recruited, as we'll see, for just the estrangements she delimits in both human hegemony and individual autonomy (and anatomy).

Without any real social diagnosis in the 1950s B thrillers, according to Sontag (217), the hazards to species and subjectivity alike are together stalled at the metaphoric level, and thus already halfway to being contained and alleviated. Beyond mass (read: nuclear) eradication, the complementary fear she draws out entails a more private psychic "invasion"—the curse of being "taken over" (221) by either bad experimental science or targeted extraterrestrial incursion: mutated from within rather than mutilated.[7] With only passing mention of the classic *Invasion of the Body Snatchers* (221), Sontag's most intriguing evidence (at least for the lineage of special effects, and though undiscussed by her as such) include certain bioorganic parables—in plots of dehumanization as anatomical disarticulation—that are delivered by implausible thrillers like *The Blob* (1958) and, before it, *The Creeping Unknown* (1955). These are films that detail alien contagions swallowing up the body itself, draining, gulping, or pulping it—rather than, as in the current CGI craze, splintering it to bits. On closer comparison, it is as if the churning larval mass that gradually sculpts itself into a perfect human replica in *The Body Snatchers* is an obverse horror drawn from the same cauldron of repulsive undulating goo. *The Blob* names (the word "imitative" in origin) an amorphous globular life form, engorged with the blood of its serial earthly victims. The unknown extraterrestrial creepiness of the previous film, titled in England *The Quatermass Xperiment*, is instead a body-devouring fungus—not likely to operate as a deliberately oblique play on the atomic "mushroom cloud," but located somewhere on a spectrum of such displacements nonetheless. Yet each invasive species of consumption in these films enfolds and dissolves the human body, one victim at a time, rather than collectively incinerating it.

It is certainly worth noting, in furtherance of Sontag's emphasis on dehumanization as an alternate specter to mass extermination, that this peculiar "imagination of disaster"—as much as with the atomically mutated Godzillas, Mothras, and the many gargantuan non-prehistoric bugs on the rampage in the period, manifesting the threat of scale itself (global) in the annals of destruction—is tied more tightly to its special effects than her emphasis only on visual credibility (and "décor," 216) might suggest. Beyond its geopolitical imaginary, disaster has its own specifically cinematic imageering, filmic then as much as digital now. The most telling effects become part of a film's cultural allegory by passing through, not entirely smoothly, the medium that flaunts them. And this is where more of Sontag's argument might be said to *meet the eye* than she explores.[8] Monstrosity conjures the body's fate in such cases as variously decomposed, liquefied, rendered invertebrate, in the fungal instance veritably ex-sponged: assimilated to an aggregate bloody mass in the one case, a parasitic and spore-borne alien vegetation in the other. Figured at first in private devolution, this disaster calls up an eventual pandemic horror more like the biological mutations feared from radioactive fallout (a facet of their threat not entertained by Sontag) than anything linked directly to mass nuclear extermination.

Given this mode of amorphous horror, this invertebrate end for a collapsed human anatomy, the contrast with the current fad of instantaneous pixel attrition—in the brittle splinter of bodies and built spaces alike—couldn't be more marked. Looking back, however, we may see a common medial thread in the threat. For there is something about the effacing blur of those globular or vegetal invasions—unshaping human anatomy from within, robbing the body of its own natural image, with its transitional counterpart in the still formless frothing pulp of the body-snatching pods in the more famous film—that may optically call up, in turn, the vulnerable plasticity of celluloid, subject in its own materiality to bleeding, blotching, and other spoilages of recorded form. In this sense, it is no accident that certain frame grabs as well as production stills from both *The Blob* and *The Creeping Unknown* tend, at first glance, to resemble the found artifacts of nitrate degeneration, both creeping and coagulated, as highlighted by celluloid artists like Bill Morrison or Éric Rondepierre: image and damage as each other's internal complements.

But the inexorable *Blob* doesn't, so to speak, stop there. This movie forces its reflexive hand in even more explicit relation to the creature's own pulsing bloody medium—and not just in association with cinema, but with filmic materiality as such. For at one overloaded moment of such irony, the formless horrific materiality of the blob intersects directly the whole apparatus of filmic projection. Here, the invasive alien predator doesn't just attack a "healthily air-conditioned" 1950s movie house called, of all things, "The Colonial." Nor is the dramatic irony exhausted when our writhing spheroid leach is sent on the rampage there, in full color by DeLuxe, during a horror double bill blazoned on the marquee: "Daughter of Horror," as if naming the genre's own lineage, alongside an unnamed Bela Lugosi starrer in presumptive black-and-white—yet taking as intertext, no doubt, the star's own signature bloodlust as the most famous Hollywood Dracula. All this would have been sufficient to make an institutional point about the derivations of sci-fi and its own mixed bloodlines. Yet the film goes so far as to have the alien organism gain entrance to the projection booth and—in its own celluloid-like translucence in front of the lens, operating as the colored "filter" of its own disclosed presence—render the entire screen image an undulant red blur, triggering the portrayed audience's mass exit. Repellant engulfment rather than pleasurable immersion: such is a countercinematic but "filmily" (filmically) realized horror in comparison with which a contemporary disintegration of imaged bodies and spaces, and of the CGI screen plane with them, seems more like the harmless pulverization of figures in gameplay than like some new monitory fable of risky computer dependence.

Crisis Update

Or is that quite right? Might there not be some pervasive displacement at work in our current technological zeitgeist, too, beyond the geopolitical, biogenetic, and climate-science anxieties so often explicitly narrativized in such thrillers, from clone dystopias to terrestrial conflagrations? From amidst these vaporous megaplots, one after another, with their increasingly hackneyed electronic effects so often brandished in excess of all narrative cause, isn't there perhaps a lurking reminder of destructive hacking itself—amid all the other associated threats to cybersecurity and systemic maintenance, including inadvertent malfunction? Invisible or not in their very real dangers, couldn't obtruded pixelation serve to picture them to the mind's eye? This is to ask whether it isn't possible, at least in the affect of reception, that current cinematic violence is structured around its own updated "imagination of disaster" passively at work in the frequently implosive quality of recognizable digital display? In this sense, intermittent pixel breakups in the VFX schemata would tend collectively to figure, across one film after another, if at a quite subliminal level, a wholesale global breakdown in the form of a computer apocalypse. Why not?—and especially for a cinema that is itself as pervasively reliant, now, on electronic transmission as is any telecommunications system that might fall victim to cyberwarfare. In the byways of the genre, as we know, one vulnerability often computes another. And with society in thrall to an electronic superstructure "too big to fail," the on-screen default—the collapse (however narratively motivated) from image to the fractured gradients of its electronic support—can tend to unsettle more than the image plane.

This becomes especially apparent for robot melodrama in a decade's line of descent for alien invasion films linking Neill Blomkamp's *District*

9 (2009) to the *Pacific Rim* sequel (Steven S. DeKnight, 2018). These are plots that conflate, in terms of Sontag's paradigm, both species threat and an individually usurped human anatomy (and psyche), figured either as a new version of the "creeping unknown" or as a willing surrender of organic immediacy. In Blomkamp's narrative, the hero's hand-become-alien-tentacle melds in biodegeneration with the machine carcass of a cyborgian weaponry, whereas, in the later plot, young military heroes (chosen for their gamer expertise) operate massive metallic robots by VR simulation from within the fortified space of the megamachines: a progressive remove of the external alien threat to prosthetic (and quasi-aesthetic) distance.

Once again the near proximity of digital extravaganza and corporal vulnerability is rendered explicit—if circuitous. And once again in *Pacific Rim: Uprising*, as in the remake of *The Day the Earth Stood Still*, a flourish of microchips serves to pixelate the looming danger itself. This happens in *Pacific Rim* when an already mountainous alien creature is grossly enlarged by what one can only call pixceleration: speeding metal-like fragments—mere abstract particles—summoned by extraterrestrial force, as if magnetized, toward its bulking form and expanding it like a specifically pixel trick of CGI build-up before our eyes. This idea is so overdone that it immediately waxes emblematic for the digital substrate of any such creature to begin with. Like every looming—and, in approach, swelling—visual nemesis in current VFX, the ominous specter of this new alien Godzilla, with all Tokyo again under threat, is thus exposed as "enhanced" bit by bit in the very bitmap array of digital *trucage*—an effect all but punned on by the agglomeration of pixel splinters as a new flaunting of armored scale(s). But what is most revealing in the film's knot of apparatus ironies—and in contradistinction to the still-"manned" robotics of *District 9*, where somatic control of the steel carapace is essential—is how digitized virtual reality (under the wired but ultimately indirect or vicarious command of the heroes) has nonetheless fused the mobile operators, at the level of psychic identification, with their own vehicular VFX "projections." The VR throttle replaces the alien appendage.

Beyond any implicit metacinematic effect, however, this narrative seems literally *embedding* its gameplay rival, as does Spielberg's *Ready Player One* in the same year, as the premise of its own screen plot. The motion picture's always encroaching commercial alternative in proprioceptive thrills, rather than the high-tech aesthetics of sheer spectacle, is thus pictured in extrapolated form by VFX representation—rather than in any way interactively engaged in the multiplex venue. In this tacit media battle, big-screen cinema—with its "bigger picture" of the thrilling scene of violence underway, a perspective not just mediated from the inside out as it is for the VR combatants—is staged to win the day. At least Spielberg's film, by contrast with *Pacific Rim: Uprising*, complicates the somatically activated but ultimately disembodied mayhem of VR with some social cautions along with the optic extravagance—and indeed some sense of a human psychological core endangered by too unguarded a vicarious overreach in such prosthetic dependence. But those cautions are themselves anodyne—and any "imagination of disaster" is again appeased by the pleasure principle of theatrical consumption. So it is that in the case of *Ready Player One* the 3-D technology of the movie's wide release marks the film's own digital gesture toward the seductive depth perceptions whose ethical and psychic risks its narrative makes a show (in every sense) of equivocating for the VR addict.

Thus Sontag's intuitions again—in extension to all such ironies of the electronic medium and its alternate commercial manifestation, as well as in extrapolation to our present technological moment at large. If VFX disintegration—executed by villain or hero alike, alien organism or defending robot—does operate in any degree, and at any level of conscious response, by transferring the splay of pixels to a lurking unease about our vast and unstable electronic infrastructure, then wouldn't a second shoe be likely to fall? Wouldn't the perils of computerization apply—across the now-familiar division of genre labor between extermination and dehumanization—not just to mass incapacitation but to the private erosion of human cognition and bodily presence in the name of prosthetic pleasures and empowerments? If yes, then yes—and again: why not? Why wouldn't digital instability as well as surrogacy begin to erode imagined corporal agency? If, increasingly, in the encroachments of technology upon ontology, we are only what we can do, it is clear that human activity is in part defined by the engines of its gesture as well as by the facilitations of its infrastructure. The fragility of wired global networks is not easy to separate from the steady cyborgization of human action as well as communication—and certainly not for a film industry whose digitized output is itself more and more remotely delivered across platforms indistinguishable from otherwise interactive screens. So that a theoretically resistant keynote of this essay is again worth sounding in just this technological connection. When manifest on screen in narrative action, the neuromuscular appropriations of VR still speak less to some fleshed body of film itself, let alone of digital cinema, than to the apparatus of the body's transferred and "simulated" organic gestures in extended (and radically postcinematic) "representation." In such rendering of—and within—VR, image may have fused with motor anatomy, but only for the futurist heroes, not the theatrical viewer. Operating still on the near side of this break with "moviegoing" altogether, nonetheless SFVFX continues, if we watch closely, to see it coming.

Intention, Purpose, Purport: A Note on Viewer Response

But from where do signs of this sort trace their source? Even before this chapter, a reader may have wanted from the concept of "apparatus reading" a clearer sense of what kind of visual texture is being read. Inscribed how—or by whom—and at what level? Though the viewer performs it—any such reading—still the question remains: to what degree is response geared to anything like intention—beyond the automaticities of machination? How does viewing enter the space, with VFX for instance, between technical design and legible (rather than just visual) purpose? Or, to put it another way: is there an aspect of *purport* that remains free, for audience registration, from any discerned authorial or technical purpose? You've no doubt guessed by now that the latter is this essay's working assumption. And Sontag's B films are a perfect testing ground. They seem in their scripts—and, as we have further noted, in their special effects—almost blindly dictated by the Cold War zeitgeist and its paranoias, rather than set on diagnosing them. The latter is up to us.

That would be enough to say in avoiding the old canard of the "intentional fallacy," and yet there is something further in play—with these and other such cases—regarding the way medium is delivered more immediately, sometimes more articulately, than its own messages. Regarding the general breaches in—and thus reflexive broachings of—the electronic apparatus per se in these final two chapters, effects are primarily just that: their causes not easily traced to any thematic intention; specialized to the hilt, yes, but specific to no coherent line of narrative (or subnarrative) inference. They are in every way designed, calculated, calibrated, but not necessarily *meant*—except for show. When what they show, however, or say reveal, is in fact something of the apparatus itself, rather just its costly panache, one may be moved to take note. Often by double take. Typically, such moments emerge only in some minor divergence from prevalent techno clichés—some extra wrinkle in the latest CGI fashion, or some arresting discrepancy in its expected process—that in either case can leverage the unexpected if fleeting grip of *trucage* on a cultural, sociopolitical, or technological matter thus materialized. Just think, for instance, of the eye-catching distortions that have come lately to inflect the title graphics of so many films, especially in the sci-fi genre, or have even bled back to tamper with the production logos themselves (as recently with *Blade Runner 2049*), as if pixel energy were itself coursing through these signature trademarks—even overcharging them to the point of digital noise and compromised iconic stability. If we should therefore see in this a kind of generalized corporate intent,[9] same with many a marked, rather than routine, burst of figurative CGI. That they are electronically (industrially) sourced is often all interpretation has to go on in an apparatus reading.

Yet in this respect the apparatus can tip its hand, hand off its optical hint, at any aesthetic level of passing manifestation—ranging all the way from design contingencies in B films through conceptually worked effects in the experimental cinema of a philosopher-cineast like Epstein. Each screen effort invites apparatus reading wherever retinal complexity has let the medium break through—speak through—the thrust of plot in the uprush of raw optical matter. Has let it, abetted it—or loosed it to sudden notice under expediency's duress. On various fronts of either narrative urgency or digressive flamboyance, and as much with photogrammic or celluloid disclosure as with the pixel reflex, anything resembling "intent" can best be seen resting on the inbuilt *tensions* of motion generation and visual aberration: again, monstration as well as its particular monsters— all apparitional when read. When read, that is, rather than just complacently (which is to say excitedly) viewed. Regardless of whose hands are in control of the apparatus at any one point, extrusions of "technique," as explored in chapter 2, need not be authored to be "asserted." Asserted— and thus potentially ascertained in their contextual force. In that mode of notice begins anything we might think to call a technopoetics of the current apparatus, as located in our ongoing attention to the ocular given of screen electronics. The current VFX Festival has thus been extended into a second and final chapter less by popular demand than by the thematic demands made on purposive *recognition*—rather than discovered intent—in the continuing output of these often formulaic spectacles. Whose succession, rather than separate success, can now be submitted to a fuller comparative review, media-historical as well as technical.

6 *Omnibus Review*

ON THE TECHNOPOETICS OF CGI

Reviewing can benefit at times from the broadest of overviews—in this case, from a metahistory of picturings from which the ever-more-blanketing scope of VFX on the narrative screen may be theoretically understood to descend: picturings, along with the shifting modes of their visibility. It isn't that our distracted gaze is ever riveted for long to anything particular in CGI cinema's field of tricked view; it is rather that our manipulated shifting glance is seldom relinquished for more than a brief letup by one-after-another insistent screen "attractions" in their (particulate) digital—and sometimes openly pixel—solicitations. We are thus part of a devolution in the history of retinal response that has, in sweeping terms, been sketched out by mediologist Régis Debray as "The Three Ages of Looking."[1] On his account, the regime of the *graphophere*—the era of art, wrested from the rule of the icon in a preceding epoch of religious idol-worship (the *logosphere*)—was an era that, born alongside the print revolution, persisted from the Renaissance into the twentieth century and, in one of its last major mutations, included the motion-writing of filmic imprint on the cinema screen. We have, however, long ago passed beyond that era's graphic (pur)view into the precincts of the *videosphere*, thus leaving behind the first two optical epochs, the iconic and the aesthetic, for the simply visual, the virtual. The idol originally induced "*a gaze without a subject*," with all looking subsumed to the immanence of the transcendental—in a piety that ultimately averted the human eye from divinity's own immediate gaze. In diametrical contrast, computerized video technology has induced a radical reversal in its hypermediated realm of "*vision without a gaze*" (551; Debray's italics on the contrast): an image stream whose remote access is channeled in address to no situated spectator.

In between idolatry and networked looking, though Debray doesn't put it this way, what lasted for centuries was the perspectival realm of focal length and POV that, if only at the end of their reign, were finally interrogated in their scopic lines of force by apparatus theory. In Debray's own terms, as opposed to an impersonal gaze or a gazeless looking, say religious subservience or image surfing, what intervened under graphic dispensation—under the sign of representational art—was an optically emplaced receipt of the picture, the vista, the view: "The era of art placed *a subject behind the gaze*: a human being" (551). This involved, mostly obviously, the art as well as the technology of perspective in both painting and film. Late in the institutionalization of the latter, it was only the advent of subjectivity theory, then, that put unprecedented ideological pressure on the implication of just this suturing-in of the participatory gaze by the privatizing apparatus of cinema. But the new flattened field of videographic VFX—often with the feel of sheer pixelated surface treatment even when in extreme simulated depth—is not to be looked at in the same way, not so much viewed as merely seen. Quite apart from the online circulation of images (and putting the specific reflections of Debray to the side here), we may say that what is left for inspection in the increasing surrender of mainstream cinema to the technical parameters of the videosphere is, once again, only the apparatus itself in its new computer mode—now, however, with the widescreen kinetic surface of explosive spectacle taking frequent priority over the focalizing eye of identified sightlines. As this essay has been proposing, one response to this blitz of images without a gaze, with image planes that can often barely be called watchable, merely radically visual, is to make its notice a matter of the *readable* instead—in all its disclosed computerized materiality.

Certainly movie after movie, for at least a decade now in the second epoch of the cinemachine, has indulged an often frenzied tendency for tipping the hand—or exposing the pixel digits—of its CGI display, its technical prestidigitation. We've already seen, for instance, the metallic substrate of the Transformers palpated into metadigital view. In *Ant-Man* (Peyton Reed, 2015), the interchangeability of microsurveillance and miniaturized weaponry in insectile form confirms a direct link between this update of the film's "incredible shrinking man" plot and the mosquito-sized drones of experimental robotics in the current notoriety of "autonomous killing machines." The film's plot thus literalizes a drastic *reduction of the human* to sheer ballistic trajectory, its results—its miniaturizing technology—then marketed to international arms dealers. It does so, further, with the improbable scientific explanation of "reducing the space between atoms": sci-fi code for the more palpable scalar shift in CGI pixelation—compression, "decimation"—whereby all of the film's seriocomic violence is micromanaged anyway.

The sequel takes us further yet into the promotional logic of production values. In 2018's *Ant-Man and the Wasp*, it's one thing to back-reference the new electronic finesse of digital scaling by including a closing episode where the lead characters are watching the clumsy VFX effects in one of Sontag's black-and-white mutant bug films, *Them!*, as the giant ants crush automobiles and fleeing passengers in their lumbering path. But to be watching this from the characters' own car at a drive-in movie—in this century?—troubled by bugs on the windshield: this throws us for a loop at first. And the loop is Hollywood-corporate as well as metafilmic. For in this ultimate self-advertising irony of scale, our heroes have shrunk their vehicle to recover the old-fashioned fun of drive-in movie going by watching the retro sci-fi on their laptop, opened at a distance on the garden grass. Here is a makeshift panoramic screen that, upon recognition by us, is immediately dwarfed in longshot by—and thus subordinated to—the frame, the fact, and the sharper definition of our multiplex screen, which neither old-fashioned amusements nor home video in any form is meant to compare (or compete) with.

With ant-men waiting in the corporate wings, that earlier metal man was unusually candid: the "not bad for ones and zeros" spoken in admiration for the digitally transformed mise-en-scène he inhabits. But beyond the CGI simulation of a robotically operated laboratory for digital ironmongery, anything approaching bioengineering is usually anathematized by these sci-fi plots—and often via the denaturing profligacy of their computerized VFX. One film above all unabashedly aligns the aura of big-budget production values with its own more naked variant of "CGI": computer *gestated* identity. In Luc Besson's *Lucy* (2014), dehumanization is a sought victory on the heroine's part, fulfilling her addictive need to fuse with the digital—as if from within her own artificially inseminated womb. There is certainly an undertone of typecasting in the title role, with Scarlett Johansson fresh from her off-screen presence as the simulated voice of a computer program in *Her* (Spike Jonze, 2013). When Lucy achieves her cybernetic apotheosis and can announce, as disembodied supercomputer in the film's unsourced last voiceover, "I am everywhere," the film suddenly feels like a prequel to *Her* as well as a companion piece to the globally wired cybernetic immortality of the posthumous hero in *Transcendence* (Wally Pfister, 2015). Certainly it rounds out the latent mass-medium fable of Jonze's film. For not unlike the projected on-screen image of an actress consumed along private lines of viewer identification and desire, the multiplied voice in *Her* can—as the hero is traumatized to discover—transact tens of thousands of erotic intimacies at once (albeit programmed and "impersonal") with paying clientele. Lucy, too, fulfills herself in this mode of empty universality. In many similar Hollywood films, to be sure, the plot exists only to "motivate the device" (as early formalism would have it): solely to justify the deployment of its VFX. But here the force of such device *is* the only plot, since Lucy spends the bulk of her time on screen striving to secure the condition of her "star presence" as contemporary action heroine to begin with—namely, disembodied digital invulnerability. Her victory coincides simply with her own constitution as screen image, in the sense less of sudden liberation than of simultaneous mass *release*.

Electronic Incarnation/Biometric Decomposition

For such are exactly the double terms in which the plot *delivers her*. After contraband drugs, unbeknownst to Lucy under sedation, are sewn into her abdomen by a Korean narcotics cartel for unwitting transport to Europe, a violent physical attack causes the mind-altering substance to bleed into her system. Its artificial distillate of prenatal chemicals—ordinarily pumped into the womb to jump-start the human embryo—now invades her adult body, breeding her own exponential superpowers in an irreversible sequence that carries her beyond all human mental and physical development, eventually beyond the body entirely. The progressive logic of biofeedback and recursive self-empowerment, though it makes no steady sense in the film's thinned-out drama, does follow—even beyond a gamer's template of level-jumping powers—a more sustained and unfolding media logic. The capacities she accesses are those of cinema itself in its own electronic enhancements. For in the dawning self-recognition of her increased powers, Lucy can first, through closed car windows, hear voices as if miked at a distance, read Asian signs as if subtitled, activate audiovisual electronics at a remote transnational remove (room lighting, telephone, Skype), and then, after controlling her entire mise-en-scène by the telekinetic manipulations of surrounding bodies as if she herself were a CGI technician, intercept countless cellular signals at will. The violence once visited upon the heroine is returned tenfold in her own aptitude for digitized mayhem, killing time and assailants both—until she can at last fuse corporeally with the computer consoles in a Paris university lab. Just before this, in a largely digressive episode where she insists to the scientists that all embodied manifestation is simply a function of time, she conjures out of thin air for them a widescreen band of moving image illustrating her point: that filming a traveling car and then making it move faster and faster ultimately makes it disappear in a serial blur.

If it weren't clear by now that her powers are precisely those of audiovisual screen technology, the media analogy turns suddenly ontological. For as the prehensile black matter of her extended body begins encircling and then vacuuming up the computer energy of the lab, main frames and all, she is able to subtract the site's entire ambient backdrop from the interrogating scientists—as if the convulsive magic that surrounds them by VFX projection (via digital green screen) had been switched off at the height of this CGI blitz. And the metafilmic overkill is not over yet. Following their entrapment in this glowing limbo, Lucy is blasted to Time(s) Square(d) by a last-ditch grenade launcher from the arriving drug lord. Yet this only fulfills her powers as the director of a postfilmic cosmic cinema when—with a biometric hand swipe—she palm-pilots from midtown Manhattan across time itself. In that most "visible" of all *trucages* in Metz's (or Epstein's) taxonomy, the altered time-space ratios of fast- and slow motion, she first stops traffic (like all screen stars) and then makes time fly. She effects, that is, an anthropological rewind that speeds back through millennia to a reprise of those pulsing and redoubling biological nuclei from the precredit montage, where the improbably geometric facets of their mitosis call to mind the digital rudiments of their own manifestation: the human cell in its new submolecular generation from pixel cells.

And as if all this weren't enough to cement the convergence of narrative with its own technical substrate, another line of medial irony—descended more directly from that pretitle image matrix of electrobiology—has worked to organize what there is of plot. Long before Lucy's once-gendered form has morphed, in the computer lab, into the swollen bioorganic power cables of a massive jack-in, viewers could well have sensed the digital subtext in the way the artificially engineered genetic fluid that has juiced her mind/body transformation has been concentrated, solidified, and minced in little blue cubelets shown in close-up like 3-D ingestible pixels: confessed source of all bodily transformation on the new special effects screen. And if not at that early stage, then certainly by the time of the subsequent VFX turning point: a cyborgian nightmare en route to a CGI rapture. When an in-flight Lucy is seen operating two laptops at once in her airplane seat, and at warp speed, to the astonishment of a nearby passenger, it is an effect achieved by seamless digital fast-forward. Here, again, is an update to Epstein as well as to the earliest modes of "visible *trucage*" in Metz: a magically empowered speed in early experimental effects that is only later, in the evolution of film syntax, assimilated to an idiom of visual figuration like time-racing-on. In this respect, Lucy's body is already computerized as accelerated image before its flesh begins dilapidating—crinkling and peeling (yes, pixelating)—by a further but equivalent computer effect of digital psoriasis: the first certain sign, by corporeal atomization, of her pending destiny. At moments like this in the scalar shift of recent VFX, the subliminal mosaic tiles of binary input are once again found shattering some sector of the image plane in a fractalized—and variably masked—acknowledgment of its own source code.

Such masking reaches degree zero in *Lucy*. For in that airborne scene of somatic fragmentation, her biologically "infected" system is becoming in panic what her anomalous powers already are in presentation: bitmapped and microchipped to death, and manifested as if in a grotesque pun on implicated digits.

Overdosed from inside her own now vitiated body by the dissolved rectangular granules of the artificially engineered mind-boosting drug, her frenetic, laptop-associated fate has by this point begun to figure global culture's widespread addiction to all multitasked digital prosthetics—for which the only cure imagined by Besson's plot is homeopathic: the human subject becoming no longer organic anatomy at all but sheer informatic functionality. In her body's rapid digital metastasis, that is, churns the film's true meta-thesis. For in that onboard globe-trotting morph of explicit (rather than just requisite) cyberdisintegration, Lucy is seen threatened precisely by what she threatens (and from here out yearns) to become: all digital, all the time.

This is the usual CGI story, to be sure—but usually not the sole plot. The imperative to up the digital stakes is typically kept in-house, a mandate to the special effects division. Here, in *Lucy*, it comes through unabashed and blatant, unfiltered by either narrative complications or the least whiff of psychology. It is all we're there for, or in any event all we get: the convergent digital telos of star value and digital production values alike. When at the end Lucy is nowhere and everywhere at once, her body entirely off-screen, her power remains wholly present—as the seductive electronic evocation of screen wizardry in general. Not just by eponymous entitlement, Lucy *is* our movie. She has grown indistinguishable from the computer projection that constitutes the film's violent mise-en-scène. This is beyond cyborgiastic. She *is* the algorithmic cinemachine. And yet this climax, too, has a softening retro touch. Installing an oddly consolatory anachronism, the impersonal sting of her destiny is mitigated by an unlikely node of familiarity in its technological upshot. In approaching this closure, as we've seen, a crisis of artificial genetics has been transferred to informatics, chemical engineering to electronic imageering—as registered most obviously when the in-flight ordeal of Lucy's dismantled organic surface is referred away as spackled, decimated image to the inherent digital collage that manifests it: the code, so to say, exposed in its own pictorial result. It is as if her poisonous blue-chip nemesis is being painfully remedied in the glimpsed crystalized building blocks of her own photogenesis to begin with—and now, let's say, its "CDI" (computer degenerated image). Live by the pixel, die by it: subsumed entirely to its mutations. Yet with any lurking phobias about a pandemic technoculture seemingly thrown over by the end, as the film pushes beyond all precedent in the machine-human interface, the disembodied goal of plot is suddenly made homely, quaint, user-friendly.

It happens so fast, it takes a few seconds of reflection to catch up with the tech letdown. For out of the last mutating abstract mass that fuses technics and flesh, supercomputer and superwoman, is ultimately "ejected" an everyday backup file. Born(e) forth as the deferred and finalized result of that artificial uterine extract is nothing less, or more, than a twinkling cosmic flash drive. Flecks of electronically encompassed starlight glint across the surface of a nonetheless dated back-up technology involving a still tactile and quasi-erotic plug-in. Or say: a still umbilical lifeline to some nostalgically concrete if (in Lucy's final divination) no longer personified source. So that after all the prolonged spasms of high-voltage molting, where the last of Lucy's corporeal feelers are seen entwining the laboratory servers in a reciprocal meltdown—achieved by computer effects that just such engines were needed to program—we have arrived here at a final parturition of the *machina ex dea*.

Digital Ingestion, Technical Digest: Lucy in the Cloud

Existence has become its own special effect in such a plot. Not just perception, as for Epstein, nor the specifics of self-imaging in a projected inner
mirror, as for Balázs, but presence itself—material form, bodily volume,
the very *there* of being—is rendered phantasmal. And so its equivocation
focuses a technological history beyond any one on-screen story—yet
one which even recent treatments of VFX tend to sideline. In a long-arc
archaeology of film imaging—in light of the longer history of imprint
technology—Kristen Whissel proposes a link between the illustrated
emblem book in the early years of print culture, where an inset image
or symbol was meant to condense textual material in a node of visual
allegory, and the not quite "show-stopping" spectacle, one might say, of
digital effects in recent cinema, operating self-consciously, as she notes
(following Eisenstein), along x, y, and z axes.[2] For these are optic episodes
on screen that in fact advance the action of the so-called picture show even
while showing forth some distillation of its main narrative drive or theme.

But my emphasis has concerned the way in which the eye is also drawn to
another aspect of picturing that gets surfaced at times—as sheer surface—
from beneath whatever narratives of threat and vulnerability those more
salient effects may help stage and channel (their "axes" operating up, down,
and across our field of view, or penetrating it at right angles, in the occupied
space of plot). Apart from any such vectored realist conviction about lines
of motion within the diegesis, however, the true cutting edge of technique
is often conspicuous as the slivered and cross-shaved field of digital visualization on the vertical expanse of the screen itself—become the figuration
of its own computer interface. Optical illusion is replaced by technical
allusion, emblem by autoallegory or electronic parable, thus bringing out
the image field's own incremental constitution and its dismemberment at
once. Such moments may be indirectly routed back through narrative less
as manifest "symbols" than as techno-optic symptoms. At which point,
by means all too easily foreseen from plot to plot, screen spectacle lapses
to little more than the parade of its own conditions—and of their own
occasional scramble for thematic motivation. On this last score (a sought
meaning behind the means) Besson's narrative certainly exerts itself less
than most. Lucy's cybernoid ordeal in fact does little more—even at the
level of digital representation—than to flay raw the constituent underlay
of her own eventual (but already essential) computer assimilation. By a
kind of mimetic loop, she is, in effect, pictured to us in somatic fracture
and dispersion, *as effect*, by the same technology into which she will eagerly

be transfigured in the end. And through which, in whatever CGI violence is done to and by her, she is mostly manifest all along.

No actual sky with diamonds for this Lucy: instead, in a twinkling black USB stick, just the reduced, handheld, pixel-sparkling version of Kubrick's totalizing black monolith as a now global (and only metaphorically astral) force field, "cloud"-based, amorphous, permeating—and here (with what a difference!) at one with the computer rather than, as in *2001: A Space Odyssey*, escaping its coercive force. Miniaturized and recycled by that self-delivered flickering flash drive, as if it contained the audiovisual data files distributed for digital projection in the movie's own theatrical release (a playback system "Lucy" by name), the film's technical sine qua non becomes in this way its own *cineschatology*: the immanent "everywhere" of screen image irrespective of the actors who might populate it—or of their fates. And realized, of course, by the ubiquitous computerization of its visual frame.

Once again, then, high-tech science withdraws from the realm of social debate into the self-fulfilling technics of VFX spectacle. Having little secure faith in the image of the human body on screen, we are asked by the film *Lucy* to sit back and settle for the fungible body, the choreographic surface, of the inclusive digital image—in the contrived dance of its transformations. But it bears emphasis, in light of this essay's recurrent demurrals from "body theory," that any such associative way of putting it reflects the screen's own tacit figuration of its image plane's ripples, welts, and gashes—not some cogent analytic paradigm brought to bear on the optic frame. For these freaks of image are derived from an essential machination at odds with the somatic contours that digital as well as filmic cinema tends, under any less duress, to picture and activate as coherent bodily forms.

Hence Sontag's dual model in extrapolation once again: species-wide lethal threat versus an individuated erosion of the human organism. If, in standard disaster spectacle, each and any given digital extrusion or glitch may obliquely figure the global apocalypse of computer collapse— to exaggerate a subliminal unease about the fractured image plane of recent narrative entertainments—then the body gone to pixels in *Lucy* is the alternate "personal" microcosm of that terrestrial anxiety in more fantastic form. At least for most of the plot. But as if to purge that dimension of fantastic excrescence from the film's own "transcendental" climax, by the end of *Lucy* the fritzing, splintering, pix-elisional heroine, with no lingering hold on personhood, has willfully *become* the network. Initially terrorized by individual "take over" (Sontag), in the long run Lucy instead spreads out over the entire framed world in the disincarnate name of her own former person. Not transfiguring the screen as flesh—far from it:

rather, manifesting the absolute contradiction of body by technology in *metadigital projection*, here, there, everywhere.

Terminatus ad Quem

A year after *Lucy*, the trend in explicitly computerized mayhem and dismemberment seems to have found one exhaustive endpoint, in its explicitly digital reflexivity, with the sixth of the *Terminator* films—even while the subsequent release of *Pixels* (Chris Columbus, 2015) reverts by parody to a global invasion of freestanding computer-game icons.[3] The world is at final risk in the latter case by the extraterrestrial simulation—and imitative violence—of early low-def computer graphics in the first generation of interactive screen-play. In contrast, species eradication in *Terminator Genisys* (Alan Taylor, 2015) is threatened by the latest "generational" advance in killing-machine robotics. Such a catastrophe is already anticipated in the opening paratext, not this time a digitally tricked logo, but, more dramatically embroiled yet, as the apocalyptically blasted and rapidly dissipated seven syllables of the very title graphic: futurist dystopian update of the old wind-through-the-pages-of-the-adapted-novel trope—including the blustery landscape of David Lean's *Great Expectations* as it takes over by superimpositions from the turned leaves of Dickens's version. Inevitably, in the later sci-fi variant, as those Terminated architectonic letters splinter and crumble in this "blockbuster" (quasi-sculptural pun all but activated), we sense the digital equivalent of reverse-action, with the ecological nightmare of lethal alien forces casting to the nuclear winds the disguised pixels that have composed the monumental 3-D lettering in the first place. Again, whether crediting this to a director's visual inspiration or to the piecework labors of a graphic effects team, its obvious intentionality is more obvious than its source.[4]

Into this posthuman landscape arrives the new robot force. The original T-800 (Arnold Schwarzenegger) must now face off not just with his familiar liquid metal ("polyalloy") enemy from earlier films (the T-1000) and then with the new "nanomachine hybrid" (T-3000) and its millionfold metallic infrastructure of magnetized glinting particles—each capable of "mimetic" shape-shifting (again the computer "chip" in fractalized pun)—but finally with a third-order digital nemesis (T-5000) in disembodied form. In all this, the real battle for dominance operates within divergent imaginations of digital VFX and its own mimetic capacities. In just these violent confrontations of the original cyborg hero with subsequent iterations of illusionist technology, the screen's own computer rendering comes under immanent analysis by triangulation. Seamless plastic flow in self-morphing molten form versus (in a more fully "sophisticated" understanding as well as futurist variant) the revealed discrete nanobits that secretly fuel its micro-*trucage*: such is the divided model that is then, in the end, upgraded (and further "undone") by the reveal of clustered but discrete pixel lumens. Three stages of violence—and of material unveiling.

And of counteractive measures as well—whether directly assaulting the lethal molecular aggregates or doing a temporal end run around them. First, a momentary stalling and "takedown" of the nanomodular composite of the T-3000, with its putative force field of numberless metallic filings, is staged to reverse its own buildup in Hollywood computer modeling. To this end, a normative biotechnology is also repurposed as weapon. The organic analysis provided by the standard MRI apparatus ("magnetic resonance imaging"), when its aperture is aimed instead against the camouflaged robot as a giant magnetic canon, peels away layers of "his" fleshless simulacrum in what amounts to the violent oscillations of a *multiple image resonance*. The effect serves to archaeologize, from within its CGI tour de force, the prehistory of filmic cinema as well its electronic destiny. For beneath the shimmer of pixelized metal bits sucked from this vanishing anatomy, we see in widescreen side view (suspending the usual melodrama of the film's 3-D axis) the staggered "skeletal" outlines of the robot's full-body profile receding behind him in a way that recalls the serial chronophotography (think Eadweard Muybridge) that led to cinema in the first place—this, as well as the sketchy origin of the present VFX in its (here reversed) phases of computer-modeled buildup.

The figure electromagnetically atomized, chipped away at, in this fractalized manner is, in this scene, all computer-chip emanation to begin with.

As if "inspired" by *Lucy* in the heroine's hands-on agony of first fingertip symptoms, yet again all *digit-zation*.

The episode is what Metz might have called the re-"diegetization" of digital *trucage*, here foregrounded as if by a histrionic glitch in its morphological code.

More interesting yet, muted rather than hypertrophic, is another reflex of the film's own production values incurred by defensive actions against the murderous human simulants. Plot can barely justify the passing fascination of this moment. In the film's half-hearted social critique, the script has tried rewriting the Reign of the Machines as a parable of computer affordance gone wrong, with the "Genisys" operating system discovered (by a return from a more distant and accursed future) as the 2017 "launch" of the ultimate "killer app" (as a corporate marketer touts it)—a commercial venture that actually launches, as if literalizing the metaphor, the high-speed machines (rockets) that all but destroy the world. Too much human technodependence has become mass-suicidal. Lucy's disembodied and computerized universality is benign (if pointless) by comparison. And the latest *Terminator* does find a way to figure the virtuality of its branching time lines by a remarkable brief wrinkle—or unfolding, even unraveling— of its own digital optics. This happens when, in sending its hero back from the mid twenty-first century to that (for us) near-future crisis point of electronic Armageddon in 2017, the film puts its own mass-market technology into momentary remission. The effect is comparable to what might have happened in *Billy Lynn's Long Halftime Walk* if Ang Lee—in the psychic blockage of some traumatic flashback, for instance—had turned off the 3-D or cut the frame rate by eighty percent, or both, and shocked us into a "normal" reception of the screen world.

The *Terminator* scene flattens out and fogs over in this fashion with an ingenious metanarrative impact. The premise is the implanting of a counterfactual memory in the service of a corrected future. With the hero's "remembering" a rural and idyllic teenage birthday party that never (before) happened, during which psychic retrofit he has been programmed to warn of a pending threat, the flashback is marked as subjective, virtual, by a misty aura that—looking at first like the hokey rhetoric of lyrical soft focus—quickly comes (un)clear as a penumbral double image. Take off the 3-D IMAX glasses at this point and the effect is unchanged. What we are seeing is simply the hyperreal of the new digital projection suddenly disengaged, suspended, reverting to the fabricated blurred rudiments of its own composite optic plane—without the technical prosthesis of that retinal gestalt otherwise bringing the overlapped differential imaging into its typically engulfing force. In a more standardized format well short of Ang Lee's innovation, it is as if one were to drop back from color to black-and-white for a memory image, allowing the medium to metaphorize its own departure from the persuasions of immersive verisimilitude and its boosted reality effects. In the lone "intelligence" of its own "machine," *Terminator Genisys* moves to delimit the plot's last best hope for defeating a pending lethal technology by momentarily pulling the plug on the film's own spectacle. The result is a kind of tacit parable by cinematic dissolution: disable the visual status of the "projected" future to lay bare its sequestered truth.

But soon enough this ongoing subtext of technical exposure is taken up again by VFX rather than its passing cancellation. Exceeding even the mimesis of nanometallic hybridity, the arch villain (the very incarnation of Genisys) finally appears in the form of computational destiny's rapidly maturing holographic avatar—and in a yet more blatantly pixelated projection. He can only be halted in his Silicon Valley headquarters, and merely for a split second at a time, by his assailants shooting out, one after the other, the overhead digital projectors that manifest him from every corner of this computational hub—only for his image to be instantaneously regrouped from another lens of transmission. Here again: the evolution of mimetic engines of destruction portrayed as a devolution to the rudiments of the film's own illusionist system. For those mimetic filings earlier lending pretend materiality to the digital fragments of the decimated nanohybrid are here revealed at yet another level for just what they are: computerized and beamed figments in simulated 360-degree (rather than just 3-D) form, or in other words coruscating fragments in a glinting bitmap simulation of a transparent humanoid frame. All told, then, in the registered violence of the lacerated or eviscerated cyborg body, digital *trucage* is ultimately parsed across plot under the manifold aspects of its simulation: form, flux, morcellated fleck, and sheer gridded scintillation. A forgivably negative review of the film in London's *Guardian*—a review skewering the lifeless mechanics of plot, dialogue, and performance in this assembly-line recycling—closes with this quip: "The War is over. The machines have won."[5] But it's really, as usual, the VFX "machinations" (Metz's term again) that retain the upper hand in the long view of our evolving cinemachines.

The next conceptual step in the manifestion of on-site holographic projection and its narratively entailed overhead sources (together with its remote alternatives) will arrive, in the Postscript, with the erotic electronics of *Blade Runner 2049*. On the way there, we can recognize again an overarching genre tendency. If the future "projected" (both senses) in classic screen sci-fi traditionally involves the very future of imaging and its screen facilitations, that tendency is extended lately into the computerized generation of its pixel composites. Yet the temporal gap of forecast seems ever narrower—certainly by contrast, for example, with the telescreen prolepsis in Lang's *Metropolis* (1926). All the while, this embedded logic of mediation connects in turn with a wider field of reflexive incidents and indicators on screen. If film declares its possibilities, for Cavell, in part through "assertions in technique," it also does so, as we've often noted, by what we might term "recessions in the optique." Repeatedly, in screen narrative, "picture windows" or "picture frames," along with mirror surfaces, are inset within the narrational frame of the motion picture—including all the spacecraft control panels and closed-circuit telepresencing consoles, and these days all the remote video feeds, dear to sci-fi in any phase of the cinemachine. All this serves to duplicate, in some degree of miniaturization, the medial display by which these optical rectangles are manifested for the theater audience in the first place. Such redoubling attaches, of course, only to the plane of cinematic immanence, as a rule, not intrinsically to its serial displacements in the figmenting of motion, whether by photogrammic or digital aggregation or by some unforeseen future process. Yet this latter technical "assertion"—and what is this but a mode of intention?—may at any point accompany the optical recession by which one plane of vision is inset within another. Such an assertion may, in other words, find itself bound up in the rectangular step back of reframed visual planarity. In any case, whether by assertion or associational regress, in the audiovisual ramification of computerized sci-fi—taking as its topic, as it often does, the overreach of computerization itself—the audiovisual future is now. And if a machinic "intelligence" is thereby "asserted" in analysis of its own transformations (combining Epstein and Cavell), its superintending functions may well be taken to *mean what we see*.

Instrumentations of Tomorrow

Based on its title page alone, this essay delivers no obvious archaeological call for the recovery of cinema's more technological aspects—in the irreversible move from filmic to digital recording—amid a steady stream of affect and interactivity studies. Instead, the title could well be taken simply to evoke all the on-screen high-tech robotic constructs that clutter and glut the narrative screen lately—and not just fortified megacraft and alien motherships, but all the prosthetic humanoids: from iron men, terminators, and transformers to their female equivalents in cyberjuiced vamps like the eponymous Lucy or the again titular Dea *Ex Machina*. Such computerized vehicles and cyberized bodies are, however, the machines of cinema in only one sense of that possessive. And yet the continuing VFX Festival has been convened precisely to show how often—as with inset viewing screens as well—such mechanisms coincide with the apparatus of their own projected image. So any undue spread of reference in the title has ended up being good enough trouble for the thesis after all.

This inquiry pursues, most actively, the machine that *is* cinema, with Epstein as initial touchstone. What machinic qualities does cinema possess—and either retain or convert in the transformation from filmic to digital implementation—that can be manifested on screen without being tethered to futurist electronics or robotic shape-shifting? And which of these can display "intelligence" in a form not unrelated to AI? Increasingly, the tech input of CGI rendering is extruded on (not from) the sci-fi screen (released rather than banished): extruded, if rarely ruminated, in the form of computer machinations narrativized to a fare-thee-well—and thus making connection, even if only implicitly visible, with their pixelated source in the underlying "machine" of digital imageering. Then, too, sci-fi is only part of the picture in this CGI epoch of pictured motion. Digital cinema seems to have entered into a new period of polarized thematics in monthly box-office competition. We get either fantasy films generating whole "incredible" worlds from a computerization as far as possible from their medieval(ized) romance setting or else apocalyptic sci-fi offloading its own electronic capacities onto malicious (or in any case nearly omnipotent) invaders astronomically advanced in the hypermachines of transport and transmit alike.

My hunch is that *avoiding* the latter fallback option in the unfiltered narrativation of CGI as intergalactic tech—unfiltered because so emphatically digitized and computer-boosted even at the plot level—partly contributed, by its deflection, to the success of Denis Villeneuve's *Arrival*: that unexpected sci-fi hit (and multiple Oscar nominee) whose climactic special effect we sampled at the start in order to achieve some brief feel for apparatus reading. We back up now to what precedes this closural moment of aerial departure rather than flight. Instead of the usual cyber-metallic sheen of typical sci-fi visitation, the original advent in question brought to earth's atmosphere a dozen weathered, encrusted spacecraft of uncertain material composition: giant ellipsoid monoliths hovering above the ground more like timeless levitated menhirs from Stonehenge than shimmering reticulated gadgetry from another galaxy. The sense of time-roughened materialization seems just right for these gradually disclosed paradoxical "remnants" from exactly the future that a preserved earth will (in the grammatically future perfect predictions of the film's closure) have eventually helped to empower. With their Neolithic mysteries of surface and material constitution, that's how those sci-fi staples, those motherships, operate at the plot level, opaque though it is. Yet the very look of these ovoid time capsules from the future serves as a visual trope not only for their own place out of time but for their relation, precisely as special effects, to the medial technology that so underplays their machine magic that it tacitly rehearses certain dated features in its own technological and genre prehistory.

This heightening of VFX consciousness by demoting its showiness is a tendency we can best return to after probing certain pertinent narrative episodes that build toward its full import. In genre terms alone, an uncertainty sets in early. It's as if the two poles of Christopher Nolan's time-bending work—the mind-game because reverse-action psychothriller *Memento* (2000) and the sci-fi spectacle of *narrativized* mind gaming through retrogenetic implants in *Inception* (2010)—are abutted here, rather than fully fused. This is manifest, in one narrative strand, by a time loop structure of tragic domestic flashback routing us through scenes of the heroine's dying daughter not yet born. The abrupt telepathic flashes—inevitably mistaken by us as flashbacks—serve to punctuate and ultimately frame an alien-visitation plot in the familiar mode of cautionary intervention for the good of the cosmos (as if it were a third version of *The Day the Earth Stood Still*), though here with the extra fillip that UFOs are only a prophecy of their own eventual need for Earth's help. In this sense, the VFX epiphanies that conjure them are imminence made immanent:

present only as visualized. They don't so much represent the future as mediate time itself.

The rest of the time-loop structure and the montage distortions it triggers—climaxed in the heroine's commitment to having the child whose fate is so grievously foreseen—seems only loosely linked to the sci-fi plot by some unspoken cliché about lived time as the acceptance of what's to come, mortally, historically. This weld is thin but at least not contradictory, and helps draw out the obvious influence from Chris Marker's *La Jetée* (1962), its own sci-fi plot turning on the question of rescue by the future only if you can accept it as your destiny; otherwise in Marker, the "barrier" of a stop-time blockage—and reversion. More compelling than this plot logic in *Arrival*, however, is the look of the film, rather than its intertextual hooks. Famously, Marker's photoroman used a montage of separate stills, rather than full cinematicity, to measure an inertial resistance to inexorable duration, whereby a past is always vectored toward a future. In his return to the photogrammic chain as the rudiment, and ultimate retardation, of all motion, forward or back, Marker might well have been reading Epstein while working this idea up.

The reflexivity of material means in *Arrival* operates quite differently. Through a combination of chastened budget and aesthetic restraint, the dialing down of VFX leaves a certain breathing room for other ruminations on the nature of the screened image in front of us: a good part of it digital too, as in other sci-fi, but low-keyed and inwardly turned. One result is that the narrated collaboration, matured into eventual flash-forward marriage, of the philologist heroine and her physicist "partner"—the wedding, in short, of lingual code and number (quite fully allegorized at the turning point, as we'll see)—figures at the plot level what the film has, so to say, internally circumscribed for actual contemplation about the verbal and optical processes that generate it. This is where the muting of digital panache both enhances the mystery of the alien visitations and educes from their sheenless forms of transport, including their sheer dematerialization on exit, a quiet technological inference: not just about the fungibility of the optic plane under CGI protocols, but about the place (so resolutely delineated by Epstein and Metz) of such generative imaging in the longer history of the film medium as inherent special effect. And yet again, such a medial subtext is enhanced by a classic framing within the frame, a "screening" structure replicated within the plot's own scenography.

In just this respect, the first glimpse of the film's trailer may seem to give the game away, even though few narrative cards are as yet on the table. The scene's literally widescreen, backlit window of monitored alien motion (another quintessential "recession of the optique" in screen display) recalls the three panoramic blank walls of the debriefing chamber in *2001: A Space Odyssey* (1968) within Kubrick's implied fourth wall of luminous 70 mm projection, like sideways cinemascopic panels awaiting the coming appearance of the cognate black monolith in the next scene.[6] But in *Arrival*, the new version of a Kubrickian extraterrestrial directive, incarnating the very force of cosmic history in its own related way, actually appears within (rather than by association with) the wide-angle screenlike aperture that is actually a protective if mutable scrim. The alien septapods, caged off there for their own biological protection, look, as a result, like nothing so much as a framed movie effect as they float into view on their squirming tentacles, photographed and filmed all the while by the human visitors to the floating spacecraft (as with the multipole camera set-ups directed at the moon crater's excavated monolith in *2001*). In *Arrival*, this mise en abyme of a "screening" room, this paracinematic interior rectangle, is embedded within one of those gargantuan impenetrable lozenges, twelve in all, whose curved forms resemble huge if occluded contact lenses for first contact. Still, the nonfuturist surface of the motherships notwithstanding, it is, from the midst and mist of an elongated interior rectangle of framed and shielded light, that alien beings emerge like they always do in sci-fi, protectively set off from spectators by the four-corned transparent shield of the strictly fictive and virtual.

But not entirely removed, even in this narrative space of apparent reciprocal quarantine. The alien's shrouding atmosphere, a dense opacity of fog, meets the transparent border at arm's reach, touched finally by the female linguist in order to make the reciprocal contact upon which she insists that translation—figured here as haptic pressure—must rest. Her "reaching out" amounts to a kind of touchpad intimacy with their own cryptic script. And yet, as far as alien communication is concerned—or, in other words, alien mediality—the linguistic and the corporeal have already begun to part ways. Two divisions gradually pertain, in fact: first between embodied speech and extruded writing in the alien "tongue," then between "language" at large and the codes of relational mathematics—with each division folded back into cinematic process in an unexpected convergence on which the plot's own climax will, we are to find, rather densely depend.

Early on, our heroine linguist discovers that the guttural sounds these beings make among themselves in their luminous chambers (their phonetic speech) bears no relation to the written script by which they end up attempting to communicate with her across its outer plane. As we hear their Dolby mumbling in off-screen space, even this exercise in an unnerving "acoustmatic" power play doesn't exhaust the metacinematic overtones of this radical divide between orality and inscription.[7] The classic division of labor in screen production between soundtrack and image track, as enacted by exaggeration in films of ventriloquism, for instance, having been reduced to digitization in the new convergence economy of cinematic delivery systems, is separated out again here as if in some historical throwback to the silent era of the cinemato-graph. In this segregation of visual from aural signal, we thus move between separate regimes of sound and script, phoneme and grapheme. This is clear when the guttural talk of the interlopers, a sound received in and over time, is sidelined by a graphic calligraphy conjured before us in what we recognize, beneath plot, as the computer-spewed CGI—rather than actual liquid filigree—of their semantic swirls, emitted in the heptapod equivalent of octopus ink.

The alien syntax is indeed circular, coterminous, all meaning released at once in the closed circuit of these glyphs as a kind of ouroboros grammar. Call it, by narrative synecdoche, a time loop code. But when a group of rogue military attack the translation chamber with a planted bomb, a multiple burst of these circular calligraphic forms is emitted (and recorded for later study). This final "message" is now up to the physicist's mathematical intuition, not the linguist's, to decode as a higher-order sign of ratio and proportion: a kind of relational pictogram, as slowly discerned. For here, in the form of a geometrically devised puzzle rather than a discourse, is a proportional rebus of sorts rather than a transcendental speech act: solved just in time as a numerical allegory. The spatial disposition of the separate closed syntactic rings (in a ratio of 8.33 to 100 across the available surface of the text-sprayed backlit barrier, now further analyzed on a backlit computer) is arranged—and then interpreted—as in itself an icon of the message itself. What is assumed, induced, is that the 12 to 1 ratio (of available interspace to marking) on the surface of the inscription figures, so to say, the big picture: namely, the global distribution of the dozen spacecraft in various sectors of Earth's transnational and contentious human sphere—thus marking off the political isolation that needs rescinding, needs consolidating as One, not a dozen, in a benign centralization of power and progressive will.

It is by dint of this wildly abstruse hint that the composite pictogram (once the physicist's insight is wedded to the linguist's previous translations) is realized to encode the collective global harmony enjoined upon earthlings in order to survive long enough to help the alien race at some unspecified point of crisis three thousand years in the future. The visitants being only temporal mediators to begin with, the medium of the spacecrafts' message rests with their spacing itself. To call this "messaging" far-fetched is putting it mildly. That it is so resolutely low-tech is the only surprise. That it is nonetheless numerical in essence, however, is the true clue to an interpretation of special effects in the fate of the ships themselves, once their message has been more like manifested than transmitted. Rather than focusing on "the ones," the positive factors in some informational code, "look at the zeros," says the physicist: the lacunae, the spacings between. His instinct amounts to a kind of digital metaphor, as he tries to discriminate the "negative space" of their patterned marks, across "too many gaps," from the false lure of "data." Binarity is thereby evoked only by displacement in a pictogram of even-handed (evenly spaced) coordination between a dozen major world hubs: a political equilibration, only to be achieved at the last possible moment, after having been blocked by an international "communications blackout" triggered by global paranoia. Only if the alien message gets through can lines of electronic mediation be reopened, textually or televisually.

Disapparition

The tables are here neatly, if obliquely, turned. Communication has been on everyone's mind from the start in this film about the heroic labors of translation. In an early bit of voiceover from an interpolated montage of TV broadcasts in response to the alien arrival, an announcer mentions that the twelve ships seem to have established no known form of communication with each other, producing neither sonic nor any other electrostatic emissions. Their own intercommunication is, in short, not what they have arrived to coordinate—except, as we find, by the decoded "message" (the indexical sign) of their very spacing out around the globe. By delayed disclosure, their arrival is meant as a catalyst to open up our world's own transnational lines of communication, only to have them ironically shut down in paranoid overreaction. As avatars of the future, the alien visitants need no mediation; they embody it: time itself as vehicle of transformative duration. Having anticipated this in "Advance Press," we now step off its further implications in the circularities of the film's elusive time-warp plot.

That early transcendence of internal messaging (among the armada of hovering spacecraft) is a detail that we may, in fact, well remember when the ultimately cracked code (the 12 to 1 spatial symmetry) of their last crowded inscription is discovered to be not discursive at base, nor grammatical at all, but in a more abstract or schematic sense digital, numeric, radically differential—available to comprehension only if factored rather than read, say "computed." And if the weightless vessels are therefore more medium than message, magic shapes of time's reversible medium itself, they seem to have contaminated their translator in the same vein, induced her flash-forward visions of the fated (destined and doomed alike) child she will conceive with the physicist before he deserts her and the ailing girl. If Einstein's quip that time is what keeps everything from happening all at once is also understood to mean, for cinematic grammar, that it keeps flashback from being indistinguishable from prolepsis, then time travel overrides this constraint.

Moreover, as a critic of Epstein's persuasion might wish to emphasize, if such anachronic montage is one of those special effects not aberrant in, but intrinsic to, the cinematic medium, filmic before digital, that is not where this film stops in its own metamedial stress. For *Arrival* brandishes a more specific mode of "truquage" in closure (Epstein's dated spelling one last time) that serves to visualize—in the negative mode of disappearance itself—the extent to which these bulking neolith-like spacecraft are "mediumized" in image as well as in astral purpose: offering, that is, with no intercommunication between them, only a collective *channel to the future*. Confirming this is a digital finesse so restrained, in CGI terms, as to invoke a much earlier lineage of trick effacements in the history of the screen medium. With the alien mission accomplished simply in keeping temporal circuits open, keeping the medium of time alive for an earth otherwise in danger of self-destruction, no special media effect is necessary to dramatize the return of such catalytic vehicles to the state of nonappearance. Coming from the future, they have been only *pending* to begin with, even in visually impending over a landscape they never touch down on. Rather than actually taking flight, now, after liftoff, they go only so far as to disappear, it would seem, into the *not yet*. In awaiting us some thirty centuries in the future, such looming tools evaporate from the now. In this way—given the absence of any discerned pixel disintegration or material crumble in these evacuating motherships—they simply evanesce. Or nearer to a film-historical crux, where their disapparition registers more in the mode of technical nostalgia than metaphysical premonition, they *dissolve*.

The film's image patterns reverse their genealogical trajectory in this way, breaking from a gradually naturalized structure of editing in the evolution of cinematic syntax. Take, for example, the look of a ghost or dream double, with its technical anomaly softened over time (Metz's point, coming up) to a mere narrative inflection or taxeme, a piece of syntax rather than a factor of spectacle. From within the same evolving optical technology, these vessels in *Arrival*—these metamedial vehicles—may seem to revert, that is, or more like advert, to one of those primal scenes of deception at the heart of film's whole phototransparent representation, long before its digital transformation. They thus liquidate themselves in present space as paradoxical throwbacks to the future. Not only do these ships look old-fashioned in their cragged stony surface, but they are digitally factored out, rubbed away, by the most old-fangled of devices: a once very special (indeed quintessential) effect that operates somewhere—in their all but instantaneous clouding and dissipation, stem to stern—between a wipe and a straight dissolve. But it is important to notice that the "intelligence" of the machine involves at this point a thinking that is not nostalgic but instead narratively strategic.

Almost by way of visual pun, as well as synecdoche, the alien mediation of temporal premonition—as in the inhabited cloud bank of their on-board atmospheric audience chamber—is more than ever mist-ified. As each ship's wear-worn bulk dissipates with a cloudy swipe rather than an accelerated whoosh before our eyes, the time-travel vehicle is swallowed up in its own dissipating fogbank, its own innate medium, before its last traces vanish into the literalized thin air of computer illusionism.[8] Yet, at just this point, and with a resonance one wouldn't wish to minimize, let alone neglect, this whole muted computer effect waxes ontological as well as epistemological as we watch. To put it in terms of the film's title, there is arrival, advent, but no real departure. There is only dis-apparition: the ships blown away, as if from within, in the spume of their own dissipated mass and magnitude. And when, instead of a warp-speed uprush, these intergalactic vehicles simply deliquesce, they do so one after another (which is to say all at once) in intercut scenes of temporal overview: narrative cinema's equivalent of a metaphysical omniscience. The point (like the VFX itself) bears iteration only for the way this floating and fading action, this recursive transformation in parallel montage, hovers—the ships literally, the inference rhetorically—at some indeterminate reversible switch point between episode and metaphor, figment and figuration.[9]

In this manner, with no communications passing between them, these transient craft (along with the singular technical "craft," in the other sense, that their VFX reveals) declare themselves as vehicles of a mediation most fully achieved in their own diaphanous fade to invisibility, terrestrial message already delivered. At the metanarrative level, this is no minor node of (reverse) disclosure. Nor for the stakes of our present discussion across various optical intensities in recent sci-fi. For this essay's convergence of discerned medial features and analytic method, the convoluted nature of *Arrival*'s climactic decoding episode stands forth as its own kind of reading lesson in address to on-screen image. Even before those aerial dissolves into atmosphere itself, that is, evoking by digital editing as they do their own predecessor in the laboratory technique of superimposition, the physicist's decipherment of the computer-screened graphic ratios (rather than grammar) of the alien glyphs is in its own way representative. The scientist of forces and flows precedes us in reading the strictly pictorial disposition of the screen as its own distributed clue: conveyed at base, as in both filmic and digital cinema alike, by intermittence itself, the on/off of an imperceptible succession on the underside of all motion. On the heels of pure geometry's ability to decode the airships' global placement for a clue to their message of harmony, apparatus reading then decodes their optical displacement, in its film-historical allusion to early *trucage*, as the sign of their parabolic status as medium incarnate. How different their return to millennial latency would have seemed if they were fumed away in disintegration by a particle system effect rather than merely subtracted from the world for now. Just that difference offers a yardstick of anachronism's power in reinjecting the lap dissolve as once again a diegetic wonder.

Implications readily accrue here for that broader measure of thematic weight borne by VFX in other films. The intensity of fleeting material apprehension invited by the alien fleet's vanishment does point, ultimately, to a sense of schematic patterning beneath the captivating visible sights (and signs) on any "tricked" narrative screen: a generative impetus machinic before scenic, and hence, under current technological dispensations, numerical before retinal. Which is to say that the physicist (rejecting the idea of a communicated formula for "travel beyond the speed of light," as first suspected) sees instead, in the alien inkings, a proportional logic beneath the illegible signifiers. He cracks the geometric code rather than translating the supposed algebraic message, reads the template (the algorithm) of image generation rather than its informational content. Such, again, is the pedagogy of the episode. In accessing the code, he too, in effect, reads the medium itself. As do we in the VFX of reverse arrival to follow.

Digitage

Probed in this way is exactly the stratum of optical fabrication that might be said, under suggestion from overt tricks of the eye, to *generalize* the otherwise *special* effect as a foundational deception. Metz's tacit extrapolation, in this sense, from the earliest "trick films" to the *trick of film* all told, is thus an account that the violence of CGI effects—or, equally, the marked suspension of such digital mayhem in *Arrival*—serves to expand rather than amend. In bringing down the curtain on this Festival of VFX and its simultaneously reviewed inferences, what remains is not that post-cinematic assimilation of motion image to "animage" adduced elsewhere (Gaudrealt and Marion) but the far more specific consideration, in light of recent screen machination, of *trucage* under the rubric of *digitage*.

The historical shape of Metz's argument entails a movement from the "diegetization" process (665) to new levels of film grammar. Having mobilized a visual effect (like superimposition) as a narrative occurrence (like dream figment), film rhetoric puts such an effect through a subsequent transformation into the mere exponent of the image. The optical device becomes a mark of "syntactic" transition (like lap dissolve) that amounts to the de-diegetization of *trucage*, which in its previous avatars offered a plot-driven marvel.[10] Think of the vanishing ghostly penumbras of early horror or fantasy film (like the flash dissolve of Frankenstein's monster disappearing, as we saw, into his creator's own mirror image in Edison) in the subsequent process of their becoming naturalized as nondiegetic ligatures of scene change. Or think of the jump cut that once represented an extraterrestrial uncanny in *A Trip to the Moon* becoming a mode of syntactic juncture in an evolving grammar of film—or as Metz sometimes calls it, a mode of "punctuation" (659).

The scope and grip of this account comes through by contrast with explanations less attached to the apparatus. Notably without reference to Metz on the features of display rendered operational, on optical deviance evolved into syntax, Ian Christie has recently built instead on Tom Gunning's influential "The Cinema of Attractions" for his own sense of transition (as Christie's subtitle has it) "From 'Tricks' to 'Effects,'" the latter including not just machinations but such profilmic illusionism as painted backdrops.[11] It is this emphasis that makes particular sense of his central borrowing from Gunning: the claim that "effects are tamed attractions." Beyond various deceptions of the set, the strictly discursive jump cut or lap dissolve (to name but two technological candidates) might well be described as a domesticated miracle, the subduing of some supernatural apparition—but only when the apparatus, not just some on-screen scenography, is engaged specifically in this long view of the historically passified marvel. In contrast to the term "effects" broadly used by Christie and Gunning, analysis here is pointed instead at what happens when the contained and markedly "special" effect, including that of binary imaging itself in the most spectacular extrusions of recent VFX, is shown forth untamed, gone feral—set free at least long enough to be actively recaptured by narrative drive.

With this annotation's own recent examples of tricked images still in view, we are in a position to rethink the triadic summary of such effects that Metz offers before coming to his sweeping conclusion (based, by a sudden and encompassing reversal of terminological priority, on the transfer from diegesis to picture plane—and with no mention of Epstein's equivalent claim): namely, that all cinema, "montage itself," is *trucage*.[12] Short of this, the "spectator who is accustomed to cinema, and who knows the rules of the game" (672), will know how to respond in distinct ways "to imperceptible *trucages*, visible *trucages*, and to perceptible but invisible *trucages*." Adding: "As to the punctuation marks, it will come as no surprise here to state that they all belong to the category of visible effects" (672). And as to the VFX of departure in *Arrival*, it is no surprise by now to say that disappearance is a perceptible trick with one foot in a seasoned means of punctuation and another in futurist magic.

Concerning the diegesis alone in all such effects, however, it is tempting to square Metz's triangle. His leading example of the "imperceptible" trick: the stunt double (664), a body you see but don't recognize as other than, say, James Bond('s). In exemplification of its "visible" counterpart: a tricked image meant to carry credence, for instance (not Metz's) the 1953 death ray in *War of the Worlds* as a superimposition upon—as if emanating from—a plastic model of the helmeted alien marauder. Instancing the "perceptible but invisible" effect (664), a tampering with the image intuited but not discerned in its actual working: the missing body in *The Invisible Man*, as in fact cited by Metz, anticipating up to a point the instantaneous vaporization of bodies in *War of the Worlds*. The serially exterminated populace in Spielberg's remake is visible at two levels, however, as we've taken time to note: what once might have been identified as the diegetic versus the photogenic level, or narratival versus cinematographic—now to be distinguished as plot space versus electronic interface. So that CGI introduces an implicit extra term, in the computer age, alongside montage and its more openly illusionist flashpoints in *trucage*. This is what I am calling *digitage*.

And what this further suggests, on reflection, is that the threefold sliding scale of optical dissimulation in Metz might indeed be conceptualized, in light of the electronic subtext of VFX manifestation, according to the fourfold template of the "semiotic square" (rather than through his not-quite-exhaustive tripartite division of optic labor). An analytic method influentially mobilized by Fredric Jameson in the cognitive mapping of a novel's ideo/logical field—and hence in isolating the "political unconscious" resulting from the unthought neither/nor of its otherwise explicit and dichotomous value system—can serve in this way, analogously, to locate the technical parameters and generative blind spot of digital production, as of the photogram chain before it in celluloid cinema.[13] Approach it as follows in cross-referencing the main categories. The acrobatic stunt double, say for Scarlet Johansson in *Lucy*, is a *presence* unrecognized: an illusion of the heroine we see without knowing we do (without sighting the deception as such). In contrast, the invisibilized body, as in the last deliquescence of the heroine's post-corporeal apotheosis, is an *absence* seen, a perceptible illusion of encroaching disapparition itself (as again in *Arrival*). Such contraries gloss each other in orienting their attempted synthesis. For bridging between these lateral poles, these pure extremes, what transpires—in the upper quadrant of manifest projection—is that predominating blend of technical ingenuity and its immanent visual form in mainstream narrative: the "special" as optic spectacle, a dimension of the visible now so widely unrecognized in its CGI illusionism that one is regularly surprised to see how many "surreptitious" digital artists are credited at the end of a drama or comedy boasting no apparent optical stunts or deceptions.

Even as the onetime body double is increasingly unnecessary in CGI production, so do all three aspects of Metzian *trucage* tend lately to conflate into the digital imaginary of the projected image field. Graphed, then, according to a semiotic template for CGI "signage" (fig. 1), the reframed cognitive picture allows us to see the missing term (the neither/nor rather than the both/and) coming to the surface in the very warping of it. In advance of any such recognition, however—and within the initial binary of a "perceptible" *trucage* when also wholly "visible" as such (the organizing alternatives in their typical intersection)—reside the standard manipulations of VFX, in fantasy as well as sci-fi: medieval wizards in flight, alien motherships, rampaging zombie armies (or ant colonies) in endless multiplication. Yet the true conceptual payoff of such a regraphing requires the further medial discernment situated by logical contraries that may be only sporadically salient. Demarcated thereby is a sector of recognition interesting not least for what it might have had to say, even in Metz's day, about cinema's unseen photogrammic series, as well as what it says now in ours about the digital undertext of screen apparitions.

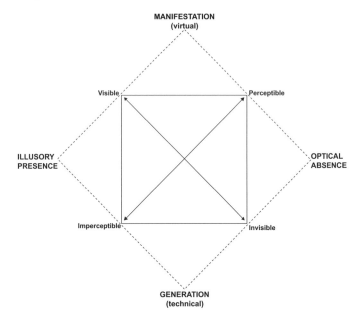

FIGURE 1

In the full gamut of special effects, and countering the upper synthesis of the manifest visual image and its perceptible technotrickery (in all the immersive virtuality of its representation), there on the underside of spectacle falls, by double negation, the *neither* visible *nor* perceptible nature of digitization itself—as, before, with the discrete serial strip and its frame-line interruptions in filmic cinema. This is the most specialized and precedent of all screen effects: a generative operation beneath the threshold of any and every view.

So convoluted as to be exemplary, an extreme case comes to mind from among the many revered rear-projection shots of Hitchcock's *Vertigo* (1958), repeatedly sealing off its characters in a world of illusions and lit-eralized erotic *projection*. This is a pattern that optically implodes after the presumed death of Madeleine, who has been impersonating the villain's wife. No sooner has she fallen (been shoved) from the mission tower than the detective who has failed to save her suffers a nightmare in which he takes her place in a blatantly artificial (and dream-justified) sacrificial fall toward the same tile roof below. As if illustrating Freud's notion that we always awake in dreams before undergoing our own death, here in *Vertigo*—just before the dreaming scapegoat would inevitably land on the tiles—the rear projection is turned off. It is as if we have plummeted with him right back onto Hitchcock's set. This is to say that the shock of the neither/nor, neither open trick nor hidden subterfuge, has penetrated to the generative depths of the apparatus in the very moment of recording. The resultant *effect* of this erased "effect" is that the hardly *imperceptible trucage* of rear-projection backdrop (though less imperceptible here, more "irreal," than with the most subdued instances in the film) has passed into a paradoxically stark mode of *invisibility* (or, say, a blanching cancellation): as nothing but the blank white backdrop of a previously tricked mise-en-scène. Aligned from top to bottom along an imagined vertical axis in that graphing of Metz, then, from manifestation down to generation, perception has passed from the virtual realization of a character's radical interiority to the site of the composite image itself on set or in lab.

The norm is very much otherwise, as was certainly the case in Hitchcock's day. What you typically see is what you get, not how it got there—or vanished. As with the earliest tricks of the Shüfftan mirror explored in chapter 3, the screen viewer today, more often than ever, sees remarkable places and things by seeing, unmistakably, the "visible" results of deception—but without seeing through them, without ridding the marvel of its mystery. Same with the disappearing acts of expunged holographic villains (progeny of *The Invisible Man*) or collapsing skyscrapers. Elsewhere, one may simply see a CGI cavern or mountain range (or plate glass window, for that matter) without sensing anything unlikely about it, anything unlifelike or *noticeably* tricked (Metz's alternate category of the optical but "imperceptible," where simulation, in fact, has often replaced the stunt double). In every case, what can't be taken as *visible* in its own underlying right, nor even *perceived* as constitutive even though known to be (algorithmic now, as before photogrammic), is the deep driver of all contemporary imaging in the coded array of its subliminal pixel grid. This is the necessarily occulted process that makes of any manifestation on screen a sheer virtuality—and sometimes returns from its own retinal repression to make just this point, as we've repeatedly seen, by making its pixelated mark on the very plane of vision. In reading the diagram, therefore, decipher the horizontal axis as capturing particular simulations, the vertical as an analysis of projection per se.

This schema is by no means a correction of Metz. Via the logical adjustment of his threefold taxonomy, such a charting merely brackets more tightly his own final claim about the illusionism of screen space (though less as a phenomenological jolt than a techno/logical deduction)—and, in consequence, marks out his theory's rebooted application to digital cinema. The spectacle one pays for may get cashed out by these means at a different level of material cognizance. What breaks through at such optical pressure points, and with a specular violence all its own, can be understood as a sudden implosion of the semiotic square's vertical axis across the vanishing distinction between marvelous event and the wonder of its underlying technical eventuation.

Optical premises can emerge as ontological cruxes in just this way, so that media history gets reviewed on the spot. While photographic film verges forward by edging out one discrete image after another in the vertical spool of photograms, digital cinema operates motion from within, with no momentary anchor in the holistic image. Instead of 24 frames per second as the standard rate of change in filmic cinema, each aggregated rather than given frame in pixel generation has hundreds of times more separate alternations per second, even on the smallest home screen. No longer a file of images, the new screen plane is generated from a computer file instead, a spray of "picture elements" both variable and distributive. And only rarely disturbed into visibility as such. In the implicit spirit of Metz's thematizations, where something structurally true about cinema, and ordinarily falsified, is avowed under special circumstances— dreamlike flow, unseen bodies, to give two of his leading examples—one notes a comparable touchstone in digital violence: sheer remorseless mutation, the image expunged and rejuvenated indistinguishably, neither wholly present nor entirely pending, always unmade and recomposited at once. Hence the semiotics of double negation. In this respect, sci-fi bodies (often di-visible men, and women, rather than wholly invisible ones) are the common scapegoats to their own optic possibility—where the science of the image becomes part of the fiction. Not just montage, but screening per se, has more openly claimed at such points the status of *trucage*: the image itself as *digitage*.

This, then, begins to explain the self-inflicted nature of recent screen violence, whereby mimesis is sabotaged by its own disruptive enhancements. Here, in such reflex moments, is how some particular (and digitally particulate) act of mayhem or decimation gets exhibited strictly at the level of computational interface: a default glimpse of electronic generation insufficiently screened *out* by narrative. Or, again: montage laid bare as digital mirage. And this without, as yet in screen rhetoric, any compensatory "discursive" turn by which a specifically computerized effect (like pixel degradation, or an equivalent of the old-fashioned "wipe" in some rapid linear rescan or unraveled interlacing) is released from diegesis to a new idiom of punctuation. CGI is mostly trapped by thematics even in its breakout (or breakdown) moments of material reduction. Digital cinema seems in this sense still a fledgling structure of mediation, aping the presentational rather than full narrational powers of its filmic predecessor in the very midst of its extravagant upgrades—and their extreme optical dismantlings.

In regard to the latter, one result is clear. Moments of technopoetics at this pitch of apprehension have a hard time getting fully regimented or integrated by plot, sci-fi or otherwise. That screen narratives so seldom know quite what do with this violation of their own diegesis in these *show-off* moments—unless, like Besson's *Lucy*, abandoning themselves entirely to them—is perhaps to be expected. And if this is where high-tech narrative cinema is tending, it's no surprise that the retro lap dissolves summoned to evict the spaceships in *Arrival*—those hovering apparitions already abstracted into objects of pure temporal mediation—would, in a

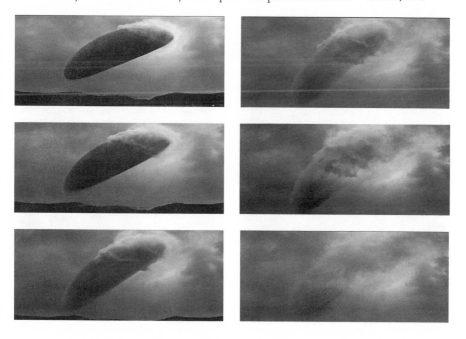

futurist inversion, enlist the digital in evoking a former *trucage* of retinal erasure in the effacements of classical cross-fade by superimposition.

If one were to say of this sequence that it offers a case of elision made legible, a "punctuation" by narrative episode itself, then this would only be to stress, yet again, how we are indeed prompted by certain plot turns of screen fiction into a concerted medial reading—as only further prompted, here, by the narrative's *prefiguring* of these particular space machines as all medium (in their material purpose) to begin with. Slowed to the point of unmistakability in deliquescence, the spatiotemporal discontinuity of the medium in Epstein—here mapped onto the analeptic leaps of time travel in sci-fi imaging, and understood through Metz's historicized apparatus theory of transitional syntax versus spectral epistemology—has parsed before our eyes, in this plot of heroized "translation," a deep grammar of the cinemachine. But noticed—it might still be useful to ask—in just what spirit? With what affective force is the apparatus itself thus read? The question may well have seemed biding its time for a fuller, or at least more direct, response.

PostScript
SPECIAL AFFX

A‍LL POSTSCRIPTS ARE PROVISIONAL, OF COURSE, ESPECIALLY WHEN APPENDED TO AN ESSAY like this concerned with the rapid mutation of a medium and its metaplots: one preoccupied, at that, with effects manifested post-script—at some generative level of the so-called production stage. So not just provisional in this case, then, but inconclusive in the other sense, defying closure from within its own evidence—like the inevitably premature "review" in the last chapter when reconnoitering the latest state of digital play in ongoing Hollywood spectacles. Here, too, in this afterword, an intended look·back must be framed by the shape and pressure of continuing screen production. In view—a constantly refocused view—of this, concerning the granular texture of cinemachination, is it even feasible to generalize at this point? What exactly is the fascination sprung from the details of "screening," in link with plot, that this essay has fastened on?

Given the retinal sensitivity, or more like susceptibility, of a certain kind of keyed-in (or at least keyed-up) film viewing—habitual on my part, from an early age—the tendency is worth dwelling on long enough to spell out. The reaction implied in much of the foregoing discussion isn't cinephilia as normally understood—and indeed it sometimes feels like the opposite: a disposition mesmerized by film moments far wide of an aficionado's checklist either of auteurs, favored titles, fleeting charms, or sustained aesthetic force. Put simply, it is, rather, a kind of screen looking hypertuned to the machining of the image per se, the generation of its particular grain or nap. One might call it a visual "touchiness" if that wouldn't send us back to the figurative haptics of current body theory.

Whatever else it may induce or contribute to, such an eye for the pressure of substrate certainly makes it easy to recover historically the allure, the speculative provocation, even the philosophical fallout of early film viewing in regard to the technical miracle of human movement both released from any living body and rethinking the very idea of embodiment in the on-screen flutter of feature, gesture, or act. And this would encourage one to imagine, further, what it would have been like to oversee the gradual if fairly rapid progress of flicker fusion—that steadily refined artifice of mechanical continuity in the projector's tooling of frame rates (via masked frame lines)—on cinema's way toward, and way beyond, sound film.

Hence, for this one postwar movie viewer, a clear motive for taking stock (after the obsolescence of "film stock" itself) of that ocular asymptote of maximal resolution in Ang Lee's experiment for *Billy Lynn*—as well as of those quite different "expressions" of the pixel in the unchecked proliferation of VFX just considered, whose estranging charge may momentarily seem to short-circuit the digital medium itself, precisely by laying it bare via the pixel epiphenomena of its algorithmic code. Registered in the long view of cinematic archaeology, yet another perturbation of the cine-machine has, in these hypertrophic effects, accessed through apparition the praxis of the apparatus itself. In this light, for any such postscript, there is more script than ever before—and this at the coded basis of the algorithmic image itself.

It should, therefore, scarcely discredit this essay's abiding emphasis to acknowledge, if it has not been amply obvious already, that its author is a bit hypersensitive in regard to "effects"—and their strictly technical affect. Not uniquely so, he's gathered from conversations with film buffs, students, and scholars over the years, but noticeably so. This essentially unschooled alertness to image grain and the receding planes of illusionism—or say (not to put too fine a point upon it) this instinctive technological fetishism—has in my case a long-arc biographical (more than physiological) explanation. As a dawning teenager looking for distraction and, most of all, immersion, I was both intrigued and aggravated by the ghostly outlines around the blue-screened Charlton Heston in *The Ten Commandments* (Cecil B. Demille, 1956) or *Ben-Hur* (William Wyler, 1959), resulting in that strange scissored-in effect that beset some of these films' most spectacular moments. I wasn't unequivocally charmed, either, even if baited, by the cheapjack sets, slapdash matte paintings, and hokey superimpositions in all those B-grade matinee sci-fi flicks I was nonetheless addicted to. Nor, in another version of that allergy to the optical cutout, was I wholly taken with those paper-thin actors and objects spaced out in supposedly three dimensional recess, like cardboard duplicates of themselves, in the crude early stages of 3-D. Its cluttered depth of field more like a storm of vitreous floaters at times, the speeding immediacy of flung tomahawks or the debris from buffalo stampedes—let alone, from the genre of choice, flailing robot arms in *Gog* or bubbling underwater turmoil in *The Creature from the Black Lagoon*—failed to reach out to me with any conviction. But I watched with an antsy fascination all the same. Relief arrived, and revelation, only from quite opposite directions in the early, then late, 1960s, with the ultrarealism of 70 mm location shooting in *Lawrence of Arabia* (David Lean, 1962) and the apotheosis of *trucage* in *2001: A Space Odyssey* (Stanley Kubrick, 1968). But that only boosted my hypersensitivity, from there out, to print quality, image resolution, aspect ratios, screen curvatures, sound fidelity, the works. And their narrative workings.

So that something like "overreaction" is admittedly one name for what results. Which is not to say "overreading," as things settle out. Primed by such tensed viewing, any considered effect of intuited visual purpose will, so to speak, discover its own intention. If from his earliest days at the movies, this viewer was always made—what's the word?—as "nervous" by rear projection as by the unpersuasive outward juts and thrusts of primitive 3-D, his attention, and hardly his alone, was thus cued not just for optical flaws but for reflective opportunities. Decades later, when movie watching is rarely filmgoing any longer, this same effects-attuned viewer, what with his history of self-inflicted discriminations in such matters, was all the more flabbergasted to discover, and only from the DVD supplement after originally seeing the movie in its theatrical run, that the moderne mansion, presumably on the German coast (doubling for the beach at Martha's Vineyard) in expatriate Roman Polanski's *The Ghost Writer* (2010), was in fact a studio set—and that its wildly "atmospheric" plate glass–windowed views of dramatically variable weather outside the chic enclave of intrigue were only green-screened, floor-to-ceiling, digital movies-within-the-movie. Braced (by gestural fake) against this "imperceptible" *trucage*, the crucified British prime minister has, so to speak, no material ground to lean on.

Invisible there, in simulation of its own depicted vitreous plane of visibility, is the same pixel scrim that breaks through to immediate notice in a dead link, like this, to a trailer for the film.

The defective web image reveals pixels exactly where we're not surprised to find them: on the fractured underside of the image they've ruined rather than realized. But with the twofold "transparency" of that actual diegetic window in Polanski's set, who could tell without being told? Who could *see*?

With other films usually, I do, like many of us, *observe* the trick, but with no sense that I'm in on anything but the film's own deliberate narrative game. For the most part, such a passively awed sense of "deception" is part of the "affect"—the cultivated amazement, a wonder sometimes turned further curious—quite deliberately instilled by movies that are themselves hypersensitized to their own production values, or say hypermedial in illusionist texture. These include films saturated in their own generative and projective technology in a tradition—span it with whatever examples of your own you might prefer—that runs from Buster Keaton's *comedial* transfusions of farce and filmic reflex to the somatic mirage, say, of Michael Keaton's engineless human flight in *Batman* or *Birdman*, from Chaplin's Tramp in industrial extremis beneath the factory floor to the pixel remixes of the *Transformers* series, from *Hellzapoppin!* to Devil's Tower in wait for the extraterrestrial advent of Spielberg's *Close Encounters of the Third Kind*.

This short volume's modest brief for a rethinking—retooling—of screen theory involves little more, I repeat, though nothing less, than putting the tool back in the image manufacture, the engine back in the illusory power it generates. This involves once again, despite its "theory" being generally overthrown, returning a sense of the *apparatus* to our receipt of the apparition. Effect in reversion to cause within the enacted (re)coils of discovered machination: that's the reflex action at stake in the whole foregoing anthology of film exhibits, as crystalized most explicitly in that extended "Festival" of digitized magic. And then there's the historical sense of return orientation as well: carrying us back from the present hypertrophic elaborations of digital cinema to the productive wonder of its founding technology in that suggestive spectrum of early German response that was already rounded out in the prewar decade before Epstein published *L'Intelligence d'une machine*.

So where (as well as what) do we get from looking back in this way? Not: where does this leave us—since things are still in technical and industrial flux from month to month. But where might all this help direct our continued looking, and not just at new movies, but at the history of the medium (the screen *media*) as such—and at the visual affect certain ingenuities may elicit? An archaeology of the cinematic "trick" certainly encourages a technological impulse in screen interpretation: again, in narrative cinema, an apparatus reading. But what about those other reflexes located in the organic system of our own nerved viewing, whether at a desk, on a sofa, or on the edge of a theater seat? Let me be unguardedly clear, since my quite narrow and modest polemic—against, say, personification rather than machination—will not suffer from it. Everything I've written about here has *affected* me strongly at the time, however ephemeral the response, however trivial or easily foreseen its narrative consequences—or, of course, however downright annoying, on the one hand, or, on the other, engrossing. Like others on the instinctive if not deliberate watch for such things, I react in particular to the *medial irritants* in that whole panoply of screen warpings and ruptures just surveyed. They come across like grit in the works, a troubling of the machine's normal scenic transparency. In the midst of whatever narrated commotion, involving whatever disintegrations of the viewing field, I am moved—in the most neu(t)ral and nonevaluative sense—by what criticism used to call the sudden "demystification" of the image plane. At such moments, one might say that cinema communicates to me the shock of its own recognition. To put it all but absurdly, this is "what's so special" about these moments: a specification of their own mediality. This is what breaks one immersive spell, at the narrative level, to tap, to plumb—and more deeply than otherwise—another: our perdurable thrall to the cinematic apparatus in whatever machine form it takes. This is a subjection not necessarily ideological, but certainly in some way "affective," even when falling far short of what one might term emotional investment in a given screen projection.

Indeed, it is exactly the value I place on a retinal response to such roughened illusionism in the exposed resistances of a narrative's carrying medium—albeit operating in frequent self-celebration lately of its own constituent computer graphics—that makes me resist alternative mystifications in theoretical parlance. Yes, my body is all there in response when faced with these and many other screen moments—held to attention, whether "thrilled" or not in the colloquial sense, by their probed conditions: the autoexposé of technique from within such spec(tac)ular deployment. I see the effect; I feel the medium working overtime to supply it, feel it in a physiological twinge of recognition, a tremulousness of ocular as well as aural response. Attention resonates, almost viscerally, to this generative impetus. But the body of such response has only a partial interpretive grip—the appeal to somatics a limited explanatory leverage—on the physical processes that move it, the factors that unsettle or block its normal circuits of audiovisual intake and phenomenological credence. The limit of this bodily claim on explanation should not be hard to recognize—in light of a competing technological paradigm and its originating instrumental base. That alternative perspective is, of course, industrial before psychosomatic. It is this framework, machinic before bodily, within which one is meant to notice the cinematic kinesis upping the ante on its own constitutive trick.

In respect to such salient flashpoints in screen narrative, it is fair to guess that the affective response to certain hypertrophic bursts of VFX technology that this one viewer readily admits to is, if not fairly widespread, at least easy to envisage when described. But this essay has had something else in mind, deferred to the film's own "mind" (or "intelligence")—terms equally suspect as those attributing "body" or "flesh" to the screen image, of course, but backed in Epstein by an emphasis on the technical functions and material substrate of the medium's own figurative cerebrations. Willingly, to vary Epstein, I'm inclined to let the machine intellectualize my instincts for me in the coils of its own representations. I'm interested in how I've been *made* to cogitate this or that aberration, some marked deviance from the norm within its own maximal exertions, some warp in the given, some extrusion of the pixel from the electronic mix, some unsparing excess of device in the very baring of it. Say, again, some intended retinal tension. And eager to let the screen context guide that inquiry. Most of all, I'm interested in what to call such a salience or glitch, such an uprush of constructedness: how to describe its overt technical inscription across the screen plane. And curious, too, about the ways its framing narrative might help assimilate it—narratographically—to one kind of rhetorical function or another, whether as local irony, metafictional pressure point, explosive limit case, or all of the above.

In short, I have absolutely no reason to deny that, like much else that happens between the screen and me, those audiovisual frissons in question—those technical frictions between image and its imageering— engage at many levels my bodily sensorium. But that's because of what used to happen between film (photogram) and screen (shimmer), and now between algorithm and pixelated frame. Affect is undeniable. But the prompt also bears scrutiny. Apart from any necessary beauty or even true ingenuity, these effects we've been looking at do take hold in reception. And when I say they get to me, I mean that they reach out, break straight through the illusion—and thereby break it back to the imagined technics of its activation. Any such recognized rupture must, of course, begin in sensation, emerge as affect, trigger some neurological attunement or dis- cord, *make itself felt*. Motion pictures move us at a sensory level, even in the most salient disintegrations of their own mobile plane. Though I trust clearer by now as bearing more theoretical weight than it could previously support, my only objection in acknowledging such special affect, as re- corded at the outset, is the tendency to transfer its corporeal excitement in the engaged body of the spectator onto some general metaphorics of the integrated screen body—apart from the individuated bodies so often dis- integrated lately on that screen. That's the main reason for taking Epstein's late book, in the paradoxical provocation of its pre-computer-age title, as a point of departure. Taken up in this sense, *L'Intelligence d'une machine* is Epstein's gauntlet thrown down to the merely ocular or perceptual in the medium's philosophical rethinking *as conceptual*—including, in the orbit of such philosophy, film's "scientific" figurations of the body in time-space rather than some loose figure of the screen as sensuous, consensual body.

Affect is real, but only in the same sense that the projected mirage isn't. In play here is the difference between the neuromuscular and the kaleidoscopic, the variable biological pulse over against the ingrained differential clockwork of a pulsional sequence or code. If we authorize the inner workings of screen art to "intellectualize" for us their own technical status in our otherwise rapt captivation by the resulting motor artifice, that gain in attention, as well as beguilement, is a value in itself. And if we leave open, to at least that extent, a further warrant for narrative interpretation, more theoretical space is thereby cleared. For this is the beginning of what it would mean in response—across media-historical time from the *cinématographe* to computer ware, from the filing-past of transparencies to the binary image file—to think *with* modernity's mutating cinemachines regarding nothing less than *l'affect d'une médium*. And thus to think through (both senses) the effects *special to those machines* from one technology to the next.

In this process of thinking *through*, a cross-disciplinary analogue is worth calling up. In textual encounter, one reads with one's body, even silently: both with retinal and cortical synapses and with the suppressed musculature of lungs, larynx, and tongue. But that's the reactive component of text production, which begins, apart from any reading act, in the alphabetic constitution of a morphophonemic script (the very fusion for Western language that the alien grammar of *Arrival* unravels). By analogy with my longstanding approach to literary writing, from the phonetic ground up, the apparatus readings of this essay are not formalist, but formative. They are keyed to what we saw Deleuze wanting to acknowledge, if rarely pursue, as the "genetic" stratum of the moving image: photogrammic long before film stock was replaced, as storage mechanism, by the housing wares of computerization. Such rudiments of the moving image, unlike the variable speeds of literary decoding, are of course first "interpreted" (in Peirce's sense) machinically, rather than optically, in their passage from increment to actual motion picture. Even when only contingently glimpsed in elusive moments on screen, still these constituents of mediality—thus effectuated before our eyes—do hold their special affect for the close looker. Only rarely, of course, does this affect, in narrative terms, rise to anything we might want to call *aesthetic* force—and thus reward close reading in some strong sense. But it can often help make a start at this. Being thus affected remains, at the very least, a test of *aesthesis*, of sense experience, in any attempt to *make sense* of our cinemachines in the fictions they still, if no longer literally, spin.

So it is, in these pages on "media and method," that the singular of the second noun has always been meant to suggest by association the rooted nature of its analytic object in a given case (in one particular *medium* or another), and at two levels: production and response alike, generativity and engagement. A medium, one versus another, is a method of communication, to be sure, and the means of reading its message can only be given by it. The method exemplified, from film to film in these pages, is simply (or not so simply) to ask *how we know what we think we see* in the apparitions of our cinemachines, regardless of whether that actionable "intelligence" is conveyed by engram or algorithm, fps (frames per second) or now ppi (pixels per inch) as well. For, recalling Panofsky via Cavell, and ratcheting the former's transfigured a prioris back from screen to machine, it is there, respectively, where we find the underlying "spatialization of time" and the "dynamization of space" that make movies move—from second to second, inch to inch, one array to the next.

Only this racing baseline—or, alternately, this compressed pixel grid—can serve to realize all other "possibilities of the new medium." Indeed once "new" for Panofsky, now history for us. Old and obsolete as film(s), nonetheless the products of narrative cinema under digitization are always learning fresh tricks from New Media. And what these technical gestures inflect, on the traditional narrative screen, they also confirm about the medium as one long trick. In attending to the move (within pictured motion) from mediating to materialized form—from strip to on-screen image track, from coded pixel to conjured visual field—our being in on the trick is one way of getting into the narrative at some formative level beneath plot. Yes, certainly, we have lost the original sense, for Epstein as well as for the early German press, in which the *cinematograph* offered a single name for the instrument and the event of display, for both engine and mirage.[1] But we can still respond to screened narrative in its optical constitution, in light of manifestations filmic and electronic alike: alike as medial substrates, that is, precisely because not identical as such—and differentiated at times, on the suddenly denaturalized screen, in the very grain of their own separate differential systems.

So a final example, focused as it is on little more than the sheer affect of human visualization by optical illusion. What evidentiary photographs meant to the overall futurist *trucage* of the original *Blade Runner* (Ridley Scott, 1982), a movie "photographed" and delivered on traditional 35 mm film stock, is only vestigially recalled in *Blade Runner 2049* via the forensic photos, hoarded by the hero, associated with the dead tree, buried bones, and woman-with-child of the mystery plot. Yet, by an almost loony *trucage*, one not just illogical but irrelevant to plot, these photos are briefly glimpsed at one point with a mobile time stamp racing ahead like a tiny digital clock at their lower right border—as if all photographic matter, however fixed, were essentially usurped by binary rhythms in the new electronic epoch.[2] A quite different transmedial counterpoint, however, dominates the new film. This time, the relation of replicant bodies to duped images is routed through the holistic mirage, and human hollowness, of the laser hologram. When the holographic female construct named (though seldom called) Joi is detached from the domestic fixture of her projection in the replicant hero's apartment and rendered remotely accessible by a portable "emanator," viewers may sense more anxieties looming—

or ironies pending, about the ontology of the imaged body—than just those worries of the heroine about damage to her new mobile unit. In Besson's *Lucy*, when the heroine disappears in body to become, in flash-drive storage, the ubiquitous availability of her global digital conscious-ness, there is a tacit link with worldwide distribution for the eponymous film itself. One might be inclined to take this comparable aspect of female upload in *Blade Runner 2049* as another form of such exhibition allegory, especially given the multiple formats of the movie's theatrical release. In yet another instance of encoded media rivalry, it would, in this vein, be easy to see the vulnerable portability and uneven shaky reception of the "emanated" rather than projected body—sometimes jammed by uneven buffering and staccato breakups or frozen by other incoming transmits—as offering a sideward and askance industry glance at the competitive new platforms for remote streaming rather than brick-and-mortar screening. Easy to see, to suspect, to interpret. But something else, more intrinsic yet to the history of cinematic technology, is there more literally—and almost unavoidably—to be *seen*. This comes clear in a prolonged episode of precarious retinal mirage centered (or decentered) on that optically generated female form in its status as machinic emanation. To this *trucage* of contrapuntal erotic manifestation, in its full technological as well as narrative context, there is no possible "overreaction," let alone overreading.

Medium in Emanation

It seems fair to say that any one viewer's special susceptibility to *trucage*, by no means mine alone, would tend to become everyone's in the relentless optic dazzle of *Blade Runner 2049*. From the electronic static of its logo-glitched credit sequence forward, the digital vampings and tamperings and transformations of this sci-fi spectacle are so little like bland electronic wallpaper, so labored and lingered over, that they command attention—and not just as preternatural décor, not just eye-popping facets of set design, but as the very sites of dynamic optical action. Enough has been said by now, concerning the throwback (and thereby recapitulative) trope of "dissolve" in the 2016 film *Arrival*, to prepare for the more hypertrophic array of translucencies and superimpositions in the director's subsequent digital spectacular. Given the way Villeneuve used special effects to nego-tiate the theme of temporal *mediation* in that preceding time-loop plot, it was no doubt to be expected that his vastly bigger budget for *Blade Runner 2049* would allow similar—even enhanced—reflections on the medium

in its manifestations by digital *trucage*. And indeed that particular effect
of superimposition deployed in *Arrival* comes, not entirely to the fore, but
into recessional 3-D prominence, in the film's abiding preoccupation with
incorporeal holography in one seemingly extraneous scene after another,
all of them marked diversions from (or, one comes to suspect, ultimate tri-
angulations with) the central issue of human replication in somatic form.

Further, this aggregate motif of holography bears a unique and curious
relation to a divided machinic format—almost a built-in technological
dialectic—in the distribution of the film, exhibited as it was not just in
standard projection but alternately in digital 3-D and IMAX 2D (where
available). Whatever business decisions went into holding the IMAX
release to 2-D, questions are certainly raised from within that platform's
hyperclarity about a film whose plot is heavily invested in 3-D illusionism via the shifting erotic and emotive lures of the hologram. For what
may seem a mere CGI sidebar to the problem of replicant bodies turns
out to map quite literally onto such bodies in a further (meta)physical
disjuncture—in that one central and eccentric scene on which these closing medial intuitions will soon bear down. Moreover, if the dissolves by
clouded superimposition at the end of *Arrival* bear a media-archaeological
relation to the quintessential *trucage* of cinema in its transition from spectacle (and its spectral tricks) to narrative syntax, from hovering phantoms
to mere fade-outs, the more complex recessional surfaces of holography in
Blade Runner 2049 take us back across a related genealogy of special effects
in regard to the conflated planes of stereoscopic process

It is a testament to the almost distracting, and certainly not dramatically essential, prominence of the hologram motif that it nonetheless stands
out so markedly from the film's ready participation in the general run of
digital knowingness that punctuates the dialogue and CGI inferences of
so many recent sci-fi extravaganzas. Villeneuve's film certainly indulges in
the usual throwaway effects, along with tossed-off visual puns, that one
has come to associate with pixel self-consciousness on the big-budget
screen—ever since *Iron Man*'s "Not bad for ones and zeroes." Here the
killing machine named "Luv" orders drone attacks, via a souped-up version of Google Glass telemetry (5.0 or beyond) that is voice activated
in its lethal digital precision—even while her own extended digits are
having their nails polished in iridescent mobile patterns by a crouch-
ing mutant, attending to this further aspect of her cosmetized replicant
body. Visual metaphors accompany more explicit dialogue ironies as well.
Earlier, when the female chief at LAPD insists on killing all trace of the
replicant Miracle—the baby "born and not made" in the film's percolat-

ing salvationist allegory—this is because any self-replication of the en-slaved simulacra would be the ultimate ontological as well as Malthusian threat. In delivering her blunter figurative explanation, and in the script's own blatant allusion to President Trump's summoned fears of an "alien" workforce, the medium shot of her emphatic declaration that "there *must* be a wall"—otherwise "total chaos"—is filmed through a barrier of its own: a rain-drenched window shaped like a wide-angle film screen under conditions of semiocclusion. This visual emblem offers an early matrix for the obsessive layering of translucent or semireflective planes in scene after scene, all the way through to Luv's underwater POV shot of the hero strangling and drowning her.

All of these rippled surfaces and scrims and diaphanes, these plastic sheetings and glass isolation chambers—including their curved holo-graphic versions in laser-molded anthropomorphic sheathing, filmy and flimsy at once—keep uppermost in mind the *sheer* visibility of sci-fi effects and their own panoply of replicated sensory phenomena. But they do so while self-consciously cordoning off these effects on the other, the far, side of the screen's own "walled"-off fictional barrier between us and the unreal. None of this emphasized optic mediation, this regress of visibility, is necessitated by plot, just by a series of technological in-jokes operating in league with visual design. The results are decidedly cinematographic rather than dramatic in impact—at least until their unstinting overkill serves to rescind that very distinction under the force of apparatus reading. Another way to grasp this tantalizing amalgam of retinal distractions is to recognize in them the charged interplay (as distinguished in chapter 6) between "recessions of the optique" and "assertions in technique": conjoint reflex actions of the cinemachine as a device of projected framed surfaces as well as generated mobile images. Here, then, in Villeneuve's motivated graphic motif, visual planarity is at a studied premium in the very force of its electronic distortions.

The most sustained pressure point for all this is unmistakably the preponderance of holography among the markers of technofuturity. We see it first in the commercial signage of downtown LA, including the translucent pirouettes of skyscraper-tall ballerinas: a new computerized leap from cinematography to what one might call choreogrammetry. As the very definition of the moving body on screen, the poet Vachel Lind-say's early notion of "sculpture in motion" reaches here its apotheosis and parody at once, as do the predictions of those contemporaneous German writers who foresaw the cinematagraph's destiny in 3-D: a telos now taken off-screen for installation in lived space.[3] In the opening shots of the urban lightscape, there is even a hologram GIF of the SONY logo (the film's own production company) being not just projected but actually *branded*, slammed again and again, weightlessly, onto the upper floors of an office tower: a case of product placement encasing in turn the whole produced fictive spectacle. Holography later generates the immersive environments out of which the quarantined "memory artist" constructs her psychic implants for replicant consciousness. And even in the film's climactic reunion scene, she delays the long-postponed moment, back-turned to her paternal visitor, in order to appreciate—in this heady sedimenting of *trucage*—the beauty of her *holographic* simulation of the snow falling by *digital* simulation (via particle system, no doubt) both there around her and over the dying hero outside.

To ask what the network of holographic special effects is meant to specify in *Blade Runner 2049* is to enter upon a telling crux in the very history of *trucage*. Harking back through the mind-over-matter holograms of *Forbidden Planet* to the freestanding 3-D broadcasts of *Things to Come* (1956, 1936), the deployment here of such conjurations and their rendered ima-geering is hard to detach, as we'll see, from comparisons between 3-D and 2-D versions of the film's own projection. Granting that holography might indeed seem a bypath and detour in the replicant plot, there is another loaded but throwaway line of dialogue, and accompanying special effect, that may actually help tether its outcroppings more tightly to the main narrative line—as well as to the undertext of VFX technique. When the power-mad blind visionary, oddly named Niander Wallace (the mandatory "wall us" off again in the name of this posthuman rather than primeval Neander?), wants to inspect the newest of his replicant mutations, about to be dropped full-grown in its newborn mucous from the huge plastic version of an amniotic sack, he says "Let's have a look": *have* one produced for him in his sightlessness, that is, rather than *taken* by him. It is only digital pictures that are in fact taken—for simultaneous transmission. This happens when a set of flying fish-like reconnaissance pods (fish-eye lenses?) emerge from behind the rippling waters of Wallace's artificial is-land chamber (amniotic in itself?) to effect his prostheticized gaze—and this only after a miniature external drive is jacked into his skull by the dutiful Luv. Can it be irrelevant that these airborne cortical relay devices for the blind cyborg mastermind circle their object like the multiple camera positions of exactly that "photogrammetry" whose digital technicians are so extensively credited in the end titles? And that they thereby transmit to the sightless villain—in short-circuited retinal registration—the kind of implied multipoint holographic assemblage elsewhere produced, explicitly as such, from the overhead projection armature in K's apartment, generating his partner Joi, in a domestic affordance trademarked indeed by the Wallace Corporation? How, in other words, can apparatus reading ignore the fact that Wallace—precisely in overcoming his visual debility—is plugged directly into the film's own optical challenge: namely, to visualize for spectators, from any and every angle, a rounded human form through the magic of microchip input?

Which brings us back to Joi *de nonvivre*, the commercial optic bride who encourages K to certify his belief in being a birthling by accepting the matching "real" name "Joe." With her body interleaved into scene after scene as if by a kind of internal superimposition, she is always on call. Whenever the control button conjures or adjourns this wifely hologram, she has emerged—has manifested, and eventually emanated at remote ranges—as the film's only heroine. It seems fair to say that rarely can cinema's own apparatus of projection, and the reading it invites, have been any more closely imbricated with the on-screen apparition of a special effect. Traditionally, sci-fi holography offers perhaps the most *visible* of "tricks" in Metz's sense: an optical illusion both within plot, as mirage, and on screen as *trucage*—and the one nearest to its taxemic (or syntactic) alter ego as mere scene change in the lap dissolve. As a 3-D superimposition, one might say, the hero's cohabiting hologram in *Blade Runner 2049* often appears like a kind of stalled fade-out, sustained in her ghostly presence only by the least glimmer of pixelated light and hue—a specter often coming in and out of "presence" when touched, as if her illusion must be credited anew, in its impalpable form, before regaining illusory body. Seldom, though, is she free from some hint of transparency around the edges, confirming her status as phantom superimposition overlain upon the recorded mise-en-scène. This fact eventually becomes inescapable when the hologram is further superimposed upon a "real" female body in an unstable interpenetration of somatic space and localized desire.

In an effect, the director reports, that took a full year's tweaking by the VFX technicians, this happens when Joi has "selflessly" hired a prostitute, a "real girl," to offer Joe a fuller bodily pleasure than "she" is able to provide. Embracing him simultaneously, the two female figures (more like figures of desire than real characters) shuffle into and out of each other's image. Here is a new wrinkle—and optic enfolding—in the history of the cinematographic close-up, achieved neither by old-fashioned superimposition (as in the throwback evocations of *Arrival*) nor by familiar CGI morphing, but by reversibly interlaced planes of computerized imageering. And achieving, in turn, a further medial suggestion. Laminated by optical and conceptual buildup according to the logic of futurist computer holography, the scene burrows at the same time into the more explicitly filmic rudiments of stereography. This eerie sequence certainly *comes across* in the crystalline IMAX format (2-D in that case) as well as in its wide-release 3-D iterations—in each mode optically unnerving and emotionally persuasive, with the female eyes of desire sometimes almost indistinguishable in their slight disjunction, one pair shifting above or below the other, or slipping sideways, four caressing hands in marginal mismatch as well. In the 3-D version, however, given the many optical reverberations elsewhere for this prolonged *trucage*—in which holographic figures are thrown into relief as if they were the mere luminous shells of other 3-D figures on the surrounding screen—the space between emanator-beamed female form and bodied woman is, in what we might call its platform context, more dramatically negotiated and imploded.[4]

There is, of course, no mistaking the point, the ontological disjunction, in the IMAX projection either. In exiting this scene of sexual and "cross-species" *menage* as an overlapping optic collage—operating like a dilatory, pulsing, and reversible match cut (to evoke once again a Metzian transfer from visible marvel to visual grammar)—the sex worker takes her leave by saying contemptuously to her holographic double, in a line that might have been K's in previous carnal frustration: "I've been inside you, and there's less there than you think." That "less," that internal vacuum beneath the epidermal figment of the laser simulacrum, is precisely what the rounded effects of her manifestations have all along, by contrast, served to evoke. But this futurism of autonomous holography is in fact media-archaeological, I want to suggest, as well as predictive. The extravagance of such a scene drags on long enough to dredge this up. Given the financial disappointment of this intended blockbuster, despite the all but universal enthusiasm of the reviews, it may well be the weird literal *introspection*, the inward-looking, of such a distended visual trope that most obviously flags the film's departure from a sci-fi action hit. But how does the departure evoke a kind of filmic reversion as well—a tacit return from the morphs of digital seamlessness to the celluloid difference of bifocal mismatch?

What, that is, does this labored special effect picture in itself that would call up media history as much as future technoptics? Premised on the near look-alike features of the two wide-eyed "women," the layered braiding of their faces may seem for a moment to suggest, if only by association, a case of 3-D gone awry, quite flagrantly botched—as if a crisis in the apparatus itself were meant to signal, and in more than one sense *deepen*, an ongoing crux of optical illusionism. The slight misalignment, that is, of the women's eyeline gazes makes their "looks" just fractionally displaced from each other in an elusive superimposition that has, in medial terms, something else than the hero in view. This perverse ocular overlap—this visual split and splint at once—has a way of recalling, in a kind of surreal default, especially in its more frequent vertical misfits, the lateral disjuncture of binocular technology in the actual operation of 3-D projection: exactly that specular gap (at the join of overlap) more obvious in the sometimes blurred deployment of its primitive versions for the 3-D sci-fi of the 1950s. In any such machining of depth perception, one image needs to be overlain by its near double to activate the stereoscopic recession that laser holography lays more convincing claim to in the round.

To be sure, this visually seductive scene of oscillating erotic objects *works* either way, as a questioning of human/oid self-presence—whether in the "image maximation" of IMAX or in the marked recessions of digital 3-D. But as distinct manifestations of the postfilmic cinemachine in its variable display options, the movie's alternate modes of exhibition may differently *expose the works*.[5] This is because the triangle at stake here is scopic as much as carnal: the very cone of vision being its off-kilter focal point in the lured POV of the male gaze. The cinemachine is worked overtime as narratographic implement in visualizing this spooky erotic stereogram. So that what results, from the throes of its latest incandescent trickery, is a case of the apparatus reading its own prehistory.[6]

In whichever *viewing* mode—via IMAX or the unique reverberations, in this instance, of digital 3-D—there is, however, only one likely *understanding*. This heavily invested but narratively expendable tour de force of CGI superimposition is certainly more pivotal, thematically, for its optic byplay than for its sexual foreplay. Despite the superficially digressive aspects of holographic presence in the film's main plot of messianic replicant birth, the ontological conundrum of the narrative, with its traumas of the "unreal," responds to medial reading on just this score of a spatial illusionism. Holography isn't some kind of false lead or laser sideshow, a mere high-tech adjunct, in the problematics of simulation. Rather, its effects are slotted into a broader problematic of surrogate being and "artificial intelligence" that includes the replicants and their implanted memories. The *transparent* tricks of holography thus mark one stage in a categorical distinction—and at times optic sedimentation—developed on a sliding scale of materialized *trucage* ranging from indiscernible replicants (the artificial self as its own body double) to the virtuality of the screen image tout court, where all presence, rather than just presence-of-mind, is a matter of similitude by visual duplication. Under these conditions of apparition, the "venom" that the filmic "irreal" could, in Epstein's view, easily unleash into our off-screen epistemology—the sense of the world as no more continuous an image of itself than was (in his day) the photogram-based motor illusion of screen action—is held in check here only by the "wall" of science *fiction* and its policed genre borders. Or in Cavell's terms—terms never more sharply drawn than in this film's parable of holographic acknowledgment and empathy—skepticism about Other Minds is cathartically performed on screen by *a* world (not *the* world) markedly not ours.[7]

Ghosts in the Machine

A contrast from the same year, another remake, seems inescapable—at least for the broadest terms of this particular essay. As long ago clear, the foregoing reflections on media and method have been launched in an effort to distinguish, across the full arc of cinema's technological trans-formations, the machinics of the screen medium from the somatics of its affect—all the while steering clear of metonymic contaminations like "flesh" or "integument" as figures for the screen interface in its supposed role as optical membrane. Given such resistance, it seems only fitting to be pinpointing this distinction at the end with films in which the flesh on screen is itself machinic (artificially engineered) rather than organic, the manufactured anatomical shell of a human revenant.

One is always urged to vigilance with ontological (in relation to techno-logical) distinctions. In *Ghost in the Shell* (Rupert Sanders, 2017), she looks like a supercharged human woman—but she isn't. In scene after scene, extravagant action sequences reveal, by visible *trucage*, the radical fiction of her own organic embodiment. Indeed, each set-piece episode begins with her stripping naked, divesting the artifice of human incarnation, clothes and all, that her image is meant to simulate. Yes, the "live-action" remake of the anime classic *Ghost in the Shell* (Mamoru Oshii, 1995) turns such issues pointedly (if pointlessly) allegorical by having all human vestments—all organic investiture—peeled away unexplained as implied encumbrances before decisive feats of violent heroism by a CGI body-stockinged cyborg. The exposed technological anatomy—tautly garbed as if for the VFX of motion capture itself—becomes here the pivotal meeting point of narrative agency and digital (special) efficacy. In the process, what was once all animation in the Japanese original is now a crossbreed of "live action" and its inherent digital mirage.

In the case of both the heroine and her damaged male counterpart, revealed beneath human costuming is thus a plastic sheathing in the hue of human flesh—the result of a mechanical operating system, as surrogate anatomy, that is so obviously CGI in actual operation that it even allows certain of these cybernetically "enhanced" characters to traverse space, not by simulated magic athleticism, but by a mere evanescent trail of jittery pixel advance: a spectral digital swoop or dash, begun in what resembles an incipient pixel breakup in the process of graphic relocation. Equally illogical in diegetic terms, the matrix for any such extraneous digital confession arrives as early as the pretitle sequence, when the robot armature for the newly transplanted brain of our pending heroine is dipped in something like a quasi-literal fleshpot of liquid tan plastic that eventually encases her (as others of her kind) like a fragile eggshell, whose splinters, cracks, and gapes eventually take starring roles in the VFX. But no sooner is she doused in this new epidermis, this fragile cyborg encasement, than a redundant bit of CGI pizzazz is tossed in. This happens when something like the new skin's unexplained transparent outer layer is shattered—in a burst of clear "plastic" fragments (of the sort that later result from the numberless glass window panes the humanoid shell will plunge or fire through)—for a little additional shimmer of revelatory computer violence. No film discussed by Evan Calder Williams in his 2017 study *Shard Cinema*, where he theorizes, in its multiple ramifications, the slow-motion window smashing trope of action cinema over the last two decades, could better confirm his thesis than the total narrative irrelevance of this shattered matter—and its medial inferences.[8] As if we weren't soon to become fully aware of the digital *trucage* by which whole chunks of these cyborgs' fleshly envelopes are gouged out or yanked off, here at the start are showily disclosed those smaller brittle fragments that evoke, by scalar inference, their own underlying pixel figments in such glitzy bitmapped effects. After which, all the other slow-mo levitations, shatterings, and the like have been, as it were, *particularized* as the infrastructural work of CGI's unique aggregate temporalities.

Digital sleights (and showy admissions) aside, this 2017 film, with its premise of a living brain implant within a mechanical body, not only joins a narrative like *Self/less*, and before it *Seconds*, in the thematics of the appropriated and recycled corpse. It also offers a bookend to the same year's *Blade Runner 2049*. Of course, whereas the cyborgs there look completely human, but have an "artificial" brain (including implanted memories), with *Ghost in the Shell* the tables are turned. True to the Cartesian invocations of its implied mind/body dualism (recalling philosopher Gilbert Ryle's famous phrase for the mistaken unknowability of the incarnate other as "the ghost in the machine"[9]), the cyborgs have a demonstrably fake body hiding a human brain. The *Blade Runner* alternative is, in terms of apparatus reading, more "philosophical" in the long run. For in our affective response to the VFX ordeals through which any and all such "characters" are put, the total artifice of anthropomorphic form and cognition alike in *Blade Runner*—for the replicants and the holograms equally—comes to seem more directly metacinematic: a superfice of illusionism, often CGI induced or amplified, behind which no human "reality" lurks. But by which audience affect is nonetheless called forth—in something like a technologically attenuated version of Cavell's own claims for the engineered screen image as a test of (or therapy for) the skeptical withdrawal from others and the world.

In returning from enshelled human mentalities to the humanoid agencies of *Blade Runner*, and thinking back to (and with) Epstein's filmic "intelligence" and the engineered wisdom of its own artificiality, its own fundamental discontinuity, we can thus orient a further aspect of holography's use in Villeneuve's battery of effects—and solicited "artificial" affect. Under the auspices of the "irreal" in Epstein, computerized laser holography would be linked to postfilmic cinema not least in its falling prey to, which is to say exploiting stylistically, the noise and crackle and breakup that the film's opening and closing titles carry to a new pitch of "channel-clearing" declaration. But the "wedding" of hologram and replicant, Joi and Joe K, is no mere shotgun marriage arranged by the VFX technicians to ceremonialize the industry's machine wizardry. It is more deeply "authorized." In Villeneuve's treatment, holography works overtime to concentrate, by indirection, the very possibility of its own manifestation in digital cinema. And, in the process, it makes the underlying discontinuity of imaged bodies in screen space a spluttering visible feature of the occupied world.

And never more confessedly, in terms of the digital substrate, than when the remotely "emanated" Joi, after a crash landing with the hero, is fritzed out—disappeared and spasmodically rebooted several times over: effacing glitches in rapid interplay with fleeting re-"incarnations." This is effected not, as before, in a more or less gauzy superimposition or fade. Seen here in semitransparency against the splattered rather than shattered glass behind and framing her, her unstable circuits result from a more explicit electronic crash and repair (dispersal followed by an openly gridded pixel fix) than in any other recent *trucage* I can recall.

It is through just these "assertions in technique" (Cavell once more) that a machinic apprehension of such *trucage*, such *digitage*, coincides with a narratography—or call it in this case an ontography—of replicant desire and the soul-sought life. *Blade Runner 2049* turns in this way on a kind of chiastic hinge, differently weighted in IMAX versus 3-D versions but manifest either way. Holography personified (the heroine in mere 3-D projection) over against a simulacral corporeality striving to debunk its own condition as such (the hero as would-be autonomous, rather than "automatonic," agent)—these are nodes of narrative motivation that interpret, as well as interpenetrate, each other at the cinematographic level, rather than being reduced to it as mere medial ironies. The "coupling" of hologram and replicant as screen characters, in their alternate forms of virtuality incarnate, thus yields to apparatus reading via their counter-pointed status as twin avatars, not just of the cinemachine per se, but of its preternatural powers of visual persuasion—with the protagonists' generated action no less compelling on screen for being at one level or another, as always, illusory. Hence, once again, the assertion *in* technique of the fabrications *of* technique—and, once again as well, given the special affect induced by such vehement *trucage*, not a vicious and airless circle but the reflective breathing room of a hermeneutic one.

Not always, of course. Sometimes we are seeing just show, rather than any telling revelation. Lucy's pixel eczema, *Ghost*'s digital sheddings, even Joi's electronic splutter, flash-fade, and reconfiguration, let alone the ex-ploded fantasy image of Pi's resurrected mother: all of this may only seem like preparation for the empty pixel apocalypse of "particle degeneration" at the end of *Avengers: Infinity War* (2018), where the trademarked super-heroes of the Marvel brand are eliminated one after another in a final digital scourge. Or more like obliterated: imploded in a pixel tornado of brown-toned fragments, dust to earthen pixie dust—or, in an alternating electronic palette in some of the exterminations, ash to gray ashen flecks. In its sharp-edged, microchipped difference from the mistily dispersing spaceships of *Arrival*, the effect is a blatant result of reverse compositing: the most obvious trick in the CGI book (and already a minor optic meme on YouTube). But whereas Joi is unabashedly electronic in her sci-fi genre, these fantasy figures are supposedly real bodies under fragmentation and effacement. They are done in according to the evil designs of the villain Thanos, who now holds all the "Infinity Stones" once dispersed into the universe with the Big Bang: an explanation conjured for us on screen like its own pixel starburst. In the film's opening episode, one of the commandeered stones is in fact turned over to Thanos encased in a radiant, handheld "cosmic cube" (a favored prop in the comic book series from which the franchise derives), looking in this form like nothing so much as a swollen and unstable 3-D pixel. With the cube immediately smashed to bits in a synecdoche for the destructive force to be unleashed by its contents at the plot level, even before the enclosed stone is revealed we thus stare straight into the secret (noncosmic) power of the so-called Marvel Universe: namely its VFX budget.

After extensive credits to this effect at film's end—and as if vouching one last time for the touchstone impact of this technology—the typical end-title coda in the series shows two more Avengers being quite literally wiped out, the last meeting his disintegrating fate in midstream epithet—and able to vent no more than "Mother—!" from the empty center of his evacuation. An epithet interrupted, of course, while at another plane an origin, a matrix, probed. If, in this same coda, the promise that "Thanos will return" may lead us to suspect that the decimated superheroes might somehow be rebooted in the next episode, we realize it would take nothing more ingenious than a fast digital rewind to reverse the pixcelerated dispersion—a magic of the sort that Thanos, once having commandeered the "Time Stone," has already used in a related execution scene. As with Chaplin saved from the coils of his own industrial cinemachine by the reverse action of the reeling track, as with Epstein probing time's new intelligence on screen in the realm of altered motion, even with subsequent electronic machinations the trick is only a flipped switch—or tapped keyboard—away.

But another inference presses, and not for the first time. For surely more has snuck up on us in these obliterations of the superheroes under the sign of an "infinity war" than just the weaponized molecular magic of a vindictive comic-book demiurge. Taking the idea of such a film as speculative fiction more seriously than its own plot might seem to encourage, we may well ask with it (a question certainly more engrossing with Joi's holographic collapses) what else could sooner negate our universe, and each of us one by one—not by bodily erasure, but by putting our everyday agency out of commission—than yet again the allegorical threat, the new "imagination of disaster," of that crashed digital grid for which certain marked pixel decimations on the VFX screen invite being taken as optic metonymies? Here, then, in respect to our condition not as somatic vessels but as social subjects under distributed computer technology, is one point, at least, where the screen's algorithmic vulnerability does, in its own way, come to render our own.[10] In registering the charge of any such parabolic disclosures, much depends, of course, on the immediate narrative force, rather than just the technical finesse, of the CGI ingenuity at play. Repeatedly, within the visually edgiest (rather than just cutting-edge) operations of recent *trucage*, the interrogated narrative *why* of a scene—all the more elusive, at times, the longer a visual insistence persists, as with that protracted episode of erotic superimposition in *Blade Runner 2049*—is a question that must be routed through the technical *how* for its answer: the machine consulted for its own best intelligence on the question. One result of which—no small yield—is that the optical rigor of apparatus theory might return loosed for new discoveries from its once too-uniform critique of a presumptively classed and gendered specular ideology inculcated by the very work of camera-induced lines of sight. At which point a new balance, both medial and phenomenological, let alone aesthetico-philosophical, might be struck between the epistemology of a screen sight and the historicized ontology of its machined image. Among others: Epstein, Cavell, and Metz in a new three-way dialogue—and debate.

The communications wing of media theory often looks first to a medium's "channel characteristics" rather than its message. Under partial guidance in this respect, and amid the characters and plots of its own screen attention, I might, in closing, abstract the method of this essay by saying, in sum, that narrative analysis as medial reading looks equally hard, instance by instance, at how the special effects of a given narrative message may serve to *channel the medium*—and, in so doing, to take the measure of its "emanations" in their full technical affect. Tracking the impact of such visual force is all (and the no little) this essay has meant, and could ever have been expected to mean, by apparatus reading—whereby, in a given medial epoch, all on-screen ghosts are recognized as hosted, in one manner of hinted technique or another, by their cinemachines. Not least in the engineered extremities of CGI sci-fi, wonderments may go so far as to make one wonder further: ponder, speculate. However instinctive our *feel* for screen process might or might not be, certain films can train us in registering not just the affective charge, but also the cognitive reflex, of their technical foundation: how we might *think*, as well as feel, about a medium's surfaced inferences.

Notes

PRELUDE

1. Screen studies, like culture at large in a different sense, is exponentially body conscious. Work in this vein of somatic theory is so familiar that it simply needs a collective setting aside here (with relevant excerpts only when directly impinging on my alternate focus) in order to clear space for a return engagement with track and/or frame, photogram nexus or pixel grid.

2. For major touchstones in this once thriving theoretical enterprise, see Jean-Louis Baudry, "Ideological Effects of the Basic Cinematic Apparatus," trans. Alan Williams, *Film Quarterly* 28, no. 2 (Winter, 1974–1975): 39–47; and, anthologized with many other representatives of this discourse, Jean-Louis Comolli, "Machines of the Visible," *The Cinematic Apparatus*, ed. Teresa De Lauretis and Stephen Heath (New York: St. Martin's, 1980). On the fading away of its disciplinary hegemony, see D. N. Rodowick, *Elegy for Theory* (Cambridge, MA: Harvard University Press, 2015).

3. See "The Scene of the Screen: Envisioning Photographic, Cinematic, and Electronic Presence," for instance, by the most prolific and influential of cinema's recent "body theorists," the phenomenologist Vivian Sobchack, appearing in the online volume *Post-Cinema: Theorizing 21st Century Film*, ed. Shane Denson and Julia Leyda (Falmer, UK: Reframe, 2016). It is symptomatic of Sobchack's rhetoric of perception that—in stressing how, thanks to "consumer electronics," the new spectator "can both alter the film's temporality and materially possess its inanimate 'body'"—the scare quotes around "body" are not likely to scare away that wing of film theory already persuaded by her often figurative approach.

4. All I wish to insist on is this: that an applied morphology of screen kinesis doesn't need to defer immediately to the palpitating (or gendered) body of reception—let alone to the mystified integument, or organless flows, of the screen field. From projector to computer, the tooling of the image makes at least as strong a claim on analysis (especially when such technical aspects are foregrounded within narrative cinema) as do the neural or emotive circuits of an embodied phenomenology of response that such mobile imagery solicits, channels, and even at times seems to mimic in its spasms, lapses, and blackouts.

5. Hence the shifting valence of corporeality in the crossfire of phenomenological and affective models, where the premise of incarnate perception seems to bleed back into figurations of the screen's own supposed body, not just the viewed bodies it typical-

ly manifests. Clarification on all this has arrived in a dissertation now brilliantly completed by Chang-Min Yu in the Department of Cinematic Arts at the University of Iowa. Building in part on his own translations from Raymond Bellour's *Le Corps du cinema: Hypnoses, émotions, animalités* (Paris: POL, 2009), Yu's thesis ("Corporeal Modernism: Transnational Body Cinema since 1968") begins with synoptic insight by identifying, as the "three-body problem," the tendency in cinema studies *not* rigorously to distinguish the variable roles of the body "on, before, and of the screen."

6. See *Between Film and Screen: Modernism's Photo Synthesis*; *Framed Time: Toward a Postfilmic Cinema*; and *Closed Circuits: Screening Narrative Surveillance* (Chicago: University of Chicago Press, 1999, 2007, 2015). Termed "narratography" in the second two volumes, as in my recent literary analysis as well, my approach has been a version of reception study that registers the microplots of narrative in the inner workings of technique, audiovisual as well as linguistic.

7. Jean Epstein, *The Intelligence of a Machine*, trans. Christophe Wall-Romana (Minneapolis, MN: Univocal, 2015); and *The Promise of Cinema: German Film Theory 1907–1933*, ed. Anton Kaes, Nicholas Baer, and Michael Cowan (Oakland, CA: University of California Press, 2016).

8. See Chapter 7, "'Animage' and the New Visual Culture," in André Gaudrealt and Philippe Marion, *The End of Cinema? A Medium in Crisis in the Digital Age* (New York: Columbia University Press, 2015), 187.

9. See Gilles Deleuze, *Cinema 2: The Time-Image*, trans. Hugh Tomlinson and Barbara Habberjam (Minneapolis: University of Minnesota Press, 1989), 215.

CHAPTER 1

1. Epstein, *The Intelligence of a Machine*, trans. Christophe Wall-Romana (Minneapolis, MN: Univocal, 2015; originally published as *L'Intelligence d'une machine* [Paris: Jacques Melot, 1946]), 104.

2. Christian Metz, "*Trucage* and the Film," trans. François Meltzer, *Critical Inquiry* 3, no.4 (Summer 1977): 672.

3. Salman Rushdie, *Midnight's Children* (New York: Random House, 1981), 189.

4. Frank Norris, *McTeague* (New York: Oxford University Press, 1995), 84.

5. In "Conclusions" to *Cinema 2: The Time-Image*, Deleuze speculates on whether the "numerical image" is destined "to transform cinema or to replace it" (265)—an issue on whose terminology, at least, the present annotations have already weighed in by resisting too liberal a use of "postcinema." The question this raises more specifically for Deleuze is whether, in connection with the time-image, digital process "spoils it, or, in contrast, relaunches it" (267).

6. See Hugo Munsterberg, *The Photoplay: A Psychological Study* (New York: Appleton, 1916).

7. See the translator's introduction to *The Intelligence* (iii) for a brief summary of this concept of *photogenie*, central to what one might call Epstein's *aesthetic theory* of cinema—as distinct from the broader *philosophical* undertaking of the translated volume, which Wall-Romana rightly sees as a direct influence on Deleuze's film theory (iv).

8. With this prevailing emphasis on cinematography's almost inhabited immediacy under the spell of *photogenie*, it is inevitable that Epstein would have been taken

up by recent arguments for cinematic corporality, as in the subtitle to the eponymous volume *Jean Epstein* by the translator of the *Intelligence* book, Christophe Wall-Romana: *Corporal Cinema and Film Philosophy* (Manchester, UK: Manchester University Press, 2013).

9. Deleuze, *Cinema 1: The Movement-Image*, trans. Hugh Tomlinson and Barbara Haberjam (Minneapolis, MN: University of Minnesota Press, 1986), 23–24.

10. André Bazin, "The Ontology of the Photographic Image," in *What Is Cinema?*, trans. Hugh Gray (Berkeley: University of California Press, 1967), I:14–15.

11. Further, although beyond Cavell's avowed scope, it is clear that any analogy between film track and synaptic circuit, assimilating to a single image the flashing past or firing off of separate optic singles, goes for the digital image as well—and with an even more intimate fit. In the photochemical phase of its long machine life (hard drives included), cinematography's difference from the naturalist understanding of perception, as well as from a digital projection still pending, consists simply in the fact that the trace of separate "snapshots" precede—and survive—their serial disappearance in the projected beam.

12. A phrase used in description of the continuous fluidity of *photogenie* in Epstein, *Écrits sur le cinema*, vol. 1 (Paris: Editions Seghers, 1974), 94, as noted by Wall-Romana, 27, in helpful connection with that technical logic of "compression" to be expanded on below.

13. Friedrich Kittler, *Optical Media*, trans. Anthony Enns (Cambridge, UK: Polity Press, 2010), where film as "hybrid medium" operates only as it "combines analogue or continuous single frames with a discontinuous or discrete image sequence" (162).

14. Concerning, in effect, two different modes of cinemachine in the distinction between celluloid film and video—closely akin to Régis Debray's demarcation, in chapter 6 ahead, between the graphosphere (writing as well as cinematic "inscription") and the videosphere—media theorist Vilém Flusser (in *Gestures*, trans. Nancy Ann Roth [Minneapolis, MN: University of Minneapolis Press, 2014]) sees film, eccentrically enough, as, at base, a three-dimensional art: comprised of the two orientations of the image itself, its optic rectangle, as well as the third generative dimension constituted by the film frames on the strip "rolling" through the projector (87) in a serial lineation, where the separate "photographs" do "trick the eye" (88) in their motion effect. In scrolling past the aperture, the actual movement of photograms is in its own right a new signifier in a more rigorous logic (or semiotics) of mediation. In the "event" (88) of projection, film thereby highlights—even while conflating—the difference between a "linear" and a "surface" code (90), as in writing versus painting quintessentially: the former "read," the latter "deciphered with the imagination" (90). Yet the two converge in filmic cinema: "The film is the first code in which surfaces move," constituting "a discourse of photographs" (90) rather than of alphabetic and lexical aggregates. The result, we may say, is synthetic rather than merely serial. In the language of general semantics, "a new kind of deciphering arises: the images of a film do not mean a scenic reality as those of traditional images do. Rather they mean concepts that mean scenes" (90). The model here is clearly "double articulation" in linguistics. Hence, again, the articulatory "intelligence" of the machine—its operative "concepts" of time and space—in its most basic montage sequencing.

15. Paul de Man, "Hypogram and Inscription: Michael Riffaterre's Poetics of Reading," *Diacritics* 11, no. 4 (Winter 1981): 17–35.

16. Despite all this, one wouldn't have been quick to guess that such insinuated and striking digital technique would later be inverted for the closing nondiegetic shot of a framed memorial photo of the poet emerging from a blackout on her dug grave—and captioned in the film's own last frame ("Emily Dickinson, 1830–1886"). There, the image is in fact reverse engineered (by the same fifteen-second morphing—and then a long pause) to recover Emily as we first saw her in the narrative. Anticipated or not, the inference is clear about the vectors of duration. Death alone anchors any optic timeline of the lived body.

CHAPTER 2

1. Mark B. N. Hansen, "Algorithmic Sensibility: Reflections on the Post-Perceptual Image," in *Post-Cinema: Theorizing 21st-Century Film*, ed. Shane Denson and Julia Leyda (Falmer, UK: Reframe, 2016), 6.3 (online volume, no pagination).

2. What emerges there is prepared for in the present chapter (on production valences rather than production values) simply by noting that a formative substrate in screen narrative is comparable, in fact, to the morphophonemic underlay of written narrative. Mostly disappeared as such into lexical and grammatical meaning, this is nonetheless what allows for just such a phonetic rebus of syllabification as *eff/ex(s)* transliterated to *FX*. The moving image has its own comparable substrate of moving and normally unthought parts.

3. There is more of a continuity across discontinuous mediations, we're noting, than always granted. Hansen: "In digital compression, as procedures like datamoshing reveal, we can no longer speak of a relationship *between* images, but rather of an ongoing modulation of the image itself . . . at the level of the pixel" ("Algorithmic Sensibility," unpaginated). For him, this is the very firstness of the first—and in these video artifacts, quite obviously so, since in such cases he can aptly demonstrate that "just as Firstness constitutes the pure quality, or better the field of pure qualitative difference, prior to the separating out of an object of perception, so too does the pixelated field of the image constitute a qualitative continuum that possesses a certain autonomy in relation to perception." A related "autonomy" is what one notes in the Deleuzian engram as well. But Hansen's point is more restrictive. What he finds unprecedented in New Media is the "extrusion of Firstness from the domain of the phenomenal," singling out "the pixel" as "the operator, in our 21st-century media culture, of a fundamental transformation of the image that, I shall argue, begins to operate *without being phenomenally apprehended.*" One way to think of the VFX flashpoint with which my essay will be frequently concerned, as well as certain forerunners in the optics of *trucage*, is that phenomenological apprehension is merely held in doubt, rather than wholly overruled. We often don't quite know if we're glimpsing the medial per se or its diegetic manifestation.

4. Hansen, *New Philosophy for New Media* (Cambridge, MA: MIT, 2004), with its own consistent emphasis on the filtering body of sensation rather than on screen technology.

5. Quotations from Conant's "The Ontology of the Cinematic Image" (extrapolating from Bazin's famous position paper on "The Ontology of the Photographic Image")

are drawn from a 2012 version available through PAL, the Duke University Center for Philosophy, Literature, and Film: https://dukepal.org/2012/04/05/philosophy-literature-and-film-two-lectures-by-james-conant-and-cora-diamond/.

6. Conant's general acknowledgement is to V. F. Perkins, *Film as Film: Understanding and Judging Movies* (New York: Penguin, 1972), in a title that, like Conant's paper, places a less materialist emphasis on the specifying phrase "as film" than, to say the least, does the present discussion. I have expanded here on a response to Cavell that I am glad to have contextualized and tacitly contested by other writers engaged with his philosophical approach in a forthcoming Bloomsbury anthology edited by David LaRocca under the suggestively double-edged title *The Thought of Stanley Cavell and Cinema*, where motion pictures may seem granted a kind of thought quotient of their own that I find inviting my particular contrast between Cavell's technical "assertions" and Epstein's machine "intelligence."

7. Cavell, *The World Viewed: Reflections on the Ontology of Film*, enlarged ed. (Cambridge, MA: Harvard University Press, 1979), 72, 146.

8. That's what I set out to illustrate in *Between Film and Screen* (see note 6 to this book's prelude), precisely by arresting for analysis the beamed transit across that eponymous median—and ultimately medial—nowhere of cast shadow.

9. Cavell suggests here, in the evolution of a particular genre, that a moviemaker would discover the "possibilities" of some technical feature only when seeing "that certain established forms would give point to certain properties of film" (31)—whether or not they are "unique properties" (31) of its *medium*. It is important to see the logical turnabout this involves. Instead of a traditional notice of the way, say, "technique enhances meaning," Cavell stresses how only "meaning can give point to technical properties" (31)—as the local potential of a medium otherwise not (and so never fully) determined in advance.

10. Cavell's terms can thus be used to reformulate a distinction in *Closed Circuits*, my study of surveillance cinema (see note 6 to this book's prelude), between *projected* narrative and *recorded* evidence, the latter tapped by the real-time transmission of forensic feeds on in-screen monitors: two intersecting modes, so to say, of world viewing, disinterested narrative reception versus the "technoptics" (my post-Foucauldian term) of visual search and seizure.

11. The precise industrial technology on call here—the "particle effect" software dating from the second decade of Industrial Light and Magic—was explained in a fall 2017 lecture at the University of Iowa by Ang Lee's special effects director David Conley, particularly enlightening on the deliberate link in such VFX design between the finesse of technique and the nuance of story.

12. Deleuze rather blithely presumes that if flicker fusion had been already perfected in the move from 16 to 24 frames per second, Bergson could have relaxed into cinema as a genuine phenomenology of the world in time: its image becoming-again before our accepting eyes. By the same questionable logic, the dubious early twentieth-century philosopher could barely have told the difference between 120 fps and life itself—with the existential seamlessness of *durée* all but achieved by machination after all.

13. See Slavoj Žižek, *The Fright of Real Tears: Krzysztof Kieślowski between Theory and Post-Theory* (London: BFI, 2001), 39.

CHAPTER 3

1. Erwin Panofsky, "Style and Medium in the Motion Pictures," in *Three Essays on Style*, ed. Irving Lavin (Cambridge, MA: MIT, 1995), 91–128.

2. In a lecture at King's College London, in the spring of 2015, exploring a comparably tardy consolidation of the term "medium" in Hollywood idiom (and in English-language usage more generally), David Trotter traced the slow emergence of the term (to mean either the process or the art of motion pictures) from its initial use in star discourse (a given film as "a medium for Garbo," say—today's "star vehicle").

3. *The Promise of Cinema: German Film Theory 1907–1933*, ed. Anton Kaes, Nicholas Baer, and Michael Cowen (Oakland: University of California Press, 2016), chock full of journeyman press commentary that one can only call deathless ephemera. For alerting me to this forthcoming publication, for inviting my commentary on its website, and for reminding me in the process of the Edison film that also figured in my remarks there, I am happy again to thank Anton Kaes. See http://www.thepromiseofcinema.com/wp-content/uploads/2015/12/Stewart-Mirror-Mirror-on-the-Wall.pdf.

4. I evoke here especially the third volume of Bernard Stiegler's trilogy, *Technics and Time, 3: Cinematic Time and the Question of Malaise*, trans. Stephen Barker (Stanford, CA: Stanford University Press, 2011), which emphasizes a cinematic model for the retentions of consciousness that actually precedes the invention of the film apparatus itself, the machine that offers Balázs its own disruptive new paradigm for an externalized self-consciousness.

5. Though only one of the articles in *The Promise* alludes to Epstein's film work, a clutch of index entries point to the number of related places in which the editors find it useful to compare sundry angles of approach to aspects of Epstein's theory.

6. Beyond that striking anticipation in Balázs of the prosthetic instrumentation of an autoreflective archive (with its latter-day apotheosis in the cell-phone selfie)—and more frequent than the stress either on forensic record or remote transmit sampled above—is the stress on screen figments in their technologically exponential (and cognitively asymptotic) approximation of *the real*. These are just some of the gathering parameters by which cinematic process is engaged in this German commentary as a proto-Bazinian ontology (and thus teleology) seen in one account, from the watershed vantage of sound synchronization, to be leading "most certainly" to 3-D, or, as phrased by its author, to "stereoscopic cinema" (272; Erich Grave, "The Third Dimension," 593–95)—while also, in its slow-motion special effects, owing a backward debt, in another piece, to the chronophotography of Marey and to earlier motion imaging achieved by mirrors in the praxinoscope (Hans Lehmann, "Slow Motion," 89–92).

7. See a schematic breakdown of the Shüfftan process here: http://metropolisvixfx.blogspot.com/2007/10/schufftan-process.html.

8. Whether with 3-D models or 2-D flats, the miniature's simulated structure or backdrop, in its mirror image, leaves space in this way for the insert of proportionately "miniaturized" actors visible when filmed in recess at a calculated distance behind that semimirrored plane held in place nearer the camera (with adjusted lighting further smoothed out so as to achieve the desired look of a continuous image field). By an in-camera effect, that is, the actors can thereby seem, for instance, overborne by some towering (rather than just secretly foregrounded and exaggeratedly scaled) image.

9. Before matte backdrops or blue screen, and long before computerized imaging, here was the anticipation by masked equivalent (in both senses: actions partially masked out by scenography in spaces wholly dissimulated) of Eisenstein's volumetric montage. This dialectic juxtaposition of different scales is projected instead, in this case, as the spectacle of monumentality—or monstrosity—rather than an overt synthesis of discrepancies. In *Metropolis*, Freder's POV shot of the Moloch epiphany is also the equivalent in personal witnessing to the telescreen (and its own inset trick effect) by which his father, the corporate overlord, accesses his only images of the proletarian underworld. Indeed, special effects and machinated surveillance tactics—operating from two sides of a supposed epistemological divide, and separately estimated in their cinematic valence by early German writers—can be found wedded from there on in the history of screen narrative. In regard to verisimilitude, however, the historical reaction at stake in the Schüfftan allusions of the German press is more specific and vigilant—if also forgiving.

CHAPTER 4

1. Henri Bergson, "Laughter: An Essay on the Meaning of the Comic" (*Le Rire*, 1900), http://www.gutenberg.org/files/4352/4352-h/4352-h.htm.

2. A reader of this chapter will soon see its sustained debt to the conference organizer, Sulgi Lie, for this articulation of comedy's inherent dialectical opposition.

3. The concept of "transposition" is developed mostly in chapter 2, "The Comic Element in Situations and the Comic Element in Words" (see note 1 above).

4. "Dickens, Griffith, and the Film Today," in Sergei Eisenstein, *Film Form: Essays in Film Theory*, ed. Jay Leyda (New York: Harcourt, 1977), 199.

5. See especially chapter 3, "Identification, Mirror," in Christian Metz, *The Imaginary Signifier: Psychoanalysis and the Cinema*, trans. Celia Britton, Annwyl Williams, Ben Brewster, and Alfred Guzzetti (Bloomington, IN: Indiana University Press, 1982), 422–56.

6. Stanley Cavell, *The Claim of Reason: Wittgenstein, Skepticism, Morality, and Tragedy* (New York: Oxford University Press, 1979).

CHAPTER 5

1. One further, albeit computer-remediated, exception occurs in *Unfriended: Dark Web* (2018), where an online cadre of friends discover that they are to become serial victims in a torture ring surfaced from the "reality"-site mayhem of the "dark web."

2. Solicited by special-issue editor Stuart Bender, this was the broad argument of an essay of mine, "Digital Mayhem, Optical Decimation: The Technopoetics of Special Effects," in the *Journal of Popular Film and Television* (21 March 2017), 4–15, several of whose examples are redistributed and amplified across this and the next chapter. And several cut for space, including an extended treatment of the ideological and political confusions caught up in the VFX logic of *Transcendence* (Wally Pfister, 2015).

3. On this widespread but often analytically leveling assumption, see Henry Jenkins, *Convergence Culture: Where Old and New Media Collide* (New York: NYU Press, 2006). Or let's say that, under this rubric, the subtitled "collisions" are not as energetic, as volatile, as they might be for screen interpretation.

4. Shane Denson, "Crazy Cameras, Discorrelated Images, and the Post-Perceptual Mediation of Post-Cinematic Affect," in *Post-Cinema* (see chap. 1, note 3), an essay adduced by Hansen in his own contribution to that volume. This failure, Denson continues in Hansen's summary by citation, "defines these images as metabolic 'spectacles beyond perspective'"—or, in other words, "as ostentatious displays that categorically deny us the distance from which we might regard them as perceptual objects."

5. Christian Metz, "*Trucage* and the Film," trans. François Meltzer, *Critical Inquiry* 3, no. 4 (Summer 1977): 657–75.

6. Susan Sontag, "The Imagination of Disaster," in *Against Interpretation and Other Essays* (New York: Picador, 1966), 209–25.

7. This is the threat of stolen humanity that Sontag never links directly, as is often done, to the creeping specter of faceless communist infiltration in the period. Yet her paradigm makes immediate room for it. In contrast to phobias of mass extermination via thinly disguised bomb anxiety, this alternate danger emerges, we might say, as *a* humanity under siege, rather than human kind en masse: usurped at its individual core rather than just leveled by global scourge. The concern in such panic is less with being slaughtered than with being "obliterated" (221) from within, wiped out: not eradicated so much as erased in one's human (anthropoid) essence. The narrative episodes to this effect, in Sontag's view, are not open critiques of a dehumanizing postwar modernity, any more than are their counterparts explicit about nuclear escalation in the Cold War. Rather, the genre in this period takes shape in pacifying allegories of each crisis, each pending trauma—raising, in order to allay, these paired common fears in the typical displacements of genre form.

8. For Sontag, those two midfifties films in the mode of lost rather than annihilated humanity, *The Blob* and *The Creeping Unknown*—those parallel fantasies of the lived body parasitically subsumed to an invasive organic will—are vague extraterrestrial variants of vampire lore: humanity penetrated and effaced from within, one embodied subject at a time, rather than collectively slain.

9. I allude here to J. D. Connor's various candidates for such reflex signaling, in the mode of studio allegory, in *The Studios after the Studios: Neoclassical Hollywood (1970–2010)* (Stanford: Stanford University Press, 2015). For the way an apparatus reading of a logo might thus connect with corporate intentionality across a whole range of VFX, though such *trucage* is not his particular focus, one returns as well to the groundbreaking work by Jerome Christensen, *America's Corporate Art: The Studio Authorship of Hollywood Motion Pictures* (Stanford, CA: Stanford University Press, 2011).

CHAPTER 6

1. Régis Debray, "The Three Ages of Looking," trans. Eric Rauth, *Critical Inquiry* 21, no. 3 (Spring 1995): 529–55.

2. Kristen Whissel, *Spectacular Digital Effects: CGI and Contemporary Cinema* (Durham, NC: Duke University Press, 2014).

3. In this vein of knowing composite materiality, *The Lego Batman Movie* (Chris McKay, 2017), with its sci-fi VFX, shifts scales from the pixel microsphere to render the interlocking cubelets of its adopted lego pieces—sometimes merely inferred, sometimes in quite explicit and signature aggregation—as the malleable "plastic" underlay

of disintegrations and instantaneous reconfigurations at the plot level, operating somewhere between a pastiche and a parody of the *Transformers* series.

4. But since *The Terminator* series is its own branded corporate franchise, the disintegrated lettering operates like the diegetically contaminated paratext in the logo allegories of other recent sci-fi openers, recalling the related work by Connor and Christensen (chap. 5, note 9).

5. Henry Barnes, "Arnie's Back but the Luster Isn't," *Guardian*, June 30, 2015, http://www.theguardian.com/film/2015/jun/30/terminator-genisys-review-arnold-schwarzenegger.

6. This recessive framing, with one screen (as, elsewhere, one photograph) dropped back from the outer narrative rectangle of screen presentation, is a recurrent touchstone of reflexive cinema, as explored across many examples of inset surveillance monitors in *Closed Circuits: Screening Narrative Surveillance* (see chap. 1, note 6).

7. On the matter of the *acoustmatique*, see Michel Chion, *Voice in Cinema*, ed. and trans. Claudia Gorbman (New York: Columbia University Press, 1994). In a variant of off-screen (or visually unsourced) sound, we hear the alien "voicings," as mere organic churning, mostly when their actual forms are not framed—or at least not clearly visible—through the mist of their inner transparent chamber, or when analyzed off-site in recorded form.

8. As detailed in an interview with special-effects expert Evan Moran, see an analytic breakdown of the logic and technology of these countermanifestations, rather than lines of flight, in the VFX designs for *Arrival* by Louis Morin, http://www.artofvfx. com/arrival-ivan-moran-vfx-supervisor-framestore/.

9. At the end, then, the alien vessels don't *leave*; rather, they are *relieved* of present duty, of presence itself (in both spatial and temporal senses). Burrowing ever deeper into reflexive inference about the cinemachine they trope, these vehicular phantoms render themselves more radically invisible than gone, thus relapsing to latency, to the future, from which they've come forth—and, by the same token and loop, reminding us of a medial past from which their *trucage* derives (in digital upgrade). Apparition is their only modality, not traverse. Once more: visual mediation in essence, time realized in space. And thus is film history folded yet again into the effect, as one valence of its specification and its special pleasure.

10. Again the two stages of Metz's metahistory of lab work: with the diegetic magic that is visible to characters within the attraction evolving into the later syntagmatic marker of a more fully articulated screen grammar that is therefore "de-diegeticized" by its new medial assignment.

11. Ian Christie, "The Visible and the Invisible: From 'Tricks' to 'Effects,'" *Early Popular Visual Culture* 13, no. 2 (2015): 106–12, with reference to "The Cinema of Attractions: Early Film, Its Spectator, and the Avant-garde," *Wide Angle* 8 (3/4), Fall 1986, reprinted in *Early Cinema: Space, Frame Narrative*, ed. Thomas Elsaesser and Adam Barker (London: British Film Institute), 56–62, with the central citation from Gunning (his p. 61) quoted by Christie on 109.

12. Metz, in the closing paragraph of the tenth (and last) numbered section of his definitive study: "Montage itself, at the base of all cinema, is already a perpetual *trucage*, without being reduced to the false in usual cases" (672).

13. Jameson, *The Political Unconscious: Narrative as a Socially Symbolic Act* (Ithaca, NY: Cornell University Press, 1981), 254.

POSTSCRIPT

1. Yet in another sense, having to do with the manifold apparatus itself rather than its bifold naming, the new affordances of computer imaging do in fact allow the generation and the playback of images on the same portable machine after all, returning by laptop engineering to the principle if not the instance of the kinetograph, though detached now from indexical necessity at the input stage.

2. The photogrammatic subtext of the predecessor film provides my first illustrated exhibit in the opening chapter of *Between Film and Screen: Modernism's Photo Synthesis* (Chicago: University of Chicago Press, 1999), 10–13; given the way futurist computerization manages there to activate a photograph as a 3-D, protocinematic space—in a genuine plot move—the overtly extraneous, self-clocked mobility of these fixed photos in the sequel, easy enough to miss altogether, may seem like an oblique digressive homage.

3. This syndrome of freestanding similitude is returned to later with the Las Vegas holograms of Elvis, Marilyn, and Frank, and then as followed up by the giant blue-haired nude Joi in her seductive come-on in the penultimate sequence, offering solace to the bleeding hero, who stands on a walkway before her gargantuan image, railed off from it in a way that calls up the protective bannister dividing the front row of banked IMAX seats from the vertical expanse of the looming screen. This optical allusion, if that's what it is, would be another pertinent in-joke—and, more, a kind of transmedial clue.

4. As singled out in a 2002 book written midway through the ongoing escalation of CGI, and looking back on the longer tradition of special effects, we note that in the Joi hologram a recurrent sci-fi tendency is being tested to what we might call its inner limit. In *Special Effects: Still in Search of Wonder* (New York: Columbia University Press, 2002), Michelle Pierson rightly observes, without invoking Metz's terminology, how the "visible trucage" of 3-D holography in film spectacles, from *Star Wars* to *Minority Report*, tends to pale in optical force compared with other, more seamless and glitch-free simulations—and thus to make the film's embedding medium of 2-D and its CGI wonders look all the better by contrast. A fully achieved evolution from the photogram to the hologram, that is, remains a technical trajectory that cinema's rectangular screen is never eager to see completed. So that one way to think about (as one must, in its decided protraction) the scene of reciprocal female superimposition in this metacinematic episode from the new *Blade Runner* is to find it coming unusually and teasingly near to closing, while still narratively preserving, the gap between technological futurity and present immersive viewing. Despite these metafilmic instances of projected optic innovation, however, the general awe induced by sci-fi effects has its undeniable emotive force. The affective fascination entailed by such effects is part of the audience "wonderment"—which may or may not prompt more pointed speculation—that Kirsten Whissel's study of CGI (see chap. 6, note 2) alludes to by acknowledging previous work in this vein, especially that of Vivian Sobchack's *Screening Space: The American Science Fiction Film* (New Brunswick, NJ: Rutgers University Press, 1997) and Scott Bukatman's

emphasis on "kaleidoscopic" sublimity in *Matters of Gravity: Special Effects and Supermen in the 20th Century* (Durham, NC: Duke University Press, 2003).

5. In both cases, a stray serendipity applies, for in view of my semiotic redrawing of Metz's terms so as to locate the neither/nor (neither visible nor perceptible) of generative digital input (previously photogram-based), the first of several VFX companies credited at the end of *Blade Runner 2049* is trademarked, just before "Framestorage," as "Double Negative."

6. One wants to contrast the momentary suspension of IMAX 3-D for the "flattened" originary flashback (and redemptive memory implant) in *Terminator Genysis*, as discussed in chapter 6, with Villeneuve's investigation (rather than effacement) of stereography's two-ply binocular effect.

7. It is at this metacinematic intersection of falsified human form and skeptical anxiety within science fiction that one can also locate the robot boy in Spielberg's *A.I. Artificial Intelligence* (2001), with the child actor's moving performance (of a self not his) serving to restage the ethical problematic at just that level of screen credence where affect and emotion always extend to the unreal.

8. Although he places no genre stress on the electronic metascience of digitized sci-fi, but surveys instead the entire field of violent action cinema since the late 1990s, see the searching and thickly documented title essay lodged at the heart of Evan Calder Williams's *Shard Cinema* (London: Repeater, 2017), 157–212. His researches are steeped in the commentary of VFX technicians in order to highlight the "threshold between a supposedly finished image and all the human work and computational procedures that went into it" (204). In the disintegrated glass transparencies of "shard cinema," his stress on its slow-mo aesthetic, together with the further fragmentations of "distributed sight" (195) and its rotary navigations, not only takes Williams back briefly to Epstein on such denaturalized movements (198) but finds in them "allegories of technique" (204). These include, most strikingly, the way the arrhythmies and retardations of such set pieces, the "ornamental dilation" (166) of their pace, evokes the scrubbing and stalling of the cursor-driven image in video replay (204)—and implicitly its further rehearsal of the CGI compositing involved in the rendering time (and "previs" editing) of such images in the first place. To this canny insight, we might add as example, one level up in the mise-en-scène, the evoked look of a motion-capture suit constituting, within plot, the very armor of invincibility in the *Ghost in the Shell* remake. As further avatars of the shard—not shattered but rather ambient—there is the spume of dust and haze, the misting "spray," the overall particle effect in film after film: an effect that "often has no real narrative explanation, looking simply like points, quanta, and pixels" (169). Like these "floaties" (170), more active fractures also *take the image to pieces* as a "glimpse backward, a refraction of the work of an image's making"—and, of course, the cost outlays of its collective labor.

9. Ryle's point, in *The Concept of Mind* (Chicago: University of Chicago Press, 1949), is that we intuit mind in a different way than we recognize bodily form or action, and that such incommensurability does not prevent functional knowledge of the former through the inferences of the latter's gesture and speech.

10. The evolution of the cinemachine from electric to electronic mediation may thus be found to invite a revived "distraction theory" in an updated variant of the Frankfurt

School paradigm. No longer sensorial cogs in an industrial infrastructure whose mechanical distractions the correlative experience of montage cinema serves to alleviate by the technical equivalents of rapid editing, we have become instead data nodes—even when not flash points of facial recognition or cyber implant—in a networked media circuit from which the dispersed optics of high tech cinema offer diversion (in both senses). With our daily surround being digitized through and through, contemporary audiences may well gravitate to enhanced distractions triggered by the eruption of one algorithmic crisis after another on the VFX screen. The model is a famous one. About both the early engines and the social engineering of cinema, Walter Benjamin's exaggerated but revealing claim for the essential cinematic "function"—sidelining all issues of intentionality—is delivered with the emphatic slant of italics: "*The function of film is to train human beings in the apperceptions and reactions needed to deal with a vast apparatus whose role in their lives is expanding almost daily.*" See Walter Benjamin, *The Work of Art in the Age of Its Technological Reproducibility, and Other Writings on Media*, ed. Michael W. Jennings, et. al. (Cambridge, MA: Harvard University Press, 2008), 26. It is exactly that "apparatus" (both before and since Benjamin's 1935 writing) whose associated local disclosures on screen we have been "reading" across the epochal break from rotary machination to binary generation, from Benjamin's "second technology" (succeeding the "first technology" of aesthetic making and the cult valuation of its tool use, 26) to the unforeseen third phase of digital virtuality and computer prosthetics, where even the aura of human self-presence, let alone of the art object, has been steadily attenuated by electronic dependencies.

Index

Page numbers in italics refer to figures.

affect, 2, 6, 26, 51, 57, 86, 119, 138, 161; "affection-image" in Deleuze, 55; technical rather than emotive or somatic affectivity, 125, 156, 158–59, 162. See also *Blade Runner 2049*

allegory: corporate, 186n9; cultural, 117, 166; digital, 76, 131, 142, 164; filmic, 94, 103; optical, 20, 71

Allen, Woody: *The Purple Rose of Cairo*, 98

Ant-Man, 125

Ant-Man and the Wasp, 126

apparatus reading, 3, 14, 23, 37, 38, 58, 88, 103, 105, 107; and *Arrival*, 139, 146; and *Blade Runner 2049*, 166, 168, 170, 172, 175; defined, 11–12, 122; double valence of, 38; and mediality, 162, 177; technics vs. somatics, 2

apparatus theory, 3, 61, 124, 153, 176; and Metz, 8, 108

Arrival, 4, 5, 139–49, 153, 162, 164, 165, 168, 175

Astruc, Alexandre: *camera stylo*, 25

Avengers: Infinity War, 116, 175

Balázs, Béla: on cinematic self-consciousness as mirror image, 62, 63, 65, 77, 131; on close-up, 52, 55

Baumer, Edward, 64

Bazin, André, 8, 45, 65; mortuary aspects of photography and film, 27, 36; teleology of realism, 52, 58, 74

baring the device, 160; as formal "motivation," 127

Batman, 148

Ben-Hur, 156

Benjamin, Walter, 189n10

Bergson, Henri, 18, 40, 41, 43, 64, 65; Cavell on, 102; and Deleuze, 9, 18, 24, 26–27, 43, 55, 59; mechanization in relation to critique of film, 79, 80, 81, 88, 183n12; physical comedy as mechanization, 1, 90, 92; on "repetition, inversion, and interference," 85–86, 95, 101, 103; verbal comedy, 87, 91, 95, 96

Besson, Luc. See *Lucy*

Billy Lynn's Long Halftime Walk, 50–53, 55, 56, 58, 135, 156

Birdman, 158

Blade Runner (Ridley Scott), 13, 163, 173

Blade Runner 2049, 4, 13, 123, 137, 163–69, *170*, 171, 173, *174*. *See also* medium; 3-D

Blob, The, 117–18, 186n8

body: as data processor, 25; in screen theory, 3–4, 121, 132, 155; somatic viewing, 25–26

Body Snatchers, The, 117

Bukatman, Scott, 188n4

Cavell, Stanley, 10, 28: on automatisms vs. automatons, 101–2; cinema as "a" world rather than "the" world, 10, 171; and skepticism, 28, 45, 101–3, 171; technical "assertions," 10, 11, 39, 41, 45–49, 58, 101, 137. *See also* film-philosophy; medium

Chaplin, Charlie, 80, 105, 158, 176; *City Lights*, 81; *Modern Times*, 81–83, *84*, 85, 99, 102

Christensen, Jerome, 186n9

Christie, Ian, 147

cinematograph(e), 1, 10, 15, 18, 24, 28, 37, 79; as projection, editing, and screening device at once, 3, 61, 63; and Weimar criticism (as *kinematographen*), 62–71

cineschatology, 132

Click, 105

comedial, 9, 158; apparatus reflex, 88; and mechanization, 79; and media archaeology, 104–5; medium in transposition to diegesis, 99. *See also* Bergson, Henri

Conant, James: on Cavell and medium, 45, 52, 58

Conley, David, 183n11

Connor, J. D., 186n9

Creeping Unknown, The, 117, 118

Davies, Terence, 33. *See also Quiet Passion, A*

Day the Earth Stood Still, The, 114, *115*, 120, 139

Debray, Régis: on transformation of logosphere and graphosphere into videosphere, 124–25

Deleuze, Gilles, 9; "gaseous state" of image, 42–43, 44; "genetic" engram, 42, 54, 59, 91, 162, 182n3; point of departure in Epstein, 27; time-image, 10, 19, 25

de Man, Paul, 33

Denson, Shane, 109

Dickens, Charles: Eisenstein on, 86; *Great Expectations* (Lean), 133; *Pickwick Papers*, 86; syntax, 86–87, 88, 105

Dickinson, Emily. *See Quiet Passion, A*

digitage, 11, 146–48, 152, 174

distraction: Frankfurt School theory and computerization, 189n10

District 9, 120

Duck Soup, 87

Edison, Thomas Alva. *See Frankenstein* (Edison)

Eisenstein, Sergei: on Dickens and Griffith, 22, 86, 185n4; volumetric montage, 185n9

Epstein, Jean: epistemological "venom" leaked by filmic illusion, 24, 28, 33, 36, 171; *Intelligence of a Machine*, 6, 8, 30, 79, 91, 94; intermittence of optical reality, 33, 45, 63, 91, 94; "irrealism," 18, 52, 53, 151, 171; *La chute de la Maison d'Usher*, 20–21, 24; "logarithmes sensoriels," 30, 45; photogenie, 25–26, 29, 51, 53; reality as extracinematic illusion, 34; reverse motion as link between experimental cinema and slapstick, 84; *truquage* ("trick"), 8, 15,

20, 28, 30, 94, 108, 111, 144. *See also* Metz, Christian; *trucage*

Ex Machina, 138

fast-forward, 36, 128

film-philosophy, 8, 10, 17, 41, 43–58, 101. *See also* Cavell, Stanley; Deleuze, Gilles; Epstein, Jean

flicker fusion, 156, 183n12

Flusser, Vilém, 32, 181n14

Forbidden Planet, 167

Frakenheimer, John. See *Seconds*

Frankenstein (Edison): mirror *trucage*, 69, *70*, 71

freeze frame, 32, 46, 48

Galeen, Henrik, 69

Gaulke, Johannes, 67

Ghost in the Shell, 171

Gunning, Tom, 147

Hansen, Mark B. N., 41–45, 182n3

Hellwig, Albert, 65

Hellzapoppin!, 80, 81, 96–97, 99, *100–101*, 103, 104, 158; and "pushing and popping" in narratology, 98. *See also* photogram

Her, 126

His Girl Friday, 87

Hitchcock, Alfred. See *Vertigo*

intentionality: as function of technopoetics, 122–23, 133

Invasion of the Body Snatchers, 117

Invisible Man, 112, 148, 151

Iron Man, 114, 126, 165

Keaton, Buster: machinic tricks, 102–3; medial ironies in *Sherlock Jr.*, 76, 81, 85, 88, 89–90, 92, *92, 93*, 94–97, 98; sight(line) gags in *Our Hospitality*, 88–89

Kittler, Friedrich, 31, 181n13

Korn, Arthur, 66

Kracauer, Siegfried, 64

Kubrick, Stanley. See *2001: A Space Odyssey*

Kurosawa, Akira, 46

Lang, Fritz: *Metropolis*, 68, 75, 103, 137, 185n9; *The Testament of Dr. Mabuse*, 72

lap dissolve, 69, 95; in *Arrival*, 4, 146, 153; as *trucage*, 147, 168

Lawrence of Arabia, 157
Lee, Ang: *Life of Pi*, 53, 54, 55. See also *Billy Lynn's Long Halftime Walk*
Leger, Fernard, 27
Lie, Sulgi, 185n2
Lindsay, Vachel: "sculpture in motion," 166
Lucas, George: "Industrial Light and Magic," 3
Lucy, 54, 138, 149, 153; cyberdisintegration, 126–28, 129, 175; digital apotheosis, 130–32; as distribution parable, 164

Mamoulian, Rouben, 37
Marker, Chris: *La Jetée*, 140
Marx, Groucho. See *Duck Soup*
medium: in disclosure, 21, 45–49, 55, 60–62, 65; and slapstick, 84
Méliès, Georges: *A Trip to the Moon*, 113, 147
Metz, Christian, 8; montage as "tapestry," 28; photogram, 29; primary and secondary identification, 97. See also *trucage*
Morrison, Bill, 118
Munsterberg, Hugo: psychopoetics of cinema, 23–24, 30, 63
Muybridge, Eadweard, 17, 134

narratography, 11, 174, 180n6 (introduction)
New Media, 1, 14, 185n3 (chap. 5); Hansen on, 182n3, 182n4; theoretical orientation for digital cinema, 40–41, 43, 44–45
Nolan, Christopher: *Inception*, 139; *Memento*, 139
Norris, Frank: *McTeague*, 17, 53

Olsen, Ole, and Johnson, Chic. See *Hellzapoppin!*

Pacific Rim, 120
Pacific Rim: Uprising, 120–21
Panofksy, Irwin: Cavell's uptake, 48, 49, 60, 162, 163
particle effect, 54, 189n8
Peirce, Charles Sanders, 18, 40–43, 47, 49, 51, 57, 80, 90, 104
Perkins, Victor, 45
phenomenology, 2, 40, 41, 183n12
photogram, 46, 108, 140, 149, 150–52, 161, 181n14; basis of photogrammar, 10, 13, 19, 22; binary element in Kittler, 31; compo-

nent of illusory continuity in Eptsein, 171; contrasted with pixel as the breakpoint in cinema history, 2, 6, 9, 15, 17, 46, 51, 123, 137; in Deleuze and Cavell, 27–28; explicit in *Hellzapoppin!*, 99–101, 103, 104; genetic element in Deleuze and Epstein, 32, 43–44, 54, 162; inferred in Chaplin, 84, 91; inferred in Keaton, 92; Metz on, 29; and retinal return of the suppressed, 10
Pixels, 133
Poe, Edgar Allan: "The Fall of the House of Usher," 19; "The Oval Portrait," 19. See also Epstein, Jean
Polanski, Roman: *The Ghost Writer*, 157, 158
postcinematic, 1; vs. postfilmic, 1–2
post-perceptual image, 41–42, 44
Promise of Cinema, The, 62–68, 75

Quatermass Xperiment, The, 117
Quiet Passion, A: shift from photographic to digital register, 34–37

Ready Player One, 120–21
Riffaterre, Michael, 13
Rondepierre, Éric, 118
Ruff, Thomas, 111
Rushdie, Salman: on filmic reality, 16–17, 28, 32, 38

Seconds: source for *Self/Less*, 72
Self/Less, 63, 173; double optical trick in, 72–73, 73, 74, 75–77
Singh, Tarsem. See *Self/Less*
slow motion, 46, 128, 172, 184n6; in Epstein, 21, 22, 23, 26, 30
Sobchack, Vivian, 179n3, 188n4
Sontag, Susan: on 1950s sci-fi threats and effects, 106, 116–18, 120–22, 126, 132, 186n7
Spielberg, Steven: *A.I. Artificial Intelligence*, 189n7; *Close Encounters of the Third Kind*, 158. See also *Ready Player One*; *War of the Worlds*
Star Wars, 3, 188n4
Steffen, Ernst, 66
Stiegler, Bernard, 63, 184n4
superimposition, 37, 103, 133, 146, 148; in Epstein, 29; evolution of, 147; in Keaton, 90, 96; 3-D holography, 170, 174; verbal, 87; in

Villeneuve, 163, 164, 165, 168. *See also* lap dissolve; *trucage*

syllepsis: cinematic equivalents, 93; in Dickens, 86; in relation to optical litotes, 97

Talbot, Henry Fox, 61

technopoetics. *See* VFX

technoptics, 169, 183n10

Ten Commandments, The, 156

Terminator Genisys, 133, *134–35*, 136–37, 189n6

Tesis, 106–7

Them!, 126

Things to Come, 167

3-D, 121, 131, 184n6, 188n4, 166–67; IMAX, 116; 1950s versions, 156; stereoscopic effect suspended, 136; 3D vs. IMAX 2D for *Blade Runner 2049*, 165–70, 174; ultra high-definition, 52. *See also Billy Lynn's Long Halftime Walk*

time: as abstraction in Epstein, 24, 40; in Deleuze, 10, 19; as function of thirdness in Peirce, 41; manipulated in *Lucy*, 128; as special effect in Hugo poem, 34

Transcendence, 126, 185n2 (chap. 5)

Transformers series, 109, *110*, 158, 186n3

Trip to the Moon, A, 147

Trotter, David, 184n2

trucage (truquage), 11, 16, 17, 21, 28, 35, 134–35, 137, 157; cinema as all trick, 15, 163, 147; and "drick" in *McTeague*, 53; historical evolution from trick to syntax, 111, 129, 144, 147, 153; "invisible," 118; and mirror illusion, in CGI, 120, 122; montage as *trucage*, 148; and remote holography, 163–65, 167; schematized by semiotic square, 148–50. *See also Arrival*; Epstein, Jean; Metz, Christian; *Quiet Passion, A*

Truffaut, François, 46

2001: A Space Odyssey, 132, 141, 157

Unfriended: Dark Web, 185n1 (chap. 5)

Vertigo: rear-projection *trucage*, 150

VFX (visual special effects), 5, 6, 8, 11, 25; scalar shifts in pixelation, 125–26, 129, 172, 179. See also *trucage*

Villeneuve, Denis, 4. See also *Arrival*; *Blade Runner 2049*

Von Ledebur, Wilhelm, 66

Wall-Romana, Christophe, 180n7

War of the Worlds: 2005 compared to 1953 version, 111–12, *113*, 114–15, 148

Whissel, Kristen, 131, 186n2

Williams, Evan Calder: and "shard cinema," 172

Žižek, Slavoj: interface effect, 50, 56, 57, 58